The Technological Unemployment and Structural Unemployment Debates

Recent Titles in
Contributions in Economics and Economic History

Studies in Accounting History: Tradition and Innovation for the Twenty-First Century
Atsuo Tsuji and Paul Garner

A New World Order?: Global Transformations in the Late Twentieth Century
David A. Smith and Jozsef Borocz, editors

Transforming Russian Enterprises: From State Control to Employee Ownership
John Logue, Sergey Plekhanov, and John Simmons, editors

The Development of Local Public Services, 1650–1860: Lessons from Middletown, Connecticut
Hannah J. McKinney

Rural Development Research: A Foundation for Policy
Thomas D. Rowley, David W. Sears, Glenn L. Nelson, J. Norman Reid, and Marvin J. Yetley, editors

Epistemics of Development Economics: Toward a Methodological Critique and Unity
Kofi Kissi Dompere and Manzur Ejaz

Economic Policy in the Carter Administration
Anthony S. Campagna

State Per-Capita Income Change Since 1950: Sharecropping's Collapse and Other Causes of Convergence
Leonard F. Wheat and William H. Crown

Work and Welfare: The Social Costs of Labor in the History of Economic Thought
Donald R. Stabile

American Trade Policy, 1923–1995
Edward S. Kaplan

Bastard Keynesianism: The Evolution of Economic Thinking and Policymaking since World War II
Lynn Turgeon

Latin America in the World-Economy
Roberto Patricio Korzeniewicz and William C. Smith, editors

The Technological Unemployment and Structural Unemployment Debates

Gregory R. Woirol

Contributions in Economics and Economic History,
Number 173
David O. Whitten, Series Adviser

GREENWOOD PRESS
Westport, Connecticut • London

331.137
W84t

Library of Congress Cataloging-in-Publication Data

Woirol, Gregory R. (Gregory Ray)
    The technological unemployment and structural unemployment debates
/ Gregory R. Woirol.
        p.   cm.—(Contributions in economics and economic history,
    ISSN 0084-9235 ; no. 173)
    Includes bibliographical references and index.
    ISBN 0-313-29892-0 (alk. paper)
    1. Unemployment.   2. Technological unemployment.   3. Structural
unemployment.   4. Economics—History—20th century.   I. Title.
II. Series.
    HD5707.5.W64   1996
    331.13′7—dc20   95-41691

British Library Cataloguing in Publication Data is available.

Library of Congress Catalog Card Number: 95-41691
ISBN: 0-313-29892-0
ISSN: 0084-9235

First published in 1996

Greenwood Press, 88 Post Road West, Westport, CT 06881
An imprint of Greenwood Publishing Group, Inc.

Printed in the United States of America

∞™

The paper used in this book complies with the
Permanent Paper Standard issued by the National
Information Standards Organization (Z39.48-1984).

10 9 8 7 6 5 4 3 2 1

For Agnes E. Woirol
and Walter R. Woirol

Contents

Acknowledgments		ix
Introduction		1
1.	The Machinery and Unemployment Debates	17
2.	Origin of the Technological Unemployment Debates	23
3.	Theoretical Disputes in the Technological Unemployment Debates	35
4.	Empirical Contributions in the Early 1930s	47
5.	Empirical Debates in the Mid to Late 1930s	59
6.	Resolution and Interpretation of the Technological Unemployment Debates	69
7.	Origin of the Structural Unemployment Debates	77
8.	Evolution of the Structural Unemployment Debates	93
9.	Peak Years of the Structural Unemployment Debates	111
10.	Resolution and Interpretation of the Structural Unemployment Debates	127
Conclusion		143
Notes		147
Selected Bibliography		183
Index		199

Acknowledgments

The research for this book was completed at the University of California, Berkeley, and at Whittier College. Much of the material was originally collected for my doctoral dissertation at Berkeley. Funding for the research was provided in part by the Institute of Business and Economic Research at Berkeley, the National Science Foundation, the Haynes Foundation, and the Richard and Billie Deihl Chair at Whittier College.

Many people have had a significant influence on the creation of this book. I would like to thank at the start Thomas Rothenberg, John Letiche, and Joseph Garbardino for the wisdom of their advice. I also would like to thank Stephen Overturf and Charles Laine for their longtime support and encouragement. Joseph Fairbanks and Robert Marks have taught me much about how to undertake projects like this, and I appreciate their advice and guidance. Two anonymous readers of an earlier draft provided many thoughtful comments and suggestions. I have used the resources of several libraries, but I would like to acknowledge in particular the assistance of the librarians and staff at the University of California, Berkeley, Whittier College, and Washington State University.

I especially thank Maureen Nerio, who has helped with much of the typing and formatting of the book. Without her willingness to spend the hours I asked of her on entering text and revisions, the manuscript would never have been completed. Haw-Jan Wu has my deep appreciation for the technical advice that he generously provided several times during the project. I also thank Kim Thomas for her insightful comments and Donna Laine for her careful reading of the text and many thoughtful suggestions for revisions.

Finally, I thank my wife Susan and my daughters Samantha and Stephanie for their understanding during those times when I would leave for a day or a week to work on the book. They will be particularly glad to see this project come to an end.

Introduction

Superficially, the issue of the employment impact of technological change is straightforward. It is obviously possible for individual workers to become unemployed due to technological change. A long list of examples, from buggy-whip makers, glassblowers, and theater musicians, down, presumably, to sliderule makers, could be compiled of industries where technological change has significantly reduced employment. No one doubts that this can happen.

When one moves beyond this initial statement, however, the issue becomes more difficult. What happens to displaced individuals? Do they rapidly—or ever—get reemployed? What are the conditions of their new employment relative to the old? What is the impact of technological change on skill requirements? And—the issue always of central interest—is it possible that on an aggregate level, technological disemployments can create a serious and lasting aggregate unemployment problem? Discussions in the history of debate about technological advances and employment address all these questions. The central concern that ties them all together, however, is the question of the aggregate employment effects of technological change.

Economists' interest in this issue dates back to the early 1800s when David Ricardo, in the third edition of his *Principles of Political Economy*, wrote that "[t]he opinion entertained by the labouring class, that the employment of machinery is frequently detrimental to their interests, is not founded on prejudice and error, but is conformable to the correct principles of political economy."[1] The machinery and unemployment debates that developed in Britain in reaction to Ricardo's claim were associated closely with the rise of industrial capitalism and the development of the discipline of economics. Coming at the height of the first wave of industrialization and involving the most prominent political economists of the time, these debates have received attention as a significant episode in the intellectual history of the development of modern capitalism.[2]

The story of the machinery and unemployment debates ends in the mid-1800s when the benefits from industrialization first obviously began to improve the lives of the British working class. The issue, however, did not disappear. The relation between technological change and employment is a fundamental dynamic in capitalism. Interest in its nature is inherent in an economic system in which the rise and fall of industries under the impact of new products and new techniques is an inevitable outcome of the processes that are the very essence of the system. As a result, as industrial nations and the discipline of economics evolved in the decades following the machinery and unemployment debates, the issue recurred. Twice in the twentieth century, popular and professional economic attention focused again on the question of the relation between technological change and employment. In the 1930s the issue was discussed under the rubric of technological unemployment. During the 1960s the issue was structural unemployment.

As the nineteenth-century debates reflected in a fundamental way the nature of the rapidly evolving systems of capitalism and of economic thought, the twentieth-century debates similarly reflected the changes in these systems over the following century. By the 1930s the Classical School economics of Adam Smith, David Ricardo, and John Stuart Mill had been replaced by the Neoclassical School economics of Alfred Marshall, Carl Menger, and Léon Walras— which in turn was challenged by the rise of modern macroeconomics under the influence of John Maynard Keynes. Concurrent with this evolution of economic ideas, the newly industrializing capitalist economies of the early nineteenth century matured and by the twentieth century were well along in the process of moving from a focus on manufacturing and primary industries toward service-based production.

In this changed environment of professional economic thought and daily economic life, the old disputes over the relation between technological change and employment took on a new cast. More empirical, they used the best data of the day with new techniques of statistical analysis. The terms and concepts of marginalist and, later, Keynesian economics replaced the compensation arguments of the Classical School. The debates focused on different strategies of policy relief. In taking on these new forms, the twentieth-century debates reflected the contemporary natures of capitalism and economics in the same way as had discussions of the same issue a hundred years before.

The past two hundred years' discussions about the relation between technological change and employment provide a unique perspective on the history and evolution of both capitalism and economics. The purpose of this study is to continue the story of the technological and employment debates into the twentieth century by analyzing in detail economists' contributions to the technological unemployment debates of the 1930s and the structural unemployment debates of the 1960s.

People read histories of economic ideas such as this for several reasons. One motivation is that they expect to learn some economics from their efforts. Histories have been written about dozens of specific economic issues, but individual readers of the history of the discipline do not read all of these studies. Rather, they select topics based on personal interests in economics. One thing they intend to get out of this exercise is a deeper understanding of concepts and issues through reading about them in the context of their development.

A second reason people read the history of economic thought is to learn something about economics as a discipline. This includes finding out who said what and when, but more importantly it involves discovering how economics works as a social science. Whether economics best can be analyzed in terms of the methodologies of science proposed by Karl Popper, Imre Lakatos, Thomas Kuhn, Paul Feyerabend, or by some other analytical framework, is an issue of lasting interest.[3] At its most fundamental, arguments about how economics works as a social science are about how economic ideas are created and progress. Discussions about these issues can be prescriptive or descriptive. Recent prescriptive analyses that review the methodological options open to economists and argue for a particular approach in the profession include Bruce Caldwell's call for a Feyerabend-like methodological pluralism, J. C. Glass and W. Johnson's support for Imre Lakatos' methodology of scientific research programs, Mark Blaug's argument for Popperian falsifiability, Donald McCloskey's claim that it is not a particular approach to empirical work or theory that ultimately drives the discipline forward but the quality of economists' rhetoric, and Daniel Hausman's argument that progress in economic thought is impeded by a too-rigid commitment to economics as a separate science which stops economists' pursuit of insights from related disciplines.[4] Blaug and McCloskey also provide examples of the descriptive approach to methodology: Blaug in several short chapters that outline the evolution of a selection of major ideas in economics, and McCloskey in rhetorical analyses of critical works by Paul Samuelson, Robert Fogel, and others. The goal of the descriptive approach is to see what economists actually do in order to understand better what works and does not work in the development of economic ideas. Such knowledge is valuable in itself, and is primary evidence for the prescriptive debates about how economists ought to act.

The technological unemployment and structural unemployment debates among economists in the twentieth century provide an intriguing descriptive methodology case study. The dominant opinion in the twentieth century—both among professional economists and the general public—consistently has been that technological change does not create any long-term aggregate employment problems. In popular articles, a casual empiric reference to the past is usually seen as sufficient evidence.[5] But economists require more than this. To be convincing to their peers, economists must provide evidence and arguments that use the logic and concepts accepted in the discipline. The fact that two periods of professional debate have developed in the past century over an issue that normally reflects a strong professional consensus raises several interesting questions. Why did a professional dispute arise? What role did data and theory analysis play in the evolution? What progress is evident in the debates, on an individual and an aggregate level? Did economists in the debates fit the image described by John Kenneth Galbraith, who once said that "[e]conomists are economical, among other things, of ideas. . . . They make those they acquire as graduate students do for a lifetime"?[6] Or were participants in the debates methodological Bayesians, constantly modifying personal prior probabilities as they acquired new information, thus always changing their views in the light of experience? These are fundamental questions to anyone seeking to better understand the endeavor in which economists are involved, and one reason to read any history of thought study is to acquire some insight into their answers.

A third reason to read the history of economic thought is to learn something about how to do economics better. By reading about what past economists have done, current economists can achieve a better sense of which approaches are effective and of what "works" in economics in convincing others.

What do the technological unemployment and structural unemployment debates have to say with respect to these reasons for reading the history of economic ideas? First of all, what has been learned?

The general question of interest in both the nineteenth- and twentieth-century discussions of the employment effect of technological change has been whether it is possible for the aggregate level of unemployment to be increased by technological advances. The 1930s technological debates took place in the context of the pre-Keynesian economic world of neoclassical equilibrium theory. Labor and jobs in general were treated as homogeneous, and no clear distinction was made between frictional, structural, and cyclical unemployment. In the framework of A. C. Pigou's *Theory of Unemployment* and John R. Hick's *Theory of Value*, wage-price flexibility and factor mobility were all that mattered. By the time of the 1960s structural unemployment debates, the context had changed. In the 1960s Keynesian-Phillips Curve world, aggregate demand was acknowledged by almost everyone as sufficient to reduce unemployment to whatever level might be desired, but at a cost of increasing inflation. The central question became whether technological change could increase the non-accelerating-inflation rate of unemployment. Labor was recognized as heterogeneous, the kinds of jobs eliminated versus the kinds of jobs created by technological change were seen as critical, and wage-price inflexibilities and factor immobilities were assumed as a fact of real markets.

Within these contexts, as an issue in economic theory, the question of the employment impact of technological change has been addressed from short-run and long-run perspectives, as a problem of partial and general equilibrium analysis, in terms of process and product innovations, under assumptions of homogeneous and heterogeneous labor, assuming flexible and inflexible wages and prices, focusing on the general level and the structure of jobs, and in an open and closed economy framework. Thorough recent theoretical treatments of the issue by Y. S. Katsoulacos and Marco Vivarelli take almost all these perspectives into account. Building on past theoretical contributions by participants in the 1930s and 1960s debates, Katsoulacos' conclusion from an examination of the short-run impact of product versus process innovations, under assumptions of homogeneous labor, partial versus general equilibrium, and competitive versus noncompetitive markets is that

whilst both process and product innovations raise the full employment ceiling, that is, the level of employment that can be attained by expansionary government policy at each level of the wage rate, for process innovation the *impact effect* may be reduction in the level of employment, whilst for product innovation even the impact effect involves a rise in the level of employment (where I mean by impact effect the short-run effect with nominal aggregate expenditure fixed).[7]

In his long-run analysis under assumptions of endogenous aggregate expenditures and homogeneous labor, Katsoulacos examines "the capital accumulation process induced by process innovation first under the assumption that prices are flexible and then for a fixprice economy. In the first case we get convergence to a new Walrasian equilibrium. In the second we find that the long-run equilibrium may exhibit dynamic instability in the sense that the transition path does not converge to long-run equilibrium but involves ever-increasing unemployment."[8]

Dropping the assumption of homogeneous labor in order to address the structural unemployment issue, Katsoulacos finds that

[i]n the short or medium run, when the proportion of skilled to unskilled workers may be treated as constant, technical change will reduce the demand for unskilled labour if the technical change is relatively more unskilled labor augmenting *and* the elasticity of substitution between skilled and unskilled labour is sufficiently low. Employment of unskilled labour may then be reduced in the presence of unemployment insurance. (Of course, this will also occur in the presence of wage inflexibility).

The assumption that skilled and unskilled labour are non-competing is less appropriate for long-run analysis. Under conditions of relatively more unskilled-labor-augmenting technological progress—and hence of a rising real wage of skilled relative to unskilled labour—more and more unskilled workers will come to consider extra training the most attractive option.[9]

Finally, in comparing general-level versus structural unemployment effects, Katsoulacos concludes that "[t]he present analysis suggests that an unfavorable *structural* effect of technical change is more likely (to occur and, I shall argue, to be sustained beyond the short run) than an unfavorable effect on the *general* demand for labour and employment."[10]

Vivarelli's analysis supports Katsoulacos' conclusions. In particular, he finds "that the relationship between technical change and employment is highly complex and comprises direct labour-saving effects, compensation forces and alternative forms of technical progress." The general conclusion, however, is that "there is no theoretical justification for the belief that . . . compensation mechanisms and new product innovation can ensure complete compensation of labour-saving displacement at every time and in every circumstance."[11]

Both Vivarelli's and Katsoulacos' books are thorough statements of what has been learned through theoretical analysis of the impact of technological change on employment. Significantly, in terms of the history of the twentieth-century debates, both books are revisions of doctoral theses. Ph.D. theses made notable contributions to both the technological unemployment and structural unemployment debates, and their appearance, a few years after the issue had begun to receive significant attention, was a sign that the issue had "arrived" as a topic worthy of professional concern.

In addition to theoretical discussions, a massive empirical literature has been published about the employment effects of technological change. Empirical studies of the issue consistently have been handicapped by a lack of critical relevant data and by the fundamental methodological issue of drawing general conclusions from specific studies. These handicaps were too great during the 1930s technological unemployment debates—especially data limitations—for empirical studies to provide more than partial insights into the issue. Statistical resources were much improved by the 1960s, and by the end of the structural unemployment debates several thorough empirical analyses of the issue had appeared.

Representative of the best of these empirical studies—and also an example of a study that originated as a doctoral thesis—is a 1966 book by Eleanor Gilpatrick. Gilpatrick's analysis warrants special attention because she explicitly connected the structural issue to relevant theoretical work. From a review of recent theory contributions and of the structural unemployment debates to date, she concluded that the 1960s disputes had been futile because of the inadequate theoretical foundation provided for almost all empirical studies.

Gilpatrick was right in this evaluation. The failure of most empirical work in the structural unemployment debates was not an extreme "measurement without theory" problem, but was due to the fact that different investigators were testing different hypotheses. Without agreement about the exact questions in dispute, empirical debates inevitably floundered. Gilpatrick correctly argued that the resolution to this impasse lay in a careful theoretical analysis of the issue which identified central empirical questions amenable to analysis with contemporary techniques and data sources.

Based on her review of recent theoretical work, Gilpatrick concluded that "[t]he key to the structural problem is the mismatching of specific labor skills demands and supplies where there is (1) limited transferability of skills and (2) limited substitutability among skills."[12] The centrality of these issues had been noted by others in the structural unemployment debates, but Gilpatrick was nearly alone in making them the foundation of her empirical analysis. From this point of view, she found she would have to prove three things in order to show that structural change in labor markets was a significant cause of recent unemployment: first, that structural change had occurred; second, that the labor force was unable to adjust to these changes; and, third, that mismatches existed between skill demands and skill supplies of labor. In her work, Gilpatrick reduced the problem to a question of "the automatic adjustment of the system through interchangeable factors, divisible units and flexible prices."[13]

Gilpatrick then tested empirically the three questions she had raised. Her analysis was mainly descriptive; only a few simple regressions were used because of limitations she found in the data. But Gilpatrick claimed that her conclusions were distinguished from the multitude of empirical studies that had been done before, not because of the statistical techniques she used but because of the careful foundation of her tests on theory-based central questions about flexibility and substitutability of factors and skills.

Gilpatrick's major conclusion from this analysis was that both structural change and deficient demand had been major causes of recent unemployment. In particular, she claimed that "structural unemployment might account for as much as half the increase in unemployment rates above the frictional minimum in nonrecession years." Although "structural and demand unemployment are so interrelated as to defy dichotomous examination," Gilpatrick argued that her tests amounted to "a refutation of the demand position. That is, we have shown considerable evidence to deny that inadequacies in over-all demand in the economy relative to productivity and labor force growth were responsible for persistently high unemployment rates from 1957 to 1964, independent of structural unemployment."[14]

Gilpatrick's study is not without its faults. In particular, despite the apparent precision of her equations, she provides only vague conclusions about the extent of structural unemployment, and she does not consider in depth the time frames necessary for working out the maladjustments she claims to have found in the economy. Gilpatrick's interpretations of the labor market changes she has found also can be questioned. But her work was done with great care and is a comprehensive and scholarly effort. Gilpatrick was not alone in criticizing the foundation of most empirical work in the structural unemployment debates and in attempting to rectify this error by deriving clear hypotheses from relevant theory. Similar approaches were taken in studies by Richard Lipsey (1965), Barbara Berman (1964), Richard Musgrave (1965), and Murray Brown (1966). But Gilpatrick's treatment is representative of the best of the empirical studies at the time, and of their results.

Marco Vivarelli's theoretical analysis of the economics of technology and employment also included empirical studies of the Italian and U.S. experiences from the early 1960s through the 1980s. His empirical findings supported his theoretical conclusions that technological unemployment is a realistic phenomenon that warrants policy attention. Vivarelli found that "[n]otwithstanding the operating of compensatory market forces, process innovations have an overall negative impact on working time." However, "this harmful effect may be more than counterbalanced by the beneficial impact of product innovations." In particular, he concluded that the aggregate level of unemployment had not increased in the United States primarily due to the rapid pace of product innovation. In the Italian case, "the labour-saving impact on working time has not been fully compensated for by market forces." However, the level of unemployment had not increased because of "a socio-institutional trend, namely the progressive and constant reduction of annual per capita hours of work." Vivarelli's policy conclusions supported initiatives to increase the level of product innovation and, more controversially, policies to encourage "the reduction of per capita working time."[15]

The general conclusion of these empirical studies is consistent with those in the best theoretical analyses of the issue. Extreme statements on either side of the technological change and unemployment issue are not warranted. To put it baldly: it all depends. Given certain circumstances—in particular a bias toward process innovation under conditions of skill immobility and price inflexibility—short- and medium-term aggregate disemployment effects are quite possible. Hans Neisser, in a 1942 contribution to the issue, perhaps stated it best when he concluded that "displacement and [reemployment through capital] accumulation are two largely *independent* factors and it is impossible to predict the outcome of the race between the two on purely theoretical grounds."[16]

Given that this is what has been learned from the twentieth-century debates about the employment impact of technological change, what have these disputes revealed about how economics works as a discipline? What has been effective, and what has not, in moving the debates forward? What methodologies, among the several that are proposed for the discipline, do economists actually use?

A first point is that there are several striking similarities between the technological unemployment debates and the structural unemployment debates. One parallel is in the origins of the two series of disputes. In each case a popular debate preceded the professional debates. Also in each case, the existence of a popular issue alone was not enough to start a professional dispute. A professional debate did not begin until it was clear that recent data trends suggested an important issue of concern. Once they had started, the evolution of the debates also exhibited several similarities. On the popular side, both periods witnessed an early stirring of interest by extremist groups (the Technocrats in the 1930s, the Ad Hoc Committee on the Triple Revolution in the 1960s), and both periods experienced similar management-labor confrontations during which major popular attacks on the issue were published (for example, *Machinery, Employment and Purchasing Power* by the National Industrial Conference Board in 1935, and George Terborgh, *The Automation Hysteria,* sponsored by the Machinery and Allied Products Institute in 1965). Also, near the end of both debates a major federal study of the issue was published (by the National Research Project on Reemployment Opportunities and Recent Changes in Industrial Techniques [NRP] in the 1930s and by the National Commission on Technology, Automation and Economic Progress in the 1960s). And both popular debates were similarly ended by a change in current economic circumstances (World War II in the 1940s and the Vietnam expansion in the 1960s).

On the professional side of the debates, there are also several noteworthy parallels. In each case it was evident that the balance of published professional opinion always was that there was nothing dramatic to worry about. The discussions were kept alive, however, by the continued publication by a vocal minority of empirical studies suggesting that recent changes had indeed created a problem. In each debate it also was the case that a major statement by a recognized economic authority of the dominant doctrine of the time played a significant role in starting the debates (Paul Douglas in 1930 and Walter Heller in 1961). In each case the debates created an incentive to collect better and more comprehensive data. In each case the foundation belief of those challenging the dominant professional opinion was doubt about the ability of the economic system to adjust to change. In each case the periods of intense debate were ended by current events rather than by a final consensus reached from formal professional analyses. And in each case the issue continued to linger on long after it had ceased to be a major professional issue, with important evaluations of past work—and a series of doctoral dissertations—appearing periodically for years afterward.

These similarities are interesting. In the case of both the popular and professional debates they suggest that there may be some general tendencies in discussions of this kind. This can only be a suggestion, however, without the evidence of other histories of issues for comparison.

The most important comparison of the two debates here, however, relates to the evolution of professional thought in the two series of discussions. A major implication of the experience of both series of debates is that simple stories about accumulation of learning through formal analysis do not adequately explain the course of events that took place.

This result is in a way disappointing. Formal analysis, both theoretical and empirical, did not have the central impact on progress on the aggregate level in the professional debates that might have been expected. Individual economists also did not respond often in a learning-from-experience fashion. It is also disappointing that the large number of studies of the 1930s had little impact on the debates of the 1960s. Only a few writers, for example, William Haber (1964), Lloyd Ulman (1967), and George Hildebrand (1966), explicitly acknowledged the contribution of the 1930s work. Even the contributions of the 1940s and the 1950s were almost completely ignored. Only a few economists in the entire 1960s debates, including Hildebrand (1966), Gilpatrick (1966), and Brown (1966), referred to the theory contributions of Neisser (1942), Hamberg (1952), or Fukuoka (1955).

Despite these facts, however, the details of both debates show several positive results that go a long way in compensating for the fact that economists did not act like storybook scientists in the technological unemployment and structural unemployment debates. Much useful information was generated, for example, in empirical studies of the micro-level effects of technological change and on the structure of unemployment. Although these data did not provide a definitive answer to the major questions in dispute, this work clearly was valuable and increased understanding of the economy. Also, the debate itself had an important impact on the quantity and quality of data available. In the 1930s this effect was especially clear. All modern aggregate productivity work of the federal government evolved directly out of the late 1930s NRP studies of technological change and unemployment. In the 1960s this effect was evident in the collections of automation and vacancy data by the Bureau of Labor Statistics (BLS). It is also apparent that because the 1960s debates focused on policy formation they helped motivate many innovative worker-training and demand-stimulation proposals.

Another reassuring result of the debates is that the general approach economists took to attacking the issue was positive in many respects. Clague (1931), Jerome (1932), Stern (1932), Stettner (1966), and Pauling's (1964) analyses of the methodological problems of studying the unemployment effects of technological changes are excellent examples. The approach taken by Roylance (1933), Jerome (1934), Gordon (1964), Eckstein (1966) and others of dividing up the major issue into key components and attacking these smaller questions one at a time also often was successful. It is also clear that when progress in the debates seemed to be stalled, an attempt often was made to diagnose and resolve the difficulty. Contributions by Lipsey (1965) and Gilpatrick (1966) are clear examples of this type of effort. The positive approach of economists is further reflected in the fact that data analysis did play a major role in the debates. Analysis of data trends was responsible for the beginning of debate in the first place. Participants in the subsequent discussions constantly tried to test their conjectures against the experience of the world, and empirical studies clearly dominated both series of discussions. The fact that simple stories cannot be told about the impact of data analysis in the evolution of the debates does not reduce the significance of these facts.

These characteristics of the debates have relevant implications for the various methodological positions that are advocated to guide economic research. The four arguments that have received the most attention in recent discussions are Paul Feyerabend's methodological pluralism, Thomas Kuhn's distinction between normal science and revolutionary science, Imre Lakatos' methodology of scientific research programs, and Karl Popper's falsifiability criterion.

The technological unemployment and structural unemployment debates do not provide strong evidence that economists are advocates of methodological pluralism. Although there were a wide variety of approaches taken in the debates—from pure theory to pure data analysis, and from a focus on individual industries to surveys of the entire economy—all the studies were within the mainstream of accepted ideas of the time (neoclassical economics in the 1930s and Keynesian economics in the 1960s). Other perspectives—from Marxian to Austrian—were certainly possible, but these were not presented in either period of professional dispute. Perhaps discussions bringing in other approaches would have helped the debates evolve in more fruitful ways, but there was no inclination to make such attempts. In terms of these debates, it is clear that economists kept the discussions within the generally accepted theoretical frameworks of the time, and did not search for insights from new perspectives.

This conclusion also has implications for Kuhn's distinction between normal science and revolutionary science. The technological unemployment and structural unemployment debates are both examples, in Kuhn's framework, of economists doing normal science. From both the neoclassical and Keynesian perspectives, technological change should not create aggregate employment problems. Only after current trends seemed to imply that such a problem was developing—and after popular debate brought the issue to the forefront of current economic issues—did professional economists begin to discuss the question. In both periods of debate, economists had little trouble in deciding on the appropriate theoretical position. In the 1930s, after a false start with the classical compensation view, a consensus quickly was reached in support of neoclassical analysis. In the 1960s, the Keynesian vision of the economy was accepted by all participants in the debate. Both debates, then, can be seen as examples of Kuhnian puzzle solving within an accepted theoretical framework. Not surprisingly, the puzzle that required solving was the same in each case. The central issue in both debates was whether enough flexibility existed in the system to adjust to changes affecting the level of employment. In the 1930s the focus was on flexibility in prices and wages; in the 1960s the issue was flexibility in job-skill transferability. An irony of this central issue—which was not commented on by participants in the structural debates—is that the Keynesian position, which was challenged by the structuralists in the 1960s debates as not acceptable because of inflexibilities in labor markets, was originally founded in part on the argument that the neoclassical view of the world was incorrect because of inflexibilities in labor markets.

There is another interesting aspect of the technological and structural debates in terms of Kuhn's analysis. Although the two disputes fit well the idea of normal science puzzle solving, they both had the potential of challenging the foundations of the accepted theoretical framework of the time. Faith was strong in the neoclassical framework that adjustments would take place in markets to compensate for the impact of technological change. Faith equally was strong from the Keynesian perspective that compensatory government policy could be used to reach full employment. The fact that conclusive studies did not appear to resolve the technological and structural unemployment debates could have led to serious questioning of this faith. The vindication of these beliefs by a return to full employment during World War II and the Vietnam War, however, eliminated the possibility of a serious challenge to accepted theory from a discussion of these issues. The fact that the central issue of concern was an anomaly in terms of accepted theory does much to explain the intensity of feelings in both periods of debate. There was a distinct feeling, particularly in the structural debates, that those challenging the accepted views were acting somehow outside the accepted normal course of professional behavior.

The technological unemployment and structural unemployment debates, then, can be discussed sensibly from the Kuhnian point of view. Because of many similarities, the same conclusion applies to the methodology of scientific research programs (MSRP) ideas of Imre Lakatos. Both periods of debates

were firmly within a given MSRP. Added insight into the debates from the
Lakatosian perspective can be derived by considering the fact that the two debates took place within the different MSRPs of neoclassical theory and
Keynesian analysis. The dominance of these perspectives was effectively
shown in the structural debates by the lack of attention given to those who attempted to frame the structural debates in neoclassical terms. It was clearly
understood during the 1960s debates that the Keynesian view was correct in its
fundamentals, and that the debate was over details of the application of this
vision. This dominance is also shown by the fact that the central ideas of the
prevailing theoretical consensus were not challenged in either dispute. In each
case, the question at issue was whether enough flexibility existed in the system
for expected outcomes to occur. But there was never any serious doubt that the
neoclassical analysis provided the correct perspective in the 1930s debates, or
that the Keynesian vision provided the correct framework in the 1960s disputes.

In terms of the MSRP view, both periods also provide examples of chal-
lenges to an existing research program. The neoclassical and Keynesian
frameworks were used to make predictions about the future that were not coming true. It was the inconsistency between these beliefs and current data trends
that created both periods of debate among economists. If these conflicts between expectations and events had continued, then a challenge to the prevailing
MSRP may have been forthcoming based on this issue. Both series of debates
ended, however, before this could happen.

The MSRP view also provides insight into the transition in the 1940s from
the dominance of neoclassical to Keynesian ideas. As Keynesian ideas became
widely accepted, the problem of the employment impact of technological
change was simply restated in terms of the new framework. By 1950, through
the work of Neisser (1942), Hagen (1942), Lange (1945), Belfer (1946), and Pu
(1949), the transition was completed. The ease with which the technological
change and employment issue was incorporated into the Keynesian view is
more understandable in terms of the evolution from one MSRP to another than
in terms of a Kuhnian revolutionary-science paradigm shift.

The debates also can be discussed from the perspective of Karl Popper's arguments about the importance of falsifiability in the stating and testing of hypotheses. The technological unemployment and structural unemployment debates would seem to provide particularly good examples here. In each case the
standard view was that unemployment would react in a certain way to changes
in the economy. This created the possibility of clearly stating falsifiable hypotheses. The record of the debates in these terms is mixed, however. On the
positive side, it is clear that attempts to test hypotheses dominated the debates.
The common approach in both disputes was to collect the best data available
and use it to defend one's own views and to attack the views of others. Dozens
of tests of the assertions of competing views were published. Most of these
contributions, however, were ineffective in moving the debates toward a conclusion. In the 1930s a major factor creating this impasse was the quality of the
data available. This was still an issue in the 1960s, but more clearly than be-

fore it is evident that the central problem was what was done with the data rather than the data itself. The attitude and general approach economists took in their work, then, at first glance looks good in terms of the criteria of falsifiability, but the results were poor in practice. The problem, as made clear during the debates in methodological comments by Clague, Jerome, and Stern in the 1930s and the theory-based critiques by Lipsey, Gilpatrick, and Perlman in the structural debates, was in the statements of the hypotheses to be tested. Frequently these statements were not accepted as valid by those holding the views that were challenged, or the hypotheses did not relate clearly to the core issues in question. These problems were recognized at the time, and the 1930s methodological studies and 1960s theory-based critiques are evidence in favor of the use of the falsifiability criterion in economics. But these more careful statements of the issues did not dominate the discussions or effectively move the debates toward a resolution.

One dominant aspect of the debates which is not adequately treated by any methodological view is that, on an individual level, there is little evidence that participants in the debates often changed their minds about the issues in dispute. This intransigence—in several cases represented by articles by individual economists dating over decades—explains much about why professional disputes often become intense. This pattern of actions is consistent, however, with the normal science and MSRP perspectives. The commitment implied by these views to a generally accepted theoretical framework would seem to be applicable on the individual as well as the aggregate level.

Recent methodological commentaries by Daniel Hausman and David Colander provide further insights into why economic debates may be characterized more by dogmatism than Bayesian learning from experience.[17] Colander argues that how economics works as a discipline can be explained by applying economic theory to the actions of economists. In particular he emphasizes the fact that economists' utility functions may contain more important variables to them than arriving at the truth of an issue, including, importantly, maximizing the number of their publications in order to keep their university jobs. Colander's economic approach to analyzing economists can be extended to explain economists' dogmatism by using another standard theory tool: benefit-cost analysis. From this perspective, it can be argued that it takes time and energy to write a contribution to a debate. Once a commitment has been made to a conclusion, one's reputation has been put on the line. Backing off or recanting comes at a significant cost. On the other hand, the costs are often quite low of creating a second publication out of the same research—with some luck, a little reworking may even result in a third and a fourth publication out of the same background work. Such benefit-cost stories are easy to tell once Colander's perspective is adopted. The strength of his approach, of course, is that for economists an analysis in economic terms has persuasive power.

Further insight into economists' dogmatism in debate is provided by Daniel Hausman's critique of economists as being too committed to seeing economics as a separate science. This is a mistake, according to Hausman, because it limits what economists do.   Researchers who incorporate into their work ideas from sociology, psychology, political science, anthropology, or other disciplines are seen as not really doing economics and thus their work is discounted.   This practice, according to Hausman, is a serious flaw impeding the progress of economics as a social science.

The technological unemployment and structural unemployment debates, then, have implications for all of the alternative methodological views that have been expressed in recent years.   The fact that the disputes do not provide decisive evidence for one methodological perspective over another would not discourage advocates of any of these positions.   The debates are only two examples, after all, and thus are susceptible to all the criticisms of drawing generalizations from specific cases.   Despite these limitations, however, the debates are suggestive of patterns that characterize economics as a social science both on an aggregative and individual level.

A third reason for reading the history of economic thought is to learn something about how to do economics.   What works best in promoting progress in understanding the economic world is a question of enduring interest.   The technological change and employment debates, of course, are only one example here.   What has worked for this question may not work well for others.   But in this particular history the following statement seems justified about what has had the most effect.   In the technological unemployment and structural unemployment debates, the greatest impact has come from statements by authorities (Douglas [1931], Heller [1961]), from detailed empirical studies that received widespread publicity (Lubin [1929], Knowles and Kalachek [1961]), and from forcefully stated, dogmatically repeated claims (Heller and Killingsworth [1962 on]).   These mark the turning points and stand out as landmarks of the debates.

This conclusion is not a very encouraging guide to doing economics well.   More useful conclusions are possible by taking a different approach.   From the perspective of a thorough reading of the literature—not as a participant but as an observer and an evaluator—what is most convincing?   The answer is clear.   The most compelling contributions were not by authorities and were not forcefully repeated claims, but works that took past contributions into account, that treated other contributions respectfully and tried to present fair statements of all sides, and that based their empirical work carefully in an appropriate (for the time) theoretical context.   Eleanor Gilpatrick's empirical study of the structural unemployment debates and Y. S. Katsoulacos' and Marco Vivarelli's surveys of the theory of technological change and employment are representative examples.   These studies convey a sense of professional integrity and thus command respect for their efforts.[18]

The following chapters provide the details that support this overview of the implications of the technological unemployment and structural unemployment debates.   As a descriptive study of the methodology used by economists, a critical limitation of these chapters should be recognized from the start.   The primary source of information used here is the published literature in the technological unemployment and structural unemployment debates.   This obviously is not a complete record of what went on. It excludes, for example, unpublished work, information about who was friends (or enemies) with whom, memos and letters, and records of informal conversations in university hallways and at conference cocktail parties.[19] A further limitation of the following chapters is that detailed reviews cannot be provided for the dozens of significant contributions to the debates. Thus, in order to tell the story of the debates, a fairly cursory outline of central points has to be made. In this outline, who said what and when is as important as whether what was said was right or wrong.

Three central questions guide this overview of the debates. Where was progress made, and how was it made? How did data and theory contributions interact? And how did individuals act in the debates, by learning from doing or by maintaining a commitment to a particular point of view? Focusing on these questions is intended to provide insight into how economists have acted, in this particular instance, as practitioners of their craft.

The chapters that follow begin this task with a survey of contributions of the classical and neoclassical economists of the nineteenth century. They then proceed to discuss the technological unemployment debates of the 1930s and the structural unemployment debates of the 1960s in detail. A concluding chapter contains final reflections upon the implications of the twentieth-century technological change and employment debates.

As a final comment, the methodology of this study of methodology warrants consideration. What follows is a search for understanding about how economics works as a social science. Recent exchanges between economists about the methodology of the discipline—including, prominently, works by Blaug, Caldwell, Glass and Johnson, McCloskey, Colander, and Hausman—provide its context. Its guiding purpose and structure can be stated in Daniel Hausman's words: "People acquire knowledge, and, to find out how, one must study what they do. There is no presumption that there [is] only one good way to learn. To find out how people have learned and to find out which methods have been successful in which circumstances, one must study what has been done and how well it has worked."[20]

1

The Machinery and Unemployment Debates

Pre-twentieth-century discussions of the relation between technological change and employment were crucial in defining the issues and influencing the course of the 1930s and 1960s debates. As a recognizable phenomenon, technological displacement of labor must date at least to man's first use of the wheel, but as a problem of major interest to economists the issue made its first appearance in the early 1800s. Discussions by economists can be found before this time, but not until the Industrial Revolution was in full bloom in Britain did the issue develop into one attracting widespread attention.[1]

Almost all of the Classical School economists of the early 1800s discussed the issue. The writings of J. B. Say, Simonde de Sismondi, David Ricardo, John Ramsey McCulloch, Thomas Robert Malthus, Nassau Senior, Karl Marx, and John Stuart Mill include detailed analyses, as do the works of many lesser-known economic writers such as Thomas Chalmers, Charles Babbage, John Barton, and Jane Marcet.[2] These early debates are of importance for a study of twentieth-century controversies over the issue for three reasons. First, these discussions developed two major theoretical approaches to argue that technological displacements could only be short run in nature. Second, four major theoretical arguments appeared to argue that technological change could lead to a lasting rise in the aggregate level of unemployment. And third, several key empirical factors were identified that are involved in any attempt to resolve a dispute over the employment impact of technological change. All of these developments were instrumental in molding the course of similar debates more than a century later.

The two major theoretical approaches developed to prove that technological unemployment would only be short run were based on Say's Law and on the wages-fund theory. Say's Law—the notion that supply creates its own demand—was used to argue that a mechanism exists in the economic system that guarantees the automatic reabsorption of any technologically displaced labor.

In his original analysis, Say argued that the use of advanced machinery "does not diminish the amount of product; if it did, it would be absurd to adopt it."[3] By his Law of Markets, then, the very existence of this equal or larger supply creates an equal or larger demand. Since there is no decrease—and most likely an increase—in total demand, Say's Law implies it is only a matter of time before any displaced workers are reemployed. In particular, three ways, which work either individually or in combination, were seen as operating to guarantee that the flow of purchasing power would be undiminished. The cost reductions caused by the technological change would be passed on in price reductions, thus increasing the demand for the product; or, if the elasticity of demand for the product was such that not all the displaced workers were absorbed, the lower prices consumers faced in the affected product would give them more money to spend on other goods; or, if not all cost savings were passed on in cost reductions, the extra profits entrepreneurs received would be used to increase their own consumption or to spend on investment goods. Say himself only argued for the first two of these effects. In a later work, John Ramsey McCulloch gave the Law of Markets theory of automatic reabsorption of technologically displaced workers its strongest classical statement when he argued strongly for all three compensation effects.[4]

The second major early 1800s theoretical argument for beneficial effects of technological change was based on the notion of the wages fund. The Say's Law approach, which guarantees an equal demand for goods after a technological change, is actually in conflict with the classical theory of the demand for labor. It was not demand for goods in the classical system but the volume of circulating capital, called the wages fund, that determined the wages and thus the demand for labor. The ultimate effect of a technological change, then, depended upon its effect on wages through its effect on the volume of circulating capital.

Classical economists who argued along this line of reasoning acknowledged the possibility of net labor displacement, but the chances of it occurring were judged to be extremely unlikely. A major employment difficulty could arise from technological change if new machines were financed out of circulating capital. David Ricardo argued this point in his famous chapter, "On Machinery," in the third edition of his *Principles of Political Economy*.[5] But capital investment was noted to be a relatively slow process, and new fixed capital was held to be financed almost always out of profits or rents. Since the amount of circulating capital was affected only infrequently, the general result was that the wages fund is maintained or increased by technological change, and thus reemployment of displaced workers eventually takes place. Ricardo himself reached this conclusion, and the same line of reasoning is found in works by Say, Mill, and Senior.[6]

The second major area of contribution of the classical discussions to the twentieth-century debates involved the development of theoretical arguments that technological change could indeed lead to a lasting rise in aggregate unemployment. The optimistic compensation theories did not arise in a vacuum.

There was a lively debate over the likely employment impact of technological change during the early 1800s, and the compensation theories were developed in answer to arguments reaching more pessimistic conclusions. The intensity of feeling generated by this issue was illustrated well in letters exchanged between McCulloch and Ricardo after Ricardo retreated from a strong Say's Law approach to a less optimistic wages-fund analysis in the third edition of his *Principles*. McCulloch was astounded by Ricardo's change of mind, and felt Ricardo had damaged the reputation of the science by his actions.[7]

The four major theoretical arguments that held that technological change could lead to a net rise in aggregate unemployment were (a) that there may be a lack of markets for the increased output, (b) that there may be a lack of capital to employ released labor, (c) that the rise in purchasing power from technological change hypothesized by the Say's Law compensation theory would not occur, and (d) that technological change led to a constantly decreasing ratio of circulating to fixed capital. The first two of these arguments were initially stated strongly by Malthus and Sismondi in the early 1800s General Glut controversy.[8] The third was emphasized by Mill and supported by Marx.[9] The fourth was the foundation for Marx's argument that a constantly changing organic structure of capital led to a constantly rising industrial reserve army of the unemployed.[10]

Briefly, these arguments were the following. The lack-of-markets argument was based on the idea that consumer wants could be satiated. Unless foreign markets could be opened—which also eventually would become satiated—there could be a lack of demand for technologically augmented production and workers may not be reemployed.

The lack-of-capital argument held that there would always be some loss in total capital in resource transfers required by adjustments to technological change. In addition, there could be severe time lags in reemploying transferred capital. In the meantime unemployment would result. If technological change were continuous or accelerating, then net unemployment may rise.

The no-rise-in-purchasing-power argument was based, in Mill's words, on recognition of the fact that "demand for commodities is not demand for labour."[11] Contrary to the Say's Law compensation theory, the increase in supply from technological change would not be accompanied by an increase in aggregate purchasing power. The supply of the output would rise, but its price would fall, so that total dollar demand would remain constant. The income increases of those facing lower prices of technologically affected goods would be offset by the income declines of those displaced by the technological change. Aggregate output and demand would continue to be equal, but unemployment would have risen.

The changing-organic-compensation-of-capital argument was based on Marx's claim that technological change constantly increased the ratio of fixed to circulating capital. Since labor demand depended solely on the amount of circulating capital, the demand for labor decreased relative to a rise in total capital. The result was a tendency to increase the level of unemployment.

The final area in which the classical debates previewed later discussions involved the identification of several major empirical questions that needed to be answered in any dispute over the issue. The initial displacement impact of technological changes was recognized as a key unknown.[12] The speed of technological innovation and diffusion was raised as an issue.[13] The ultimate disemployment impact as determined by the elasticity of demand of affected products was seen as a major factor.[14] The important role of occupational or geographic mobility was discussed.[15] The implications of possible skill effects of technological changes were mentioned.[16]

Despite the recognition of the importance of these empirical questions, however, the analyses of all the classical economists were primarily deductive. The only empirical evidence used in the machinery and unemployment debates was in a few brief references to the widely known historical experience of the cotton textile and related industries. At the time, detailed statistical evidence simply was not available to make convincing arguments in answer to the empirical questions raised, and as a result the debates that took place were concerned mainly with disputes over assumptions and details of deductive analysis.

After 1870 the nature of professional discussions about technological change and employment changed. In effect, the problem disappeared as a concern to economists. Discussion and analysis of the myriad effects of technological change continued to be an important topic, but because the general upward trends in investment, production, employment, and living standards were supported by evidence that could not be denied, the employment effects of technological change ceased to be seen as a relevant problem.

A common theme in economic treatises of the late 1800s became that trends over recent decades, in spite of dramatic technological advances and serious cyclical fluctuations, had been in general favorable to laborers. Looking at widely read works of the time in the United States, it is not difficult to find examples of this view. Arthur Hadley, for example, found that "machinery has not displaced labor. On the contrary, there has been a conspicuous increase of employment in those lines where improvements in machinery have been greatest."[17] Arthur Perry found that "as a matter of fact and experience, it has not been found true that the introduction of improved processes, the substitution of Nature's forces for human muscle, has deteriorated the condition of laborers generally. Exactly the reverse has usually taken place."[18] David Wells, in his comments on recent technological advances, found that "in the United States there is little evidence thus far that labor has been disturbed or distressed to any great extent from this cause."[19]

In the face of recent favorable trends, professional discussion of the unemployment impact of technological change in the late 1800s was limited. John Shield Nicholson published two editions of a small book on *The Effects of Machinery on Wages* that emphasized the negative side of the question.[20] But Nicholson was almost alone.

Despite the lack of concern about the employment effects of technological change after the mid-1800s, economics did experience two major developments that had significant influence on later discussions of the issue. These developments were the first scientific analysis of unemployment as a separate issue of economic interest, and the use of marginal analysis to provide a new theory to explain the automatic reabsorption of technologically displaced labor.

The beginning of analysis of unemployment as a distinct issue of scientific interest came in the years around the turn of the century. Writing on unemployment in 1894 and looking at the state of current knowledge, Sidney Webb concluded that, "I fear that if we were given full power to-morrow to deal with the unemployment all over England we should find ourselves hard put to it how to solve the problem."[21] Writing in 1909, however, Webb found that the "problem is now soluble, theoretically at once, and practically as soon as we care to solve it."[22] What had happened in the fifteen-year period between Webb's comments was that an impressive structure of studies of unemployment had been built, to be capped in 1909 by William H. Beveridge's classic study entitled *Unemployment: A Problem of Industry.*[23] The theory of unemployment before this time, generally accepted by the public and professional economists alike, held that individual unemployment was due to personal faults, and that ability and willingness to work would always guarantee employment. The contribution of Beveridge and other interested social scientists at the turn of the century was to debunk this theory and to replace it with a scientific analysis of the causes of unemployment. By the 1920s a large body of literature existed for each of the various causes and cures that had been proposed for unemployment, and the resulting interest in the subject, in conjunction with the increasing empirical orientation of economics in general, motivated the first efforts at the collection of detailed current employment statistics.

The second important late 1800s development relevant to later discussions of technological change and employment was the development of marginal analysis. In its application to questions of employment and technological change, neoclassical theory provided a third approach, in addition to the classical Say's Law and wages-fund theories, to explain why technologically displaced workers would soon be reemployed. As developed by Alfred Marshall, John Bates Clark, the Austrians, and the Lausanne School, neoclassical theory took full employment as the characteristic equilibrium condition of an economy and viewed technological change as one factor among many that may disturb that equilibrium.[24] Like all disturbances, technological change was seen as setting in motion price adjustments that guaranteed a new full employment equilibrium. These price adjustments, operating on the principle of substitution and the search for best methods of production, took care of the four major classical reemployment problems that had disturbed Ricardo, Mill, Marx, Malthus, and others. The movement of commodity prices, on the one hand, took care of all problems connected with a lack of markets. Changes of relative factor prices, on the other, assured that no long-run unemployment could take place due to a lack of capital or because of a constant level of purchasing power after technological changes. The Marxian decline-in-circulating-capital argument was held to be simply wrong and irrelevant.

In discussing the relevance of the theory of reabsorption based on neoclassical analysis, Joseph Schumpeter was later led to comment that "the controversy that went on throughout the nineteenth century and beyond, mainly in the form of argument pro and con 'compensation,' is dead and buried. . . . It vanished from the scene as a better technique filtered into general use which left nothing to disagree about."[25]

Up to the 1920s, the optimistic conclusions of neoclassical theory, in conjunction with continuing confidence in long-run trends in production, investment, and employment, reduced professional concern about the employment effects of technological change almost to nonexistence.

2

Origin of the Technological
Unemployment Debates

The beginnings of the technological unemployment debates of the 1930s can be traced clearly in the popular and professional literature of the late 1920s. The issue of technological unemployment arose because of two events: the publication of the first comprehensive productivity data in the United States in 1926–27 and the onset of a recession in 1927. No other factor had equal importance in the initial identification of the issue.

Through the early 1920s there is little evidence of any popular or professional concern with the employment effects of technological change. A few isolated articles considering the topic appeared. The most notable of these from a professional point of view was a series of studies of the impact of technological change in specific industries by George E. Barnett. Such studies had appeared periodically for years and were a reflection of the inherent interest in the topic in an economy open to continuous technological transformation. But there was no suggestion in this early 1920s work of anything more than a continuation of past endemic concerns similar to those reflected in J. S. Nicholson's books in the late 1800s.[1]

Widespread concern over technological unemployment emerged only after the publication in late 1926 and early 1927 of the first good productivity data in the United States. These data appeared in three separate studies by the Bureau of Labor Statistics (BLS), the Bureau of the Census, and the Bureau of Foreign and Domestic Commerce.[2] The motivation for these first productivity studies had nothing to do with unemployment concerns about technological change. Rather, reasons for labor losses besides turnover or absenteeism, and the question of factors affecting the trend of real wages, were the main issues stimulating attempts to produce good productivity data. The fact that the American Federation of Labor at its convention in 1925 adopted a "new wage policy" of tying wage demands to productivity also was a factor cited by the BLS as a reason for beginning its productivity studies.[3] The novelty of these data in the mid-1920s is indicated by the fact that the Bureau of Labor Statistics reported that up to mid-1922 it had "never heretofore made output per man per hour the subject of special investigations."[4] Another sign of the newly developing interest in productivity data is that the Census data as originally reported included only separate output and employment series. The obvious output-per-worker ratios were not derived. The BLS, however, quickly exploited this new source of information and in a June 1927 *Monthly Labor Review* article combined the two Census sources into a productivity series.[5]

The results of these first productivity studies were dramatic. The numbers suggested that there had been enormous productivity advances just since the end of World War I. The BLS data indicated a rise in labor productivity in manufacturing from 1919 to 1925 of 59 percent. The Census and Commerce data showed increases of 40 percent and 41 percent over a similar period. The Commerce data also showed productivity increases of 9 percent in railroads, 27 percent in mining, and 18 percent in agriculture.

These results were startling even to the authors of the studies. Ewan Clague, who supervised the BLS work, wrote that

many people today are aware of the fact that great improvements in machinery, processes, management, and output are taking place; but, except for a few magazine articles from time to time, very little has been done to express this advance in productive efficiency in comprehensive terms. Some people have hesitated to accept as typical of industrial production as a whole the surprising figures of improved output in particular plants or establishments. And yet, even when we deal in mass figures, the facts stand out clearly and unmistakably. We are at the present time experiencing what is perhaps the most remarkable advance in productive efficiency in the history of the modern industrial system.[6]

General productivity trends were the main focus of analysis in these three statistical papers. A breakdown of the productivity data into its employment and output components, however, revealed other significant trends. The Commerce data, with a base of 1918–20 = 100, showed in 1924–26 employment in manufacturing at 91.5, employment in mining at 100, employment in agriculture at 95, and employment in railways at 91.5. The BLS employment index had manufacturing at 92 in 1926 compared to 110 in 1920. The Federal Reserve Board's (FRB) employment index had manufacturing at 92 in 1926 compared to 99 in 1920.

The apparent association of rapid productivity advances with employment declines almost immediately led to the stirring of popular concern about a problem of technological unemployment. In January 1927, before the publication of the Commerce and Census data and just after the first publication of the BLS data, an article appeared in *Nation's Business,* asking "Need We Be Afraid of a Job Famine?" Also in January 1927, Secretary of Labor James J. Davis was quoted as claiming that there was a danger of lack of employment due to the rapid adoption of new techniques of production.[7]

Shortly thereafter, in mid-1927, the United States entered a recession. The resulting dip in employment served to raise popular technological change concerns further. A September 1927 *Nation's Business* article, written to follow up the January article, reported that the editor had received mail from all over the United States arguing various points of view on the issue. In his Labor Day message of 1927, Secretary Davis again repeated his concern about labor displacement problems in a speech that was widely reported in labor, business, and popular periodicals.[8]

By the winter of 1927–28, then, the question of technological unemployment had become a major popular issue in the United States. An October 1927 editorial in the *New Republic*, for example, reviewed recent indexes of employment and productivity and claimed that the tendency for employment to decline "was marked even before there was any falling off in the indices of output itself. . . . Now that production itself is slackening, more unemployment results, and a vicious circle is begun. . . . Reports from various sources indicate that there is a large and growing number of genuinely unemployed." An early 1928 editorial in the *Journal of Commerce* claimed that "this country has upon its hands a problem of chronic unemployment, likely to grow worse rather than better. Business prosperity, far from curing it, may tend to aggravate it by stimulating invention and encouraging all sorts of industrial rationalization schemes." A January 1928 article in the *Railroad Trainman* claimed that "the rapid development of machinery in the past few years has thrown so many men and women out of employment that it is impossible for other employments to absorb them. As a result in what is regarded as among the most prosperous periods in the history of the United States there are thousands of men and women heretofore gainfully employed who are walking the streets in search of a job." Lewis Corey in a March 1928 article in the *Annalist* concluded that "the bulk of [current] unemployment is the result of improved technology." It is an "unemployment developing gradually, almost unawares, like creeping paralysis, in the midst of unprecedented prosperity, the by-product of improved technological efficiency." Corey stated succinctly the facts that had to be accounted for. "Between 1910 and 1920 there was an increase of 3,500,000 in the gainfully occupied, 3,000,000 of whom were absorbed in manufacturing, transportation and mining. But since 1919 these industries, instead of absorbing other workers, developed 1,200,000 surplus workers of their own." By mid-1928 the concept of technological unemployment was firmly entrenched in the public mind.[9]

With the onset of recovery from recession in mid-1928 the issue of technological unemployment faded as a popular concern. It did not disappear, however. Regular popular contributions continued to appear throughout the months leading to the Great Depression.[10] The trends noted in the first major productivity studies held firm, with the index of manufacturing employment in 1928, for example, at 87 in FRB data and 87 in BLS data (1918–20 = 100).

Most of the articles already noted were on the alarmist side of the issue. An equally large number appeared on the optimistic side.[11] None of this was particularly new. Popular concerns about the employment effects of technological change had arisen periodically for decades. In none of the post-1850 decades, however, had professional economists become more than tangentially involved in these discussions. The 1920s technological unemployment debates turned out to be different. By 1930 several professional analyses of the issue had been written, and a series of debates that were to last through the depression had begun.

The reason why the late 1920s popular debates over technological unemployment led to professional involvement is that the productivity studies of 1926–27 that were the primary foundation of the popular debates suggested trends that did not conform with generally accepted economic thought about the employment impact of technological change. The heritage of the past one hundred years of economic ideas had been to believe that the long-run employment effects of technological change would be positive. Short-run problems of adjustment could well exist. However, adjustment would take place. No net unemployment would occur.

This was clearly the dominant professional view in the late 1920s—as it had been since the 1820s, and as it is today. The best data on recent trends in the late 1920s, however, did not support this sanguine view. The result was a tension between expectations and current trends that soon involved economists. Some economists tried to explain why expectations and current data did not conform by noting the limitations of existing data. Some tried to show that there was nothing to worry about by using other data besides the three major productivity series. Others, however, had less confidence in the standard optimistic view, and supported the negative implications of the three productivity studies' data trends. The net effect was the beginning of a professional debate over the issue of technological unemployment.

Professional analysis of the new productivity data began soon after its publication. Analyses in 1927 included studies by Paul Douglas, Rexford Tugwell, E. Dana Durand, Woodlief Thomas, Sumner Slichter, and John D. Black.[12] The dramatic nature of the data was noted clearly in these discussions. Paul Douglas, for example, concluded that "the past six years have witnessed in this country the most extraordinary increase in per capita productivity in manufacturing and mining which has probably ever occurred in a similar space of time."[13] Rexford Tugwell wrote that "with all this data at our command, to say nothing of the evidence of observation open to anyone familiar with manufacturing and commerce, does it seem an exaggeration to say that we are in the midst of a new industrial revolution?"[14]

In none of these first 1927 studies, however, were the unemployment or employment effects of technological change given more than passing notice. Woodlief Thomas and Rexford Tugwell did not mention employment problems at all in their work. Their sole concern was to present the data and to try to discover the causes of the rapid productivity advance. The few employment comments in other papers were brief and optimistic.[15] A typical reaction was that the employment data in the three productivity studies were misleading because only the four sectors of agriculture, manufacturing, railroads, and mining were covered. John D. Black, for example, in a December 1927 discussion claimed that "it is hard to believe that there was an actual decrease of 7 per cent in the number of workers in agriculture, manufacturing, mining and railway transportation in this short period [1920–25]. . . . But, of course, it is entirely possible that the 7 per cent have been absorbed by the expansion in construction, in transportation other than railroads, and in retailing and other forms of merchandising." In support of this argument, Black offered the evidence of a likely continuation of rising trends in Census of Occupations categories that were evident from 1880 to 1920, and "common observation" of the recent rise in the number of service-related occupations in the economy.[16]

These comments were the limit of economists' concern with the employment implications of recent technological change in 1927. In 1928, however, they began to pay attention to the rising popular concern about technological unemployment. The transition from a lack of interest in the issue was a gradual one. A group of papers on productivity trends, for example, by Paul Douglas, Sumner Slichter, George Soule, and R. P. Flakner at a February 1928 American Statistical Association meeting ignored employment problems. In a criticism of these papers, however, John R. Commons claimed that the crucial factor in recent technological trends was the number of people unemployed, and that any analysis which ignored the employment problem was not telling the most important part of the story.[17]

The timing of Commons' critique was significant because it was not long afterward that professional articles approaching the technological unemployment issue began to appear. These articles took two approaches. One group was aimed at a popular audience and at current popular concerns over technological unemployment. These articles appeared in popular journals. The second group was aimed primarily at a professional audience. The approach in this second group was to critique recent data in detail. Both kinds of articles appeared throughout 1928 and 1929, with the professionally oriented articles becoming more prevalent as time passed. Both kinds of articles displayed the tension between the negative evidence of the best data and the generally accepted optimistic view about the beneficial effects of technological change.

Looking at the popular-oriented articles first, most economists who opted for this approach attempted to show that the long-run effects of technological change would be positive. When they got down to examining the recent evidence, however, they had difficulty in explaining the issue away in a convincing fashion. Almost every popular-audience writer was led to conclude that recent trends were indeed pessimistic.

One of the more pessimistic evaluations of recent trends, for example, was made by Sumner Slichter in a February 1928 article. Slichter claimed that "far more important than the cyclical drop in production has been the steadily increasing efficiency of techniques. . . . *The present [unemployment] situation is not primarily the product of cyclical causes.*" Slichter, in examining the evidence of recent BLS and Interstate Commerce Commission (ICC) employment data and FRB employment and output indexes, concluded that "we are confronted with an extremely grave problem—the problem of reducing the cost of technical progress. We are obtaining more and better equipment only at the price of a heavy investment in unemployment and human misery."[18]

An April 1928 article by Irving Fisher provides a similar example. Fisher gave a strong case for the long-run benefits of technological change and argued that monetary factors were primary causes behind current employment problems. But, like Slichter, Fisher was led to conclude that "increased productivity per worker, aided by improved machinery and organization and more willing labor, is partly responsible for the anomaly of growing unemployment during an extended period of increased business activity." The reason Fisher gave for this conclusion was, simply, that "the best available statistics seem to agree with this finding."[19]

Other examples are provided in 1929 popular analyses by Ewan Clague, William Leiserson, and W. Jett Lauck. Using BLS and Commerce productivity data as his primary sources, Clague was led to conclude that "if inventions and improved processes spread faster than the workers can adjust to them, then it is clear that jobs are being destroyed faster than new jobs are being created. The rate of invention is greater than the rate of adjustment. . . . This undoubtedly describes the situation in the United States during the past five years."[20] Leiserson found after a review of recent trends that "as long as conditions make the drive for efficiency and reduced costs necessary, and it is accompanied by technological and managerial improvements such as have marked the last five years, we may expect the same tendency to continue—increasing unemployment with increasing prosperity."[21] After a similar review of recent data, Lauck found that "early in the year 1928, it became evident that full and regular employment for industrial workers was the most vital problem which had developed from the new era of industrial efficiency and unprecedented prosperity. . . . It soon was apparent that this unusual unemployment situation was the result of mass production and the unprecedented mechanization of industry during recent years."[22]

A final example is provided in a September 1929 article by Wesley C. Mitchell. Mitchell made every effort to set a positive tone in his analysis, with the title of his article being "Machines Make Jobs." Basing his analysis on research reports in the National Bureau of Economic Research (NBER) book entitled *Recent Economic Changes*, Mitchell claimed that there is "a marked trend toward elimination of unemployment, and there is no reason to believe this trend will not continue." The only support he gave for this claim, however, was his belief that "the rate of [technological] change will be slower at least for a time," and that "the decline in the birthrate, limited immigration [and] the natural expansion of business, are factors that should help to narrow the gap between jobs and workers." Despite this optimistic prediction, Mitchell concluded that recent data did show that "so far the number of new jobs had lagged behind the number of jobs wiped out. It probably will continue to lag. . . . We have no guarantee that the new jobs created will correspond in exact number and timing to the jobs eliminated. We may have not inconsiderable periods of unemployment on as large a scale as ever in the past."[23]

As is clear from this sample of professional reviews of recent data trends, economists' popular-reply efforts in 1928–29 to set a positive note and to downplay fears of technological unemployment were not completely successful. It was widely felt, as William Leiserson noted, that "the remedies for this and other kinds of unemployment are now well known."[24] Detailed proposals for programs such as unemployment insurance, national employment offices, old-age pensions, and retraining programs were made by all economists who wrote on the issue. But as evidenced by continuing popular concern with the issue, success in dispelling popular fears was limited.

The fact that the quality of economic analysis in these popular articles was at times poor did not help. At one point Ewan Clague came close to advocating universal monopoly to control problems of overproduction. In another, Clague seemed to be arguing that there was only so much work to do in the economy.[25] Sumner Slichter at one point implied that only one-third of the Say's Law analysis of labor reabsorption applied in the modern world.[26] Despite these deficiencies—or perhaps because of them—the results of these popular articles had the effect of motivating a more detailed professional look at the problem.

In the articles that took a more professionally oriented approach to the issue in the late 1920s, the same conflict between data and expectations is evident. The data did show a fall in employment in four major sectors and a coincident rapid rise in productivity. But a simplistic linking of these two trends in a cause-effect explanation—as was done in the popular debates—was not acceptable to most economists and led several of them to consider the problem in more detail.

The first professional attack on the question involved attempts to prove that workers were being rapidly absorbed in sectors other than the four that showed employment declines. This view was widely expressed, but as indicated in J. D. Black's December 1927 paper on the issue, through 1927 the argument rested almost totally on casual empiricism and the extrapolation of decennial Census of Occupations trends evident from 1880 through 1920. The only current employment series available in the United States through 1927 were for the manufacturing, agriculture, mining, and railroad sectors, and all these series showed declining employment since 1920.[27] Because of the lack of specific supporting information, the argument for rapid labor reabsorption was a controversial one.[28]

In response to this lack of concrete information, in mid-1928 Lawrence Mann of the Department of Commerce undertook an investigation of recent employment flows among occupations. After updating decennial occupations data through 1927, the Commerce study reached the conclusion that "there has been an increase of over 2,800,000 workers engaged in transportation, distribution, professional service, and personal service as compared with a decrease of about 2,000,000 in agriculture, mining, manufacturing and United States government service." In addition, the study concluded that "it is probable that there have also been large gains in employment in a number of other industries for which it is impossible to make estimates."[29]

This seeming confirmation of the fact of rapid labor reabsorption received wide publicity, and the Commerce data were soon repeated in popular articles on the issue.[30] There were, however, problems with the Commerce study. Data sources for 1927 were at best incomplete, and later versions of the same study consistently revised the positive job-creation gap downwards. In a 1929 article, for example, Mann claimed only a 2,500,000 instead of a 2,800,000 increase in the number of jobs in growing industries, as opposed to declining employment in other industries "by a somewhat smaller number."[31] Even more significantly, no account was taken in the report of the fact that the labor force had grown by an estimated three to five million workers over the same period.

The inadequacies of the Commerce study, and its rapid circulation as confirmation of the argument for rapid labor reabsorption, soon led to professional economic comment. The most notable response was by the Brookings Institution. When asked by the Senate Committee on Education and Labor in mid-1928 to undertake a study of the current unemployment problem, the Institution decided on an investigation responding directly to the Commerce occupations-flow study. According to Isador Lubin, director of the Brookings study, the Commerce investigation claimed

that the "newer" industries had in fact taken on more workers between 1920 and 1927 than had been discharged by manufacturing and agriculture. The conclusion arrived at was to the effect that industry had been absorbing the discharged workers and that labor had reached the state where it was sufficiently mobile to move easily from one line of economic activity to another. Under these circumstances, it seemed that prevailing estimates of unemployment might be too large. The Institute accordingly undertook to make a survey of dispossessed workers in order to see just how many dispossessed laborers were being absorbed by American industry.[32]

At almost the same time, other economists were led by similar considerations to begin their own investigations of the technologically displaced. By December 1929 results of displaced worker studies were available by Lubin and by Robert J. Myers.[33]

Although different in details of organization, the Lubin and Myers studies were both in the tradition of the earlier case study work by George E. Barnett. The Lubin study, for example, covered 754 technologically displaced workers from a wide variety of industries and occupations in three cities. The Myers study covered 370 skilled cutters displaced from the Chicago men's clothing industry. Both studies reported very similar results. In each case it was found that workers experienced a considerable period of unemployment, with the time lost averaging between four and six months. There were also a significant number of workers who were unemployed for more than a year, and since a considerable number were still unemployed at the time of the surveys, not all of the losses due to unemployment had been recorded. Of those who did find work, about half experienced a cut in income. It was also found that younger and, especially, older workers suffered the greatest hardships.

The results of the displaced worker studies were conclusive in demonstrating that a significant unemployment problem did exist—at least for some technologically displaced workers. No one questioned this aspect of the results. As with all case studies, however, whether these results were indicative of a widespread or growing technological unemployment problem was not clear. These same data were eventually used by advocates of both sides of longer-run questions to support arguments for both eventual reemployment and for lengthy unemployment. That the data could be slanted in either direction was clear even from different presentations of the Brookings results by Isador Lubin. In a December 1928 paper Lubin took a distinctly positive approach. In contrast, in his mid-1929 official Brookings paper, Lubin's conclusions almost all emphasized the negative side.[34]

The attempt, then, to resolve the expectations-versus-data conflict caused by the 1926–27 productivity studies by doing further empirical studies led to an impasse. The newly collected data were not good enough to counter the pessimistic productivity study trends or long-run enough to counter the optimistic general attitude about the impact of technological change.

A second major professional approach to the issue in the late 1920s also had little success. Analyses taking this approach used already-collected data and attempted to include the recent productivity and employment trends as part of a larger interpretation of recent economic change. The most notable work in this respect was done in the NBER-sponsored surveys included in the 1929 two-volume work *Recent Economic Changes* and in a 1928 article by Sumner Slichter.[35]

Recent Economic Changes was an outgrowth of the continuing work of the President's Conference on Unemployment of 1921. The goal of the 1929 report was to survey the economy as a whole and to describe the major developments that had taken place since World War I.[36] The various surveys, each concerned with a limited area and written by a noted expert, focused on reporting recent facts and drew few conclusions from recent trends. Nonetheless, the theme of the impact of recent technological change appeared repeatedly. In all the reports, the dramatic rise in productivity since 1919 as recorded in the new productivity studies was taken as an unquestioned fact. In general, however, and in conformance with the usual theme of contemporary popular comments by economists, an optimistic view was taken of the relative importance of these advances in creating an unemployment problem. Dexter Kimball, for example, emphasized that there was "nothing new" in the present situation. Henry Dennison claimed that although "the *rate* of change may now be such as to introduce new considerations and demand new measures," he found "no immediately pressing problem of this sort." Wesley Mitchell emphasized the broad results of the past century which demonstrated that "'labor-saving' machinery has turned out to be job-making machinery." Mitchell also noted, however, that a careful look at the best data available showed that since 1920 "the supply of new jobs has not been equal to the number of new workers plus old workers displaced."[37]

The sum of views in *Recent Economic Changes* was to repeat the traditional analysis that although productivity advances had been dramatic and hardships had occurred, there was nothing fundamentally to be concerned about. The analysis provided by Sumner Slichter in a paper presented at the December 1928 American Economic Association convention argued this same point. Slichter, however, had his own distinctive reasons for drawing this conclusion. In a detailed empirical analysis of the past decade, Slichter claimed that demand shifts and perverse factor price movements were primarily responsible for the current chronic unemployment. With respect to recent technological change, Slichter claimed that "the relationship between labor's productivity and its displacement is more indirect and more complicated than many commentators assume." He argued that BLS productivity index studies and the Day-Thomas Census data series showed no significant relation between rapid productivity advance and employment declines. Rather, he found a close relation between employment declines and market declines which accounted for the major share of the shrinkage of employment in the manufacturing, mining, railroad, and agricultural sectors. In addition, Slichter claimed that recent displacements of workers had been due to the fact that, since 1920, the relative movements of wages, producer-goods prices, and long-term interest rates had "made it profitable for employers to shift to a combination of productive factors which involves the use of more capital and less labor." This disemployment effect had spread across all industries. Slichter also reaffirmed his belief in the Say's Law analysis of released purchasing power which proved that it is impossible for displaced workers not to be absorbed eventually. To date, however, Slichter admitted that "the impossible has apparently occurred" and reemployment has not taken place. Slichter explained this anomaly by claiming that recent shifts in consumer demands had been toward goods that also require more capital-intensive production. As a result, Slichter concluded that the final impact of recent technological changes had been not so much a cause of the current unemployment situation as an exacerbating factor to more fundamental causes simultaneously at work.[38]

The overall status of professional-oriented analysis as illustrated in these articles was little different from that achieved by current popular-oriented professional articles. The general opinion was one of long-run optimism. Yet no one could demonstrate that the current data trends were illusory. The major support economists had for their optimism was that the evidence used to argue for growing technological unemployment simply was not reliable. At the time, the sources available for a careful study of technological unemployment were extremely limited. There were no good unemployment data (estimates of unemployment in early 1928 ranged from 3.0 to 5.8 million), and the state of employment data was not much better. The story was nearly identical for production data. Statistics were available for only a few sectors. All current output indexes dated from after 1920, and all of these were thoroughly revised in the late 1920s. By 1930 rough national income data were available only through 1925. With respect to productivity, the major sources were the three government studies of 1926–27, all of which were severely limited with respect to length and breadth of coverage.

The effect of professional work in 1927–29, then, was to add little to a careful understanding of the recent relation between technological change and employment. A few good points were made. The Mann, Lubin, and Myers studies were excellent attempts to attack the issue directly through original data collections. The Slichter argument—that a study of trends industry-by-industry showed that output changes and not productivity changes were the key to employment changes—also was well taken. Other major arguments, however, including Slichter's that changes in tastes were the main problem, Mitchell's that technological change would be less rapid in the future, and Dennison's that product invention would soon outpace process invention, were not very convincing or reassuring reasons to believe that things would get better.[39] At base the problem for economists in their 1928–29 analyses was one of a conflict between evidence and expectations. By tradition and several decades of past experience, expectations were optimistic, yet at the moment data trends did not support these beliefs. The general view was that things would get better and that traditional expectations of labor reabsorption would soon be reaffirmed. Before this could happen, however, the Great Depression began.

3

Theoretical Disputes in the Technological Unemployment Debates

By the start of the depression, little progress had been made by economists toward resolving the technological unemployment issue. Analyses of existing data were inconclusive, and collections of new data had added little. In the first years of the depression both of these kinds of professional work were given increasing attention, and new directions of analysis were begun. The question of technological unemployment, of course, was not the major concern during the 1930s. The issues of recovery and relief were of first importance to everyone. But technological unemployment remained a lively subsidiary issue among the greater concerns, and a large number of popular and professional discussions of the issue appeared.[1]

A brief review of some contributions on the popular side of the issue will illustrate the concern generated by the technological unemployment issue throughout the 1930s. An early depression popular review of all current employment, output, and productivity data by Michael Scheler, for example, concluded that "these facts prove that the machine, taking all favorable factors into consideration, steadily displaces more men and women than industries old and new, can absorb." Harry Laidler, in a similar early depression review, concluded that recent data showed that "the net result has been a decrease in demand for workers in proportion to the supply and a consequent increase in unemployment." Organized labor also drew attention to the issue during the depression. According to testimony by William Green early in 1930, "normal" unemployment had risen to a level of 9 percent in 1928–29 "during this intense period of machine displacement and technological unemployment." Green claimed that technological unemployment had become endemic in the economy and was a significant part of the depression unemployment. To L. E. Keller, also writing in 1930, recent technological changes had created a situation where "we now have a serious unemployment problem even in times of prosperity which is only intensified by industrial depression." Writing in May

1930, Theodore Knappen found that up until 1927 jobs in new industries were created at about the same rate as they were destroyed in old industries, but "in the recent past, the tide has changed. The machine is now increasingly building up a surplus of labor and a deficit of employment. . . . The robots are rolling up a permanent surplus of labor, a perpetual roll of unemployment." By 1931, then, the long-run aggregate unemployment impact of technological change was a well-developed popular issue. As a 1931 Senate report concluded, "the real issue is not whether technological displacement causes workers to lose their jobs. It undoubtedly does. The real issue is whether over a period of years the continual introduction of new and improved machines and processes is causing a total net increase or decrease in mass employment. . . . On this issue there are two opposing points of view, each held by large numbers of earnest people."[2]

These concerns were heard throughout the depression. In the early 1930s, suggestions were made for a moratorium on technological change through a holding action by the patent office. The rise of Technocracy in 1932, with its emphasis on the issue of technological unemployment, became a famous episode in American social history. Particularly radical views were expressed by a mid-1930s movement to tax machinery.[3] The National Organization for the Taxation of Labor-Saving Devices, although never a significant voice in anybody's politics, was the strongest lobby in this movement. As late as 1939 proposals to tax machines were introduced in both the U.S. House and Senate.

The strongest positions on the optimistic side of the technological unemployment issue were taken, predictably, by organizations of manufacturers. The National Industrial Conference Board (NICB), especially in the writing of its president Magnus Alexander, continued the opposition to all claims for widespread technological unemployment that it had begun in 1928–29.[4] The NICB presented one of the most detailed popular literature attacks of the entire decade on technological unemployment arguments in its 1935 book entitled *Machinery, Employment and Purchasing Power*. Other interested groups took similar positions. The Machinery and Allied Products Institute, for example, published a series of short pamphlets on technology and employment in 1936 and 1937.[5]

Almost any selection from the popular periodical or labor literature of the 1930s will include an article or two on the unemployment impact of technological change. This literature is interesting in itself and conveys well the concerns and fears of the time. What is relevant here, however, is that it was a background factor in continuing professional discussions of the issue.

During the period that these popular debates were going on, more than sixty significant contributions were made to the professional literature concerning technological unemployment. The empirical aproaches begun in the late 1920s were expanded, and beginning in 1930 a new direction was taken. A distinct theoretical literature developed, which received regular contributions until the 1940s.

The initial contributions to the theoretical literature were in 1930 articles by Paul Douglas and Willford King.[6] The King and Douglas papers both were directed primarily at a popular audience and presented fundamentally the same views. Douglas' more detailed paper, however, had the distinction of leading to a series of replies by other economists, and the entire series of theoretical debates that followed can be traced to Douglas' contribution.

Douglas' analysis was published in the American Federation of Labor journal *The American Federationist* in August 1930. Douglas was writing specifically to question "the common belief . . . that improvements in technology and in administration do throw men permanently out of work." He acknowledged that recent employment and productivity data "seem on the surface to lend support to these views," but he claimed that a full treatment of the longer-run question was necessary before any reasonable conclusions could be drawn. To do this, Douglas used a modernized version of the Say's Law argument for labor reabsorption. In his analysis, Douglas first assumed a situation where all cost savings are passed along in price decreases. He then considered the various cases of elastic, unitary-elastic, and inelastic demand, and analyzed what would happen to consumer purchasing power in each situation. The cases of elastic and unitary-elastic demand provided no employment problem, so Douglas directed the bulk of his attention to the possibility of inelastic demand. Here he found a case "which apparently confirms the contention of those who urge that industrial advance causes technological unemployment." But Douglas found that a careful analysis showed that there was little to fear. According to Douglas, consumers would buy less in total dollar demand of the affected product, but now they would have extra dollars which they would either spend or save. If they spent the money, demand for other goods would rise; if they saved it, the bank would invest it and it would be spent on capital goods. In the end, "not only are new opportunities for employment built up . . . as the old opportunities shrink, but they are built up to an equal degree to that by which the older opportunities decay. For every man laid off a new job has been created somewhere, and the ratio between monetary purchases and employment is still the same as before." Douglas thus concluded that "in the long run, therefore, the improved machinery and greater efficiency of management do not throw workers permanently out of employment nor create permanent technological unemployment."[7]

Douglas' addressing the issue in terms of concepts more associated with Classical School economics than with the Neoclassical School seems an odd one. Yet this version of the Say's Law compensation argument was the most widely accepted theoretical approach taken by economists in 1930. It was not the only one that could be found; alternative approaches, however, were only of secondary importance.[8] There was a near-unanimous acceptance of the Say-Douglas analysis as adequately explaining the economic mechanisms at work.

This conclusion is illustrated well by several contributions presented at a December 1930 symposium on technological unemployment sponsored by the American Association for Adult Education. This group of papers is significant in that it identifies economists who were recognized as important participants in contemporary professional discussions of the issue, and because it reflects the state of professional thought on the issue at the end of 1930. Papers were solicited before the symposium from non-participants Paul Douglas, Elizabeth Baker, Isador Lubin, Rexford Tugwell, and Charles Beard. Sumner Slichter contributed an additional paper at the meeting.

The paper presented by Douglas to the symposium was a considerably shortened version of his earlier *American Federationist* paper. No new points were added to Douglas' analysis.

Rexford Tugwell's contributed paper was also theoretical. Tugwell's position, however, was as a critic of accepted economic theories of the automatic reabsorption of technologically displaced workers. According to Tugwell, the Say's Law formula to explain away the problem of technological unemployment depended crucially on the assumption of free competition. In his view, the acceptance of "so questionable a fact . . . caused a neglect of damaging evidence for which we are now beginning to pay." Tugwell felt, therefore, that there were "serious reservations to be made to the conception of automatic operation of the economist's formula."[9]

Sumner Slichter's paper at the symposium also was mainly theoretical. In it Slichter presented an analysis similar to his March 1929 *American Economic Review* article. In this article, Slichter specifically attacked the idea that technological change was a major cause of recent unemployment. Slichter felt that there was no doubt that the 40 percent rise in manufacturing productivity and the 9 percent rise in agricultural productivity from 1919 to 1929 "has had something to do with the shrinkage of employment in those industries. . . . But this is not the whole story. In fact, it is hardly half of it." Slichter presented his 1929 argument about taste changes and recent perverse price shifts to support this contention. He claimed that "every economist will maintain that labor-saving devices do not permanently reduce the volume of employment. No one can read the history of the nineteenth century and doubt that economists are right" in this analysis.[10]

As indicated by these analyses, by the end of 1930 the traditional optimism of economists about the impact of technological change had been reinforced through theoretical analysis of the problem. There was wide agreement that the classical Say's Law absorption argument provided the correct approach. Even Tugwell, who disagreed with this theory, acknowledged its preeminence. This general agreement held firm through 1930. It was not to last, however.

New directions in the theoretical literature began to appear in the summer of 1931. Between mid-1931 and late 1933 a dozen significant theoretical analyses by nearly as many different economists appeared in various journals. These articles critiqued the Say's Law analysis from several different points of view until, by mid-1933, a new period of consensus began to emerge.

These theory debates began in the summer of 1931 with a series of articles specifically concerned with the merit of the Say-Douglas analysis of labor reabsorption. The first contribution appeared in June 1931 in an expansion by

Rexford Tugwell of the argument he first had presented in 1930 in his article for the Adult Education symposium. Tugwell now attacked the 1930 theory contribution by Douglas in detail. Tugwell felt that Douglas made a serious error in finding "that the problem is purely a temporary one of bridging gaps between jobs," and emphasized that such a conclusion "is directly antithetical to the conclusion from the reasoning used here. I should say that more and more workers are being thrown out of employment and the permanent group of unemployed is increasing in size. . . . A difference of opinion so deep as this must arise from faulty reasoning on one or the other side." The faulty reasoning was, according to Tugwell, that Douglas erred in thinking of unemployment only in aggregate terms, when the kind of new job a worker is forced to take was as important as whether he got one or not. In addition, Tugwell found that Douglas accepted Classical School assumptions and did not consider their relevance to modern conditions.[11]

Two months after the appearance of Tugwell's critique, a second and more constructive criticism of Douglas' analysis appeared by Alvin Hansen. Hansen argued, first, that the Douglas paper was not an accurate interpretation of Say's Law. Second, and more important, he found that Douglas' analysis contained a flaw. With respect to the first error, Hansen noted that, as originally formulated, Say's Law said nothing about how technologically released productive factors would be put back to work. "The Say-Mill-Ricardo analysis assumed without question that idle productive resources would ere long be set to work to produce goods." As Hansen noted, this was assumed to be true because a freely flexible price system and competitive market for productive agents was presumed to exist. The classical economists were concerned instead with whether there would be a market for the new production, and Say's Law was their answer. They were not concerned with whether released factors would find reemployment. Yet this was precisely what Douglas was trying to prove. As to Douglas' fundamental error, Hansen claimed that this came from identifying the demand for labor with the demand for goods. Hansen noted that labor-saving improvements do not increase total purchasing power because the gain to consumers, producers, or retained workers is exactly offset by the loss in purchasing power suffered by displaced workers. Hansen admitted that displaced workers may be supported by charity or relief, but he claimed that these are just transfers of income. There was no net increase in purchasing power, just a release of productive power. Hansen thus claimed that Douglas' analysis was wrong in assuming such an increase, and that as a result the forces working for the ultimate reabsorption of displaced workers must be sought elsewhere. Hansen found that these forces did exist in wage and credit policies. He claimed, however, that such policies were crucially dependent on institutional factors. He traced through in detail how these policies would have to work to guarantee reemployment. Hansen's major conclusion was that "under certain conditions of institutional control of credit and wages . . . we cannot definitely assert that labor displaced by technological improvements will eventually be reabsorbed into industry."[12]

Tugwell's criticism of Douglas was not productive in that it did not provide an alternative approach to analyzing the issue. Hansen's critique was more constructive, although again an odd one in the 1930s world of neoclassical theory. In effect, all Hansen had done was to provide the John Stuart Mill critique of the Say's Law compensation argument—the theory of technological unemployment was still stuck in the nineteenth century. The Hansen and Tugwell critiques, however, did have a clear effect on the professional literature. In response to their analyses, theoretical confrontations among economists quickly expanded. Where the theory articles of 1930 were infrequent and presented harmonious repetitions of a common theme, the theory discussions of 1931–33 were numerous and were, in most cases, attacks on another economist's views. By the end of these two years of give-and-take over the issue, a new consensus began to emerge. In effect, the late nineteenth-century neoclassical analysis of technological change and unemployment was rediscovered, and the theoretical literature was at last brought up to date.

This process began at the December 1931 American Economic Association meetings, where Alvin Hansen expanded his range of criticisms to attack two additional mistaken views on the subject. Hansen began by noting that the Douglas "orthodox view has been roundly criticized from the standpoint of price rigidity by numerous adherents of the institutional school." Hansen claimed, however, that the institutional view also was wrong. Hansen noted that it was not essential that prices be lowered to the extent of newly lowered costs. If wages were freely flexible, reemployment would take place as long as some areas of investment were not under total monopolistic control. The theory advanced by Sumner Slichter was the next target of Hansen's criticism. In Slichter's view, technological unemployment had increased because wage rates remained constant while the prices of capital goods had fallen sharply. Hansen claimed that this view, "while on the right track . . . does not go far enough in the analysis." In particular, Hansen argued that the relative productivities of factors matter, not just their prices. Technological change disturbs relative productivities, thus disturbing correct factor pricing. "As a rule, labor is the factor which becomes over priced in consequence of the lag required to adjust relative factor prices." In this sense, Hansen noted that Slichter is right, because it is flexibility of prices that is crucial. In all cases, Hansen asserted, for reemployment to occur a basic flexibility in economic institutions is necessary; in particular, "the complete absorption of the displaced labor presupposes, as a necessary condition, flexible capital and labor markets." Hansen concluded "that we cannot afford to assume a too easy optimism with respect to technological unemployment. The increasing rigidity of modern economic life consequent upon price controls . . . points in the direction of a slackening in the rate at which displaced labor can be reabsorbed into employment."[13]

At the same December 1931 meetings, Sumner Slichter also returned to the subject of technological unemployment. He criticized the optimistic Say-Douglas approach to technological unemployment and defended his theory of recent relative factor price movements. In this paper, however, Slichter was considerably more pessimistic about the problem of technological unemployment than he had been in his earlier analysis. Slichter now claimed that displacement of labor was a serious problem. "Occupational statistics for agriculture, manufacturing, mining and transportation show plainly that changes in technique and markets have produced displacement on a large scale." Slichter also evidenced a change in view by his criticism of "the extraordinarily optimistic assumption that each labor-saving device, by reducing the cost of producing goods, releases exactly enough purchasing power to create a new job for every one it destroys." Slichter had once supported this argument, but he now felt that there was no reason to believe an exact number of new jobs would be created. Slichter then repeated his perverse-price-changes argument to claim that "unemployment may be serious and chronic. In fact, displacement may become more or less cumulative." As a result, Slichter concluded that technological change can affect not only the kind and location but the number of jobs.[14]

These theory debates continued in 1932 when Gottfried Haberler argued that Hansen's analysis "tends to exaggerate the disturbance caused by the introduction of improved methods of production." According to Haberler, Hansen's error could be exposed by considering a monetary rather than a credit economy. Assuming that the quantity of money and the velocity of circulation remained constant, Haberler claimed that a close analysis of adjustment over time periods showed that purchasing power actually was created. Haberler claimed that his analysis showed that if "there is an increase of demand in general for other goods, prices and wages will go up somewhere and the displaced workers can be reabsorbed, as Professor Douglas contends." Haberler acknowledged that a decrease in the velocity of circulation at the beginning would invalidate this argument, as would displaced workers keeping part of their money longer than usual. "But such assumptions are highly precarious."[15]

Hansen then replied to Haberler's critique. Hansen acknowledged that ungrounded hostility to technological change was clearly to be avoided. "But I think it would not only be deplorable but dangerous to assume that technological unemployment can quite well take care of itself regardless of what sort of a social structure we are building. My view is that the more rigid our economic life becomes, the more difficult the reabsorption process will be." Hansen noted that in his orginal paper he had shown how displaced labor would be reabsorbed if the credit system functioned normally. "But the credit system does not function normally in a depression period. . . . This is precisely the reason why it is important to see clearly that the 'setting-free of purchasing power' does not automatically come into play." According to Hansen, Haberler's analysis in terms of a cash economy essentially made no difference. Hansen also claimed, contrary to Haberler, that in a depression the velocity of circulation may well slow down. Finally, Hansen noted that in the case where prices were not lowered and producers kept all the gains from technological change, Haberler's argument would not apply at all.[16]

The Hansen-Tugwell-Haberler-Douglas-Slichter exchanges all took place in American economic journals. The significance of the technological unemployment issue at the time is shown by the fact that a similar series of theoretical debates occurred simultaneously in Europe. This literature began in 1932 with an article by Nicholas Kaldor in response to a book on technological unemployment by Emil Lederer. Although the problem of technological change and employment was receiving widespread attention in Europe, the non-English literature was essentially ignored by American and British economists. Emil Lederer's 1931 theoretical attack on the problem, however, was notable enough to draw a response from Kaldor.[17] Kaldor's major objection was that Lederer's argument was based on a case that could not take place in a competitive society. In effect, Kaldor found that Lederer had proposed a case that "sounds very strange to people who were brought up on the marginal productivity analysis." Kaldor acknowledged that if Lederer's assumed case were true, and wages were rigid, unemployment would be prolonged or even permanent. Such unemployment would always occur when wages were out of equilibrium with labor's true marginal productivity. But Kaldor found no good reason for blaming invention for this fact. Kaldor argued that factor price-productivity relationships could also be affected by changes in factor supplies or by changes in factor prices with supplies remaining the same. As a result, Kaldor concluded that "it seems to us that the attempt to link up economics with common sense has failed. It is only 'pure common sense' to regard Technical Progress as the cause of unemployment and depression when all over the world, on a scale which compelled everybody to take notice, workers were dismissed simultaneously with the introduction of far-reaching technical changes." Kaldor found that Lederer's "gallant attempt to fit theory into facts" failed mainly because Lederer's basic assumption of technological change as an independent variable ignored the possibility that both technological change and unemployment could be dependent on a third cause: interference with the price system. In Kaldor's words, "to blame Technical Progress for a lack of adjustment due to rigidity is putting the cart before the horse."[18]

In early 1933 Mentor Bouniatian engaged in another attack on Lederer's analysis, this time with reference to Lederer's analysis of the classical reabsorption theories. In doing so, Bouniatian produced a spirited defense of the Say-Douglas automatic reabsorption argument. After a detailed review of all of Lederer's arguments against the classical reabsorption theories, Bouniatian was "led to the conclusion that none of the arguments advanced against the theory of equilibrium can stand up to strict scrutiny. However rapid it may be, technical progress cannot give rise to unemployment or become in any way harmful to the economic life of a country."[19] Four months later, Emil Lederer responded to Bouniatian's article.[20] Lederer found Bouniatian to be wrong because of his concentration on a stationary economic system. In a static economy Lederer acknowledged that equilibrium would clearly be reestablished, but claimed that it was in a progressive state that the real problem lies. Lederer took on each of Bouniatian's arguments and showed where they were in error.

At the end, he reviewed his dynamic model to claim that, even in the most favorable possible conditions, inventions that reduce labor costs in existing products could create serious disturbances.

The early 1930s series of confrontations over the theory of technological unemployment concluded with a January 1933 article by Paul Douglas on Technocracy. With respect to the Technocrats' emphasis on growing technological unemployment, Douglas claimed that the technocratic analysis ignored "the forces which work towards the reabsorption of labor" and he repeated his earlier analysis based on Say's Law. But Douglas went on to acknowledge recent criticisms that had been made of this view. In particular, he noted that there is an important factor "which classical economic theory . . . tends to overlook." Douglas acknowledged that Hansen and Haberler had shown that workers thrown out of employment "have their incomes cut off and purchasing power reduced," and that although the effect of an increase in purchasing power has a head-start, its "passage to ultimate reemployment" is often slowed down in bank deposits and tills. "In practice the decline in purchasing power may get there first and thus create rather prolonged unemployment. To this extent, therefore, the Technocrats may be right." Douglas, however, was not ready to adopt a negative view, and he repeated his conviction that "the recuperative forces are real and have in the past generally been adequate."[21]

In these major theoretical articles through 1933 it is evident that the theoretical consensus of the professional literature in 1928–29 had disappeared and had been replaced by a confrontation between individual views. It is also apparent, however, that there was progress in the theory debates. In a period of two years, all of the arguments of the past century were relived and rediscovered. To the Douglas restatement of the classical Say's Law analysis, Hansen added John Stuart Mill's criticism that the demand for goods is not the demand for labor. Then, in conjunction with Hansen and Haberler, Kaldor brought the analysis up to date by restating the issue in terms of neoclassical marginal productivity analysis.

Progress in the professional discussions is also indicated by the fact that here the theory debates stopped for a period of several years. From late 1933 to the end of the depression, no other significant discussions occurred in the theoretical literature. A new theoretical consensus had emerged out of the debates of 1931–33 to replace the consensus of 1928–29. The Hansen and Kaldor analyses were convincing. Neither the extremes of the Douglas reabsorption position nor the Lederer displacement position were correct. In the place of the Say's Law purchasing power analysis, the marginal productivity approach had gained a position of predominance. Price flexibility and the proper functioning of credit and monetary institutions were the key in the reabsorption process. Only if these functions were interfered with was it possible that reabsorption would not take place.

That this view had emerged as a new consensus is evident in several mid-to-late 1930s comments on the technological unemployment question.[22] It is also clear that the new consensus helped to open up other areas of investigation.

The extent of rigidity in modern pricing systems in particular became a major issue. The subject of administered prices and price flexibility, for example, rose to a peak of professional interest in the mid-1930s as Gardiner Means began publishing his famous studies of administered prices in 1935.[23]   Other related areas also expanded as debate faded over the relevance of different theories of reabsorption.   John R. Hicks, for example, provided a careful consideration of the impact of technological change in terms of modern economic theory in his *Theory of Wages*.   Hicks assumed reemployment would take place by referring to Kaldor's 1932 analysis for confirmation and concentrated instead on the problem of the distribution of the ultimate gains in the national product.   Before the end of the decade, Hicks' analysis of inventions in turn received attention, in particular in work by Joan Robinson and A. C. Pigou.[24]   These discussions again assumed reemployment of all displaced factors of production.   A third area of theoretical concern that placed a great deal of emphasis on employment problems of technological change in the mid-1930s was business cycle theory. By 1933 cycle theory was one of the most intense areas of economic interest, and many theories gave technological change a central role to play.   In particular, theories emphasizing oversaving or underconsumption were widespread long before Keynes gave respectability to these previously heretical notions.[25] Keynes' *General Theory* in 1936 soon returned these theories to a position of relative obscurity, as it was Keynes' theory of cycles, and not that of Douglas, Schumpeter, Adams, Clark, or Mills, that received attention in the years to come.   Although many of the mid-1930s cycle theories emphasized the role of technological change, they disagreed significantly about what exactly was going on.[26]   Almost invariably, however, they agreed that no automatic compensating mechanism for technological unemployment existed if wages and prices were inflexible.   As such, they provide further evidence that the application of basic tenets of marginal analysis to the issue of technological unemployment helped move theoretical discussions of the question out of a period of debate in 1931–33 to a period of consensus in the mid-1930s.

The theoretical consensus that price flexibility would guarantee an automatic cure for technological unemployment is illustrated well by a 1939 article by Edna Lonigan.   In her analysis, Lonigan viewed the theory of technological unemployment as an issue of such general agreement among economists that she found no reference to past theoretical debates on the issue to be necessary. As to the general question of the total job-supply effects of technological change, she offered three basic propositions.   First, "technological change, whether due to mechanization or to managerial organization, tends constantly to accompany rising, not falling employment."   Second, "the normal tendency of technological change is to *increase* the openings for new employment."   And third, "if technological progress is *not* followed by rising employment, it is a result of some malfunctioning of the price system or of debt, capital and investment, not of invention."   She asserted that these last two statements were unassailable theoretical facts.   "If prices and investment are functioning soundly, that is not technological but price unemployment.   It would be better if it was called 'price unemployment' to indicate its real origin." As with almost all economists writing on the subject after 1933, she concluded that "if our society wants to retain technological advance, it must give up stable prices. It must not only accept, but force, price changes that are equal *in full* to technological gains."[27]

The only significant theoretical contribution to take a different approach to technological change in the late 1930s was the stagnation thesis. This theory—developed by Alvin Hansen—again, however, was based ultimately on the notion that price inflexibility was the root cause of current economic problems. Hansen felt that the development of new industries was a key factor in future growth. But here he found that price inflexibility comes in. In his view, current institutional developments, including powerful unions, trade associations, the growth of monopolistic competition, competition by advertising and persuasion instead of by price, and the tendency to shelve patents, were all significant restrictions on investment and growth. With this source of relief shut off, Hansen could only conclude pessimistically that "it remains still to be seen whether political democracy can in the end survive the disappearance of the automatic price system."[28]

Technological unemployment was not a major concern to the stagnationists. For them, it was too-slow rather than too-rapid innovation that was the problem. Reaction to the stagnationists was not long in coming. William Fellner in particular effectively attacked the technological argument of the stagnationist thesis.[29] Yet the development of the stagnationist thesis was significant in that it again emphasized the importance placed by economists in the late 1930s on price flexibility as an automatic adjusting factor in the economy. From the mid-1930s on, the neoclassical analysis of technological unemployment had created a firm consensus in the professional literature.

4

Empirical Contributions
in the Early 1930s

The history of professional empirical discussions of technological unemployment during the 1930s is quite different from the rapidly achieved theoretical consensus during the decade. The dispersion of empirical views at the end of the decade was very much like that at its beginning. In this literature, although a great deal of work was done and new data collected, there is little evidence of clear progress toward a final consensus.

The relative ease of achieving a theoretical consensus compared to making progress in the empirical debates is a central feature of the technological unemployment debates. The reasons why this was so have much to do with data limitations at the time. Accurate current data on even such basic macroeconomic variables as employment and unemployment did not exist until the 1940s. The relevance of access to comprehensive employment data for any empirical study of technological unemployment is obvious. Data sources were much improved over past decades, however, so where the machinery and unemployment debates of the 1800s were almost purely theoretical, the technological unemployment debates had an extensive empirical component. Given the absense of key data sources, however, economists contributing to this literature struggled to arrive at conclusions that were convincing to their peers.

A review of major empirical contributions during the 1930s illustrates this course of the empirical debates. As will be recalled, during 1928–29, two empirical approaches had been begun by economists. The first was to collect new data to test claims about the experience of technologically displaced workers. The second was to evaluate existing statistics in order to analyze the employment impact of recent technological change. Neither approach during 1928–29 was successful in dispelling technological unemployment concerns.

During 1930 several further empirical attacks on the issue appeared. Appropriately—given that his 1930 theory paper began the 1930s theoretical disputes—one of these papers was by Paul Douglas. In this article, Douglas suggested a major innovation in empirical attacks on the question of technological unemployment. Douglas presented this paper at a December 1930 meeting of the Taylor Society. Beginning with a citation of the by-then familiar employment and productivity trends, Douglas stated that these data suggested that "during the last decade some very unfamiliar changes have been occurring."[1] Douglas repeated his earlier theoretical argument to demonstrate that there was really little to worry about, but he acknowledged that Lubin, Myers, and others had shown that serious short-run dislocations did occur. Because of these problems, Douglas claimed that it was desirable to have the ability to predict likely problem areas. In order to do this, Douglas proposed a study to estimate the elasticity of demand for 150 goods over the period 1909–29. In his paper, Douglas presented preliminary results for nine goods. Douglas' proposal was ambitious and his method original. Despite his professed intention of using this method to make a broad empirical study of technological unemployment, however, these preliminary results were all that appeared. The study was never completed.

A look at the criticisms that were made of the Douglas paper at the same Taylor Society meeting indicates why. Elizabeth Baker criticized Douglas on the basis of data from her recently completed case study of the printing industry. According to Baker, the Douglas formula depended crucially on good estimates of output and price, yet the heterogeneity of the product in printing was such that no meaningful output or price index was possible. Sumner Slichter criticized Douglas on two additional points. First, Slichter pointed out that the Douglas formula required, in addition to accurate price and output data, a good index of the general price level and of total output changes. Slichter claimed that the obvious inadequacy of existing data for these latter indexes made such calculations impossible. Second, Slichter claimed that the Douglas method was not justifiable theoretically. Douglas' approach assumed that prices were cut as productivity rises, but Slichter noted that this was not always the case.[2]

The level of professional interest in technological unemployment was reflected in several other empirical papers in 1930. The most important empirical work published during the year was expansion of original data collections similar to those begun by Lubin and Myers in the late 1920s. Studies by Elizabeth Baker and by Ewan Clague and W. J. Couper were published in 1930, and several other large-scale individual worker studies patterned on the Lubin-Myers example were begun.[3] The International Institute of Social Research in New York, for example, began a series of studies that concentrated on the experience of unemployed workers. And at the University of Minnesota, the Employment Stabilization Research Institute was formed to make studies of the economic aspects of employment and the characteristics of the unemployed.

The Clague-Couper and Baker studies were important in that they provided clear support for the results found by Lubin and Myers. The Clague-Couper study reported on the fate of 1,206 workers technologically displaced in the late 1920s from two United States Rubber Company plants. As did Lubin and Myers, Clague and Couper reported a considerable loss of time, income, and skill.

Elizabeth Baker's work was different in conception. Patterned on the work of the BLS and the earlier studies of George Barnett rather than that of Lubin, Myers, or Clague-Couper, Baker focused on the printing industry for an in-depth technological history. Her main concern was with the employment impact of recent technological changes on an industrywide rather than an individual-worker level. She found in her research that total employment had risen rapidly in the industry, but that the occupational mix had changed dramatically. As a result, although many displaced workers were transferred to new jobs, a significar t number had been forced from the industry.

In later references to the individual-worker effects of technological change, the contributions of Lubin, Myers, Clague-Couper, and Baker were by far the most often quoted studies. Although this work was only a fraction of the total worker case studies completed during the depression, they were the major sources concentrating specifically on groups of technologically displaced workers. Although carefully conducted and honestly reported, the limitations of these studies for drawing conclusions about the aggregate employment effects of recent technological change were obvious to all. The individual-worker and individual-industry studies provided important information about the displacement of individuals, but they did little to create movement toward a consensus on the aggregate questions of interest.

The final important empirical contributions in 1930 were presented at a late-year symposium on technological unemployment sponsored by the American Association for Adult Education. Isador Lubin's paper was the most empirically oriented of the group. In addition to the standard review of trends in manufacturing, mining, agriculture, and railroads, and a review of the evidence presented by Lubin, Myers, and Baker, Lubin made two original empirical points. In reply to the argument that the gains of recent technological change had been going to producers rather than to wage earners or consumers, Lubin claimed that the fact that consumers had gained "is evidenced by the declining course of wholesale prices for semi-manufactured and finished products from 1923 to 1929" as seen in BLS indexes. Lubin found that "the resulting savings were not, however, an unmixed blessing to American labor." To support this argument, Lubin made his second original empirical argument. Lubin presented New York State data on the ratio of common laborers applying for work to jobs available to show that skill effects of recent technological change were significant. The index had risen steadily in 1923–29 despite two business cycles and was higher in 1929 than in the peak years of 1924 and 1927. As a result of this evidence, Lubin concluded that "the oft-repeated assertion that [the displaced worker] is reabsorbed by other growing trades and industries still calls for definite substantiation."[4]

Elizabeth Baker's paper at the symposium began with the caution that we know very few facts "about the rate of displacement, the nature of the displacing process, and the labor-saving power of industry." But she found that important recent progress had been made in this empirical work. For example, a primary question of interest to her was "whether technical advance dissolves the need for skill among workers." If it did, then retraining was not a vital problem. "We have strong evidence, however, that skill in some industries is of increasing importance." Baker gave evidence from two examples, commercial printing and a chain and conveyor plant in England.[5]

During 1930, then, attempts to overcome the lack of factual information about technological unemployment were continued. In these empirical efforts, two important difficulties in making inferences about the problem were clearly identified. First, the lack of critical basic data sources made it difficult to make estimates of the extent of the problem. Second, the difficulty of theoretically justifying those inferences that could be made also limited the impact of empirical work. Paul Douglas' 1930 Taylor Society paper illustrated both of these problems well.

During 1931 attempts to overcome these difficulties and to produce more useful empirical analyses continued. The highlight of the 1931 contributions was a careful evaluation by several economists of the methodological problems of empirical investigation of the question. By the end of the year, the problems of an empirical attack on the question of technological unemployment had been clearly stated, and a serious attempt to resolve these problems had begun.

Contributions in 1931 also suggested that the empirical discussions were becoming more contentious. In particular, several 1931 studies were noticeably more pessimistic than had been reviews of the same data in the past. One such review of existing data in 1931 was made in an International Labour Office (ILO) publication on *The Social Aspects of Rationalisation*. In the section on employment effects in the United States, a detailed review of all past studies and available data led to conclusions similar to those voiced by economists in 1928–29, but with a distinctly more negative slant. The final conclusion was that technological unemployment is only temporary. However, the study claimed that workers are constantly being displaced, so that a growing pool of ever-changing technologically displaced workers can exist. It was concluded that "this appears to be what has happened during the past few years in several countries where rationalisation measures have been adopted at a very rapid pace."[6]

Another 1931 ILO study, by Harold Butler on *Unemployment Problems in the United States*, gave half of its volume to a discussion of recent technological change and its employment effects. Again contrary to most previous reviews of the same data, Butler's conclusions were decidedly pessimistic. Butler focused on the question of whether there had been a significant impact of technological change on "normal" levels of unemployment. The data Butler reviewed on this question included aggregate employment indexes, BLS industry productivity studies, Commerce occupations-flow data, and displaced worker studies by Barnett, Baker, Lubin, Myers, and Clague-Couper. From this review Butler reached several conclusions. First, he found that the worker case studies "arrive at sufficiently similar conclusions to suggest that a real social problem has been created by the recent rapidity of technological progress." Second, Butler found that there is good reason for believing that the lag in reemployment "is either more important than has hitherto been supposed, or more important than has been the case in the past." And finally, it appeared probable to him that "'normal' unemployment is tending to become higher now in the United States and in some other countries, and that this state of affairs may persist for some time to come."[7]

The conflict of opinion over the problem of technological unemployment that was becoming more evident among economists in 1931 was reflected in the fact that other interpretations of the same data used in the ILO studies reached different conclusions. R. C. White, for example, in a June 1931 article reviewed all the evidence in technological unemployment studies by Clague, Barnett, Myers, Lubin, Douglas, and others in reaching an optimistic conclusion. White had two major objections to recent pessimistic studies. First, there was the data problem that available sources were severely limited in time (since 1919) and scope (four major sectors only). Second, there was a theory problem. According to White, past pessimistic views had ignored the fact that it takes time for the technologically unemployed to be reemployed. As a result of these two problems, White felt that technological unemployment had been misunderstood in past studies. "Its essential characteristic is the shift in occupations, not a relative reduction in the total number of occupations."[8]

As these conflicting conclusions from reviews of exactly the same data indicate, in the early 1930s it was not possible to reach a consensus on aggregate issues on the basis of existing statistics. There was a clear need for well-conceived original empirical work. As it turned out, such studies were in process and were soon to appear.

In doing this new empirical work, the fundamental problem had to be faced of presenting an acceptable theoretical justification for any conclusions that were reached. The response to this problem in 1931 was an attempt by several economists to develop a careful methodological foundation for future empirical studies. Three important papers specifically concerned with this issue were published in 1931.

The first methodological paper was written by Ewan Clague as part of a BLS study of current employment statistics. Clague's approach was to classify and critique past empirical studies of technological unemployment in order to suggest improvements. Clague found that several approaches had been used in past studies, but that "although some progress has been made in each of [these] lines . . . , it is safe to say that comparatively little has been accomplished."[9] In particular, according to Clague, the productivity index approach used in 1927 by Durand needed closely comparable output and employment data, but these were often technically impossible to provide. More important to Clague, however, was the fact that productivity gains were only indirectly connected to unemployment. Clague found similar theoretical problems with BLS productivity case studies. The most difficult theoretical problem here, however, was in generalization of results from specific cases. With respect to the approach of doing displaced worker studies like those done by Lubin or Clague-Couper, Clague noted that identifying workers as technologically displaced was often open to question and that problems of generalization were even more severe because of the small samples involved. Clague's recommendations were for a continuation of work similar to all types of past studies, but with improvements through lengthening the time periods covered and expanding the size of economic areas surveyed. As for new studies, he concluded that the best possible approach was to concentrate on individual industries. Clague argued that a comprehensive study of an industry's technological history, of trends in the size and composition of its output and employment, and of the fate of its displaced workers would combine the good points of past studies while avoiding their greatest faults.

A second 1931 methodological discussion was presented by Boris Stern. Stern had authored several BLS productivity case studies and wanted to convey "the difficulties with which one is confronted in this comparatively new field of research and to emphasize the need for a generally accepted definition of the terminology and the scope of this type of study."[10] Stern used two of his own BLS studies to illustrate his points. To meet the difficulties he found, Stern suggested the following rules: limit each study to one industry only, and define technological change broadly to include all changes in product, production, labor types, or equipment that raise productivity. Using this procedure Stern claimed that measurement of the employment impact of technological change was not overly difficult. To supplement currently existing data, Stern suggested a series of studies based on his rules of groups of related industries, followed up by studies of the fate of displaced workers.

The third important 1931 methodological paper was presented by Harry Jerome.[11] Jerome found that the problems of estimating technological unemployment were: first, to know the technological changes in an industry; second, to know the effect of these changes on labor productivity; third, to know the effects of this productivity advance on labor displacement; and fourth, to know the effects of this displacement on unemployment. Jerome claimed that all these questions must be answered in any adequate study of the problem. The problem at the present time, however, was that there was no data base from which to answer these questions. Jerome noted that productivity indexes told little about the causes of productivity advances or about their employment effects. Productivity case studies got at the causes and at displacement effects, but did not give any idea of the effects of displacement on unemployment. Jerome thus concluded that the best approach was to do plant case studies covering a substantial proportion of several industries over a long time period with follow-up studies of displaced workers. The only available study that Jerome felt came close to these requirements was Baker's study of commercial printing. In order to provide evidence for reasonable estimates, however, Jerome claimed a substantial number of similar studies would be needed.

As these methodological comments and the fact of contradicting interpretations of the same data suggest, by the end of 1931 the problems of making convincing empirical judgments about the aggregate employment effects of technological change were widely recognized. Progress might have been made in the empirical debates if the prescriptions of the methodological studies were followed in creating new data collections. This was not done. Instead, empirical contributions in the mid-1930s continued much along the same line as before, with the focus on reevaluations of existing data sources.[12] The inadequacy of this approach reinforced the contentious attitude evident in the early 1930s literature, and by the mid-1930s a clear professional debate was evident in the empirical literature.

An important example of what still could be done in evaluating existing data sources appeared in a 1932 book by Frederick C. Mills entitled *Economic Tendencies in the United States*. Mills' book was a descriptive survey of economic trends comparing the experience of 1922–29 to that of 1901–13. The book was an impressive collection of all the best data on the most important aggregate trends since 1900. In his consideration of technological unemployment, Mills constructed from existing data sources wage-earner accession and separation indexes on an industry level in manufacturing from 1899 to 1929. By ignoring intra-industry transfers, these data understated the problems of worker transfers. Even so, Mills found that for three five-year periods from 1899 to 1914, an average of 21 out of every 1,000 manufacturing wage earners were separated from industries, with an average accession rate of 149 per 1,000. For three two-year periods between 1923 and 1929, the comparable figures were 49 out of 1,000, and 45 out of 1,000. As a result, Mills concluded that "not only was the rate of separation much higher than it had been over longer pre-war periods; it was higher than the accession rate, which may be taken as an index of employment opportunities in manufacturing industries." In light of the great output advance that had taken place in both periods, Mills concluded that a significant change in manufacturing production had taken place. In his words, "the turn-over of men, the shifting of labor among industries, the enforced displacement of labor—these were becoming more prominent features of industrial progress than they had ever been before." Another important empirical contribution by Mills concerned price flexibility. In the concurrent theory debates about technological unemployment, price flexibility had emerged as a key factor determining employment adjustments to technological change. Mills' detailed review of price data since 1890 showed that there was a distinct trend toward decreasing price flexibility. This trend was clear in 1890–1914, disturbed by the war in 1914–21, but had reasserted itself in 1922–29. As a result, Mills found that although accelerating change served "to intensify the demands for flexibility and adaptability . . . these demands were made . . . at a time when elements of structural rigidity and inflexibility were apparently growing in strength."[13]

It is clear that Mills' views were on the pessimistic side of the technological unemployment issue and that these conclusions were based solidly on his empirical investigations. The originality of his data analyses and the care he gave to creating the best possible data series were impressive. But there were problems with Mills' work. His results were sensitive to his choice of end-points for his survey periods, and all of his data were only from the manufacturing sector.

The problem of reaching a professional consensus about the aggregate employment effect of technological change because of the inadequate scope of existing data was reinforced in a series of empirical articles in the *Journal of the American Statistical Association* (*JASA*) in late 1932.

The first article in this series, by David Weintraub, examined existing data for 1920–31 from the manufacturing, mining, and railroad sectors in reaching an optimistic conclusion about the impact of recent technological change on employment levels. Choosing existing FRB output and employment indexes and NICB hours-worked indexes for his sources, Weintraub's goal was to assign total employment fluctuations either to output or to productivity changes. He did this by first calculating an output-per-manhour index for all manufacturing covering the period 1920–31. This gave him an index of the employment requirements necessary to produce an output equal to that of the base year 1920. By comparing the trends in this index with trends in an output index covering the same period, Weintraub concluded that from 1922 to 1929 manufacturing output had grown enough to absorb most of those displaced by efficiency gains. Turning to a similar examination of railroad data, Weintraub found that the situation in the 1920s had been very different. The railroad data showed an employment decline of about 130,000 due to efficiency gains, and of about 100,000 due to output declines. An examination of bituminous coal mining data showed a trend similar to that in railroads. Weintraub then followed with an examination of the depression years 1930–31, which suggested that about 10 percent of the manufacturing employment decline of three million was due to technological advance, with the rest due to output declines. All of the railroad employment decline of 500,000 in this period was found to be due to output declines because productivity was stable. Weintraub's final conclusions generalized these results. In particular, he found that the evidence for 1920–31 "is not conclusive enough to warrant the statement that the increased output per man-hour has resulted in a permanent displacement of workers," although "temporary displacement played an important role in the fluctuations in employment."[14]

Weintraub's conclusions using the same data sources clearly were more optimistic than Mills'. Weintraub was supported in this view in another empirical paper at the same conference by Willford King. King began by admitting that "it is clear . . . that there is such a thing as technological unemployment." He claimed that evidence collected by Lubin, Myers, and Clague left no doubt about this fact. King thus found that there were only two issues in dispute. First, in normal times, was it true that automatic mechanisms existed to guarantee that "even though these inventions cause considerable labor turnover, the net volume of unemployment ascribable to technological forces tends to be very small?" And second, was it the case "that technological advances in industry are responsible for the plight of a large portion of the persons now included among the unemployed?" To answer these questions, King made use of decennial census data. First, King found that the proportion of the population gainfully employed since 1890 had not fallen, thus that there was no evidence of hidden unemployment. Second, of those in the labor force in 1930, King noted that recent Census of Unemployment questions asking workers to give reasons for their unemployment showed that technological unemployment was very small. Third, figuring manufacturing unemployment in April 1930 at 15.8 percent, King calculated that, of this number, 8.3 percent was due to output declines and that "an allowance of 3 or 4 percent for technological unemployment in this field, in April, 1930, would seem to be an outside limit, the most probable amount of this type of unemployment being far smaller." Thus King concluded that after two centuries of rapid technological change, "the cumulative effect observable in 1929 was that technological unemployment was almost negligible in amount." As to the second question he raised, King acknowledged that since 1929 it was probably true that a "considerable fraction of those now out of work lost their jobs because of technological changes in industry." But he claimed that this unemployment was not due basically to technological change but to "the evils resulting from our antiquated and unsound monetary system."[15]

King's analysis prompted two replies. F. B. Garver had three methodological comments to make. First, he found that King's evidence of a constant percentage of the total population being gainfully employed was no surprise in a nation without unemployment insurance. Second, King's evidence that few workers in the Census of Unemployment said that they were technologically unemployed was not surprising. Garver noted that workers can be displaced due to improvements in the same industry hundreds of miles away, by the substitution of new products, or by a cessation of hiring forcing new workers into other industries. Third, Garver claimed that the logical necessity of the orthodox theory King claimed to support was not convincing. Garver noted that the traditional Say's Law approach had been accepted "chiefly because it seems to have agreed with the facts in the past. Improvements have not in the past caused unemployment and real wages have risen." Garver pointed out that "the more recent productivity theory" has demonstrated that cases may exist where wages must fall to get reemployment. If wages did not fall, unemployment would result due to technological change.[16]

Boris Stern concluded the series of articles at the conference with a statistical argument against King. After a note similar to Garver's about the inadequacy of Census of Unemployment data, Stern presented data from a BLS study of six tire plants from 1921 to 1931 to show that output and productivity, although not independent, were "at constant war with one another." From 1922 to 1929 Stern found a continuous rise in output which served (except for 1926) to absorb all those displaced by efficiency and to add to total hours worked. In 1929–31, output and hours fell sharply but productivity still rose. On the basis of these trends, Stern concluded that from 1922 to 1925 there was no unemployment at all. In 1926 all of the decrease in hours worked was due to technological change. In 1927–28 there was no unemployment. In 1929–30, he claimed that 43 percent of the unemployment was due to technological change. In 1930–31, he found that 73 percent of the unemployment was technological.

Stern made these estimates by comparing the actual decrease in manhours to the decrease in manhours implied by a constant rate of output per manhour applied to the actual change in output. In 1929–30, for example, output fell by 15 percent. This implied a decline of about 5.135 million manhours. Actual manhours fell by about 9 million. The difference, or 3.865 million manhours (43%), was held by Stern to be due to technological change. Stern admitted that the tire industry may be a special case, but he claimed that many other BLS surveys showed similar trends. The major point he wanted to make was that there was abundant data to suggest that the proportion of technologically unemployed "is very large, much larger indeed, than that intimated in Dr. King's paper."[17]

The Mills and *JASA* articles were not the only empirical contributions during 1932 and 1933, but these represent clearly the state of the debate at the time.[18] The focus was on evaluations of existing data, but given the limitations of these sources, strongly conflicting interpretations were possible. The creativity of this work in coming up with new configurations and tests from the same data was impressive. But these tests were often ill-conceived—as Garver's critique of King showed well.

A final article from 1933 by Leo Wolman also presents this picture of the contemporary state of the empirical analysis of technological unemployment. According to Wolman, the measurement of productivity change and unemployment, and accounting for causes of unemployment, "are related economic problems on which a tremendous amount of work has been done during the past fifteen years." Yet despite the fact that "material, then, on both the output of industry and the volume of unemployment exists now in greater abundance then ever before . . . there is still wide difference of opinion among close students as to precisely what has happened, say, in the last twenty or thirty years. These differences of opinion, moreover, are not the result of hair-splitting but of real difficulties which cannot be disposed of by any amount of argumentation." Wolman's intent in his article was to identify the problems involved in making an empirical attack on the problem. First, he considered the question of how to approach the problem. He noted that a mere list of labor-saving devices would clearly not be adequate since it is aggregate forces that matter. Yet Wolman claimed that in an aggregative approach the severest data problems are met. Output data are "still defective in quality and comprehensiveness," and as one goes back in time to make comparison with current trends, "the defects in the current data are often multiplied many times." In addition, Wolman claimed that because of the war and the rise of the automobile industry that the past twenty years have "in so many respects been unusual" that many atypical influences must be considered. Thus the events of 1922–29 may reflect "temporary forces" much more than "persistent long-time trends." Another difficulty Wolman found in aggregate work was that the length of periods chosen for comparison and the economic conditions during terminal years have "often powerfully influenced, if not determined" past conclusions that have been drawn. In addition, Wolman noted that "every novice in economic statistics knows" it is impossible with current data to know the amount of unemployment.[19]

In making these points, Wolman summed up effectively the state of professional empirical studies through the early 1930s. As he noted, a considerable amount of new data had been collected and applied to the problem and several major studies had appeared. Yet these data remained inadequate for a careful study of the issue, and thus real differences continued to exist among economists about the interpretation of recent trends.

In addition to data limitations, methodological problems continued to bedevil the empirical work that was done, with notable examples including Mills' choice of time periods for his contrast between prewar and postwar trends, and King's use of Census of Unemployment data to estimate the volume of technological unemployment. The empirical techniques used to estimate the amount of technological unemployment also remained rudimentary. As illustrated by the work of Stern and Weintraub, the most sophisticated method of analysis was simply to compare trends in indexes of output, hours worked, and output per manhour. The difficulty of tying these trends to a careful definition of technological unemployment was admitted readily, but still this was the typical method used. Regression analysis was first proposed as a method to study the problem in 1933, but its initial use in an empirical article addressing the issue was a few years away.

There were, however, a few areas of advance. The reality of technological unemployment was acknowledged, mainly due to the displaced-worker studies by Clague, Lubin, Myers, and Baker. It also had become a generally accepted belief that technological unemployment had grown worse during the 1920s. The fact that technological change aggravated depression unemployment also was acknowledged. But on the central question of whether this technological unemployment had been, was now, or would be to any significant extent an important economic problem, there was sharply divided opinion.

5

Empirical Debates
in the Mid to Late 1930s

During the mid-1930s, empirical work appeared less frequently than in the early years of the decade. The recognition that not much more could be done given current data reduced empirical contributions in number, although it did not stop them. The fact that after 1932 the economy began to recover from the bottom of the depression also mattered. Given that the basic information available for analyzing the question had not changed, conflicting interpretations of available data continued to dominate the discussions that appeared. The only notable change in the empirical debates at the time was that sufficient information now was available on the experience of the 1930s for the debates to shift their focus from the 1920s to the depression years.

The late 1930s saw a change in this experience. The recession of 1937–38, which increased unemployment from 14 percent to 19 percent, revived public interest in the issue of technological unemployment. This renewed concern was supported by the publicity received by popular organizations arguing for radical economic policies. For example, groups lobbying for reducing the pace of technological change by taxing machines, including the American Technotax Society and the National Organization for the Taxation of Labor-Saving Devices, were at the peak of their activity in the mid to late 1930s. The late 1930s also saw the publication of three major government-sponsored series of studies dealing with the technological unemployment issue.

A consequence of these developments was a new surge of professional interest in the technological unemployment issue at the end of the decade. Despite these new studies and the new empirical information made available by the late 1930s government investigations, the fundamental problems of doing convincing empirical work remained the same—inadequate data sources and insufficient attention given to asking carefully focused questions. As a result, the professional empirical debates remained contentious, and little progress was evident toward resolving the disputes.

The first major empirical study to appear in the mid to late 1930s literature actually provided new information for the debates. This study, Harry Jerome's 1934 NBER-sponsored book entitled *Mechanization in Industry*, was based on detailed field studies, mail surveys, and reviews of existing data for approximately two dozen manufacturing and two dozen nonmanufacturing industries. From these surveys, Jerome drew several conclusions. First, he argued that the process of technological change was too complex for uncontrollably rapid change. Second, Jerome found that "changes in the rate of mechanization, although limited, are not negligible." In particular, he found that the 1920s was a period of unusually rapid change. Third, Jerome found evidence of "a substantial amount of skill displacement and technological unemployment." However, he did "not find convincing the evidence or theoretical arguments sometimes advanced to demonstrate an inherent tendency for mechanization to create an ever larger body of unemployed."[1] Jerome concluded that the truth of the matter was that there is a lag in absorption and that when the pace of mechanization is faster, the changing pool of technologically unemployed grows. Jerome specifically warned that these judgments concerned the effects of mechanization alone and not all possible sources of efficiency change. In particular, he noted that the productivity effects of management and business reorganization were not considered.

Outside of Jerome's contribution, the basic data available for an analysis of recent relevant trends did not change in the mid-1930s. The only important change in sources was the fact that a long enough period had now elapsed for inferences to be made about depression trends as well as about predepression trends. Several empirical studies took a close look at these more recent data.

One representative study of depression trends was published by Frederick C. Mills in early 1935. Mills concentrated on manufacturing sector data in making a detailed comparison of the depression years with earlier periods. Mills found several important depression trends and interpreted them along the same line as in his 1932 book *Economic Tendencies*. In his 1932 book Mills had claimed that unemployment in the 1920s was in large part due to a lack of adjustment to recent rapid technological change because of growing rigidities in the economic system. Mills now found that "there is some analogy between the situation prevailing in manufacturing industries from 1933 to 1935 and that which prevailed from 1922 to 1929." Mills claimed that the maintenance of profits and prices in the face of rapid productivity gains in the 1920s "tended to reduce marketings and so contributed to the unstable situation existing in 1929." He now found that recent movements of prices "at a time when such goods were over-valued, retarded a needed expansion in the volume of sales." Mills' major generalization from these results was that the "experience during the last ten years seems to justify one general conclusion. The immediate passing on to consumers of a major part of the benefit of increasing industrial productivity in the form of lower prices, contributes directly to the maintenance of industrial operations on a high level, and to the raising of the standard of living of the people at large."[2] And, he claimed, this had not been happening recently.

The pessimistic tone evident in Mills' work was repeated in another 1935 article evaluating depression trends by Alfred Kahler. Kahler's goal was to make an empirical test of the theory of technological unemployment. In Kahler's judgment, a look at the best available data covering manufacturing over 1899–1934 showed a distinct break in trend in 1920. His detailed look at productivity data for 1920–35 showed "an extraordinary increase . . . distributed over the entire period." Kahler found that depression trends alone suggest that "a considerable part of the depression unemployment was brought about only after the break in the period of prosperity and as a result of the increase in productivity which then set in." Using the same method as Stern and Weintraub did of comparing trends in indexes of output, manhours, and output per manhour, Kahler estimated that "a portion of the present unemployment corresponding to [20%] is directly traceable to mechanization or rather to rationalization in general." Kahler also criticized Weintraub's claim that up to 1929 reabsorption nearly fully compensated for all manufacturing displacement. Kahler claimed that when a labor force growth of 17 percent and the fact that manhours worked actually fell in the 1920s were considered, it was clear that Weintraub "is incorrect, therefore, to speak of a successful compensatory movement in manufacturing, even with reference to periods of prosperity." As to developments since 1929, Kahler felt that it was doubtful whether manhours would ever again rise in manufacturing to even the 1920 level. He acknowledged that compensation could take place in other sectors, but he cited Jerome's 1934 book *Mechanization in Industry* to show that mechanization had been more rapid in areas outside manufacturing. Kahler's final conclusion, then, was that "we believe we have shown that the labor displacement theory not only holds out certain interesting theoretical possibilities but also deals adequately with one of the most active elements in our economic structure."[3]

Two other substantive empirical analyses in the mid-1930s—one by Wladimir Woytinsky in 1935 and another contribution by F. C. Mills in 1936— provided similar reevaluations of existing data to reach pessimistic conclusions about technological unemployment trends.[4] These studies were balanced by the appearance of optimistic evaluations on both the popular and professional level. Optimistic attacks on negative views by nonprofessional groups were particularly intense in this period. For example, a lengthy, optimistic empirical publication by the National Industrial Conference Board (NICB) entitled *Machinery, Employment and Purchasing Power* appeared in 1935. The Machinery and Allied Products Institute also published a series of strongly stated optimistic pamphlets on the issue in 1935 and 1936. Professional optimistic analyses of note were published by Mordecai Ezekiel and by the Brookings Institution. Ezekiel's study added nothing new to the debates in terms of data or approach. The 1936 Brookings study is notable, however, because in it one of the first attempts was made to use national income data as the primary base for a study of technological unemployment. Using an update of NBER national income data to 1929 made in the 1934 Brookings book entitled *America's Capacity to Produce*, a comparison was made of productivity trends in manufacturing versus the rest of the economy. The major conclusion was that although manufacturing productivity gains had been from 3.5 percent to 4 percent annually since 1919, for the whole economy the advance was only about 1 percent per year. Thus concern over recent productivity advance was greatly exaggerated. In the same vein, it was noted that most examples of rapid productivity advance had been taken from a limited area of the economy. It was claimed that only about 25 percent of the labor force was in areas likely to be affected significantly by productivity advance.[5]

In the late 1930s the pattern of a low-but-steady frequency of conflicting professional exchanges about technological unemployment was broken by a major resurgence of popular interest in the issue. This revival began in 1937 with the downturn in the economy and with the publication by the federal government of three major federal investigations of recent technological change and its effects by the National Resources Committee (NRC), the National Research Project on Reemployment Opportunities and Recent Changes in Industrial Techniques (NRP), and the Temporary National Economic Committee (TNEC). These three studies collected a massive amount of relevant data on the effects of recent technological change. With these empirical contributions and improvements that were being made simultaneously in other statistics, the late 1930s was a period of dramatic improvement in basic data sources.[6]

These data advances, however, only reinforced the conflict between empirical results and optimistic expectations that had been evident in professional discussions throughout the depression. In 1937–38 almost every empirical analysis that appeared was pessimistic. Included among these studies were analyses that ranged in coverage from individual industries to the entire economy.[7]

Representative of this work were continuing studies by F. C. Mills. In a 1937 paper, Mills argued for a better methodological approach to a study of technological change and employment.[8] Because conditions varied so greatly within sectors, Mills argued—similar to the 1931 methodological studies by Clague, Stern, and Jerome—that an intensive study of plants or industries promised the best results. Mills presented a technique for doing this work, based on his 1936 paper on the distribution of productivity gains among workers, producers, and consumers. Mills' method again involved the standard approach of comparing various indexes of output, employment, and productivity. He gave an illustrative example covering the meat-packing industry from 1923 to 1935. This example was inadequate, however, to do little more than suggest how Mills' technique might be used.

Mills followed these proposals with an expanded study of the manufacturing sector in a 1938 paper. After a detailed survey of trends since 1899, Mills reached the conclusion that "the record of changes in production and productivity from 1919 to 1929 explains, in some degree, the decline in employment opportunities already noted." In his analysis of trends since 1929, Mills added another reevaluation of existing data to the debates. For the period 1927–35, Mills attempted to divide between output declines and productivity advances the responsibility for employment remaining below its 1929 level. Using the standard methodology of comparing trends in various indexes, Mills reached a figure which "represents 49.0 percent of the total decline of employment (in man-hours) between 1929 and 1935. Without going into the causal relations involved, this may be taken to measure the loss of employment directly associated with rising   productivity, with reference to the level of output actually prevailing in 1935." This figure was much higher than Kahler's 1935 estimate that 20 percent of recent manufacturing unemployment was due to technological change mainly because Mills and Kahler constructed their output, employment, and productivity indexes from different primary sources. Where Mills used Census data, Kahler used FRB, BLS, and NICB data. This difference between Mills' and Kahler's estimates is a perfect example of the data problems that kept the technological unemployment debates from being resolved. Mills cautioned that his results were only suggestive because the situation was so complex. But it was clear that his personal position was that technological unemployment was a real and significant contemporary problem. By 1938 Mills had made arguments in support of this position a half dozen times. One consequence of firmly adopting a position on one side of the debates was also illustrated well in Mills' 1938 paper. At one point, Mills remarked that an examination of records of separate industries showed that output, employment, and productivity movements seemed to be closely associated. This result was used by Slichter in 1928 and White in 1931 (and later by Fabricant in 1941) as a primary source of evidence in support of optimistic conclusions about technological unemployment. Mills, however, cursorily dismissed this evidence by stating simply that "these relations . . . call for more extended investigation." Mills' reluctance to accept as relevant a central piece of evidence that was in conflict with his personal views is a clear example of what was emerging as standard practice in the debates: economists tended to become committed to particular views and not to be receptive to information challenging their positions.[9]

Mills' 1938 article illustrates well the continuing problems in the empirical literature of evaluating existing sources of data about the topic of technological unemployment. The most important empirical contributions of 1937–38, however, added new information to the sources in existence. These contributions were made in the aggregate studies of the NRC and the NRP. The National Resources Committee report on *Technological Trends and National Policy* contained comprehensive chapters on technological histories and social effects for nine major economic sectors and a detailed survey of current aggregate trends.[10] The aggregate analysis was written by David Weintraub and Harold Posner of the National Research Project and was also published as both an NRC and NRP report. In this work the national income approach to the issue was developed to its greatest extent to date. The purpose of the study was stated to be to bring the best data available to bear on the question of whether "any economic changes [have] occurred during recent years and especially during the last two decades which justify the dark prophecies of ever increasing unemployment that have become current of late." The first problem was to consider carefully existing data and possible methodologies. In this review, Weintraub and Posner used the best data available on employment, output, hours, productivity, national income, and prices for as many sectors as good estimates existed. With respect to the fate of individual workers, they concluded that the data were not adequate to make reasonable judgments. They found the "scattered and inconclusive" studies by Lubin, Myers, Clague-Couper, Baker, and others were suggestive, as was Mills' turnover data, but judged these studies to be too few for valid generalizations. To provide a better estimate of the relative extent of displacement and absorption, Weintraub and Posner presented an alternative method of approaching the problem. Their method was new in that it treated the national economy as a whole. It was basically the same as that used by Stern, Weintraub, Kahler, Mills, and most others in the empirical debates, however, in that trends of various indexes were compared. Weintraub and Posner took actual output levels from two years and used productivity levels from the first year to calculate what employment in the second year would have been if productivity had remained constant. They then compared this employment with actual employment in the second year to yield what they called a figure for "unrealized employment." For 1922–29, they found that "'unrealized' employment constituted from one-fifth to one-half of the unemployed man-power in the years when over-all productivity was increased." They acknowledged that this did not measure the number of technologically unemployed. But they asserted that it did suggest that "it is reasonable to conclude that in any given year a considerable proportion of the unemployed consisted of workers who had been [technologically] displaced." As a result, they concluded that since the future outlook is for continuing productivity advance and "since our economic system has not evinced an ability to make the necessary adjustments fast enough, it may be expected that the dislocations occasioned by technological progress will continue to present serious problems of industrial, economic and social readjustments."[11]

These pessimistic conclusions were reinforced by later NRP findings.[12] As in previous work, however, these new empirical approaches also had problems with the methodological assumptions they made. The December 1938 American Statistical Association meetings, for example, presented a range of views on the methodology of the NRP work.[13] Harry Magdoff of the NRP staff defended the "unrealized employment" approach as a reasonable method of attacking the question of whether current unemployment was fundamentally different from that in the past. This measure of technological unemployment was attacked in detail, however, by Arthur Wubnig. Wubnig first noted that while technological change did affect productivity, it was only one of many influencing factors. Thus the NRP assumption that productivity changes were due to technological change was wrong. More important, Wubnig argued that the NRP's link between productivity changes and reemployment difficulties was not proven and plainly unjustifiable as an assumption. Wubnig's points were well taken, and seriously qualified the value of the NRP's work.

The extensive government-sponsored studies of the technological unemployment issue, then, foundered on the same difficulties as had previous empirical studies. One other attempt to address the issue in a new way in the late 1930s had the same result. Beginning in 1937, practitioners of the then still-novel skills of econometrics turned to an analysis of the issue. A model to attack the problem was first proposed by D. I. Vinogradoff in *Econometrica* in October 1933, but no data were used.[14] In 1937, however, J. J. J. Dalmulder used U. S. data covering 1921–31 to estimate a model of his own.[15] Dalmulder was more interested in justifying the use of econometrics to attack the problem than in deriving results, but his illustrative examples showed that a period of from sixteen to twenty years would be needed to return to full employment in response to a significant exogenous productivity increase. The most careful econometric work on the issue, however, was presented by Jan Tinbergen and Paul de Wolff in a 1939 paper. Using U. S. data from 1910 and 1919–32, they formulated a long-run model with a chief interest in "studying the consequence of technological development for employment and the consequences of some of the best-known devices to improve employment." After a careful explanation of the model and data, Tinbergen and de Wolff were surprised to find that "the remarkable result obtained by our calculations is that [increases in labor productivity] are unfavorable to employment. This stands in contrast to what is known as the compensation theory." A number of indirect influences, including price and income changes, were included in the model, but they found that "our results show that these repercussions are not able to compensate for more than 50% of the direct influence."[16]

The application of new techniques of analysis by the econometricians had no noticeable impact on the debates. In the last years of the 1930s the range of views expressed about the technological unemployment issue in the empirical professional literature remained as wide as ever. TNEC hearings in 1940 on *Technology and Concentration of Economic Power* provided a compendium of contemporary views, with testimony by economists Corrington Gill and Isador Lubin defending the optimistic case in reviews of recent professional contributions.[17] The intensity of professional interest in the question at the time and the continuing substantive divergence between views are illustrated by three major studies of the issue in 1940–41 by Solomon Fabricant, Spurgeon Bell, and John M. Blair.

Fabricant's evaluation of the employment impact of recent technological change was the first project in a NBER series expanding upon the work of the National Research Project. Using NRP work as a base, Fabricant revised, expanded, and published the best manufacturing statistics to date. In 1940 he completed work on output data. In 1941 he published a survey of results on *The Relation between Factory Employment and Output since 1899*. Overall Fabricant found no consistent aggregate relation between his indexes. When he looked at individual industries, however, a major conclusion was apparent.

First, Fabricant found a high correlation between output and employment movements. Second, he found a similar correlation between output, employment, and worker-output ratio changes. In fact, worker-output ratios declined the most where output and employment were up the most. Third, he found that an examination of the stages of development of an industry showed little pattern in worker-output ratios beyond a continuous decline. Fabricant acknowledged that the implication of these results for debates over technological unemployment was not decisive: "Technological unemployment, i.e., the fraction of total unemployment that may be ascribed to a particular set of the several factors making for unemployment, remains so complex and theoretical that it can scarcely be estimated with existing statistics." But Fabricant concluded that his results suggested a more optimistic relation between productivity and employment than had been commonly assumed.[18]

Spurgeon Bell's study was part of the continuing Brookings Institution studies of the distribution of income in relation to economic progress.[19] Bell presented a detailed survey of output, employment, productivity, wage, price, and profit trends for five manufacturing industries and four major sectors. Bell's stated purpose was to determine the actual facts of the distribution of productivity gains since 1919 among workers, owners, and consumers. Using the by-now familiar national-income-per-manhour approach for this work, Bell reached several conclusions. In all sectors, he found a remarkable rise in productivity. He also found that employment in all sectors had declined materially. He found that the volume of output did not rise proportionally to productivity and that total wages had fallen considerably from 1923 to 1937. Bell's conclusion based on these trends was that the gains of productivity advance should go to price declines. If gains went to wages or capital, as he claimed to have found in recent trends, then no gain in employment would result.

Bell's analysis was unsatisfactory in many respects, and in a severely critical review Mordecai Ezekiel demonstrated clearly the problems that continued to bedevil the empirical literature. Ezekiel acknowledged that Bell had presented an impressive amount of important data in analyzing the problem. In drawing his final conclusions, however, Ezekiel found that "the author makes little use of data. . . . The book turns to a purely theoretical (and highly oversimplified) analysis." Ezekiel found that "solely on the basis of this theoretical discussion, the general conclusion is suggested that a part, at least, of recent unemployment has been due to shifting productivity gains too much to higher wages and higher profits and too little to lower prices." As a result of its failure to provide a satisfactory link between empirical trends and theory-based conclusions, Ezekiel concluded that Bell's study was highly disappointing. Given that Bell's conclusions were not justifiable, Ezekiel turned to a consideration of what actually could be said about the issue using Bell's data. First, and in support of Bell, Ezekiel found that the lower-price, higher-output nexus was much more marked in the 1920s than in the 1930s. Second, and opposed to Bell, Ezekiel found that most productivity gains had gone to profits in the 1920s, and to wages and prices in the 1930s. Ezekiel noted that these facts threw little light on Bell's thesis that price declines were the best policy. "He may be right—but not because of the facts he has brought together."[20]

John Blair's analysis was part of the TNEC monograph studies and capped off the depression discussions with one of the most pessimistic empirical analyses of the entire debate. Blair's thesis in this paper was that depression-period technological change had caused a significant unemployment problem, and that automatic economic mechanisms to offset this unemployment did not exist. Blair used a range of case study and aggregate data to support these conclusions. First, Blair reviewed the extent of recent productivity advances. Using Census data for 1909, 1914, and 1919, and other data for 1923 to 1939, Blair found that in manufacturing, railroads, and coal mining, productivity had reached all-time high levels in 1939. For the period of 1923–29 Blair found that output and productivity had moved rather closely together. In 1929, however, he found that the pattern had radically changed as output fell and productivity continued to climb. Blair used data for forty manufacturing industries from NRP reports to support these conclusions. Blair next presented a list of types of labor-saving techniques. Blair's purpose here was to point out the wide range of changes that caused labor displacement, and each example was illustrated with recent instances of change. Turning to the effects of these recent technological changes, Blair then presented recent output and manhour data for twenty manufacturing industries. In each case, he found output was nearly the same in 1929 and 1936–38, yet in nearly every case sharp decreases in manhours were evident. Blair found that an examination of sectoral data for manufacturing, railroads, and mining yielded the same results. Blair then cited NRP case studies and the earlier Lubin, Myers, Clague-Couper, and Baker results to show that "technological unemployment is likely to be long-term unemployment." In view of all these negative effects of technological change, Blair claimed that it was to be hoped that automatic forces existed in the economy to compensate for them. Blair's look at these forces, however, again yielded negative results. His data on hours-worked trends showed a pattern of steep declines followed by a plateau, and Blair concluded that there was no immediate large-scale further reduction in sight. Blair also found the value of new industries to be suspect. He argued that new industries go through initial periods of rapid employment growth very quickly. If the new goods are substitutes, they cancel employment elsewhere. If they are capital-saving, they reduce investment demand. With respect to the compensation mechanism of price reductions, Blair reviewed his recent doctoral thesis results to show that concentrated industries do not use prices as an output expansion policy. As a result of all these trends, Blair could only conclude that "in the absence of effective offsetting forces economic and social distress may be expected to accumulate. . . . Today a state of unbalance exists, and it seems likely that under present conditions unbalance will continue and perhaps become ever more pronounced."[21]

Fabricant's NBER study, the Bell-Ezekiel exchange, and Blair's government-sponsored TNEC analysis are an effective way to end a discussion of the

1930s empirical discussions of technological unemployment. The range of views at the end of the decade was as pronounced as at the beginning, and, if anything, even more forcefully stated. Despite the appearance of significant new empirical techniques in the debates (econometrics) and of major efforts to collect more data on the issue (the NRP and NRC studies), progress in arriving at a resolution in the empirical debates was limited. Many of the new empirical arguments, sources, and techniques appeared in just a short period right at the end of the decade, so it would be expected that it would take a while for their importance to be assimilated. What might have happened with a few more months for the effects of these contributions to work their way through the literature cannot be known, however. World War II soon changed all the economic issues of interest, and the technological unemployment debates were quickly forgotten.

6

Resolution and Interpretation of the Technological Unemployment Debates

World War II ended the popular technological unemployment debates. Interest in the issue disappeared for the first time in fifteen years as government agencies that had been concerned with finding jobs for workers turned their attention overnight to finding workers for jobs. Productivity change became a concern not for its rapidity but for its retardation.

World War II also effectively ended the professional empirical debates of the 1930s just when the lines were drawn most clearly between alternative interpretations of past and current trends. Only a handful of professional papers approached the question empirically after 1941, and no significant original analyses were made.[1] A conclusive empirical analysis had not appeared. Rather, as a current policy problem, the issue simply ended. The pessimistic empirical analyses of the depression quickly became irrelevant as the long-run adjustment of employment to productivity-induced job opportunities that had been confidently predicted for fifteen years finally was accomplished, and the appeal to historical precedent which was the major foundation for this confidence was justified once more.

Although World War II ended the empirical debates among economists, it did not stop the theoretical discussions. As a problem in economic theory, the question of the employment impact of technological change transcended immediate policy concerns. As a result, several significant contributions were made during the war. At the beginning of the war, the mid-1930s theoretical consensus among economists that price flexibility was adequate to compensate for all problems of technological unemployment held firm. In the early 1940s, however, the spread of Keynesian ideas began to weaken confidence in the price flexibility mechanism.[2]

In 1942 the implications of Keynesian analysis for the theory of technological unemployment were identified clearly in an exchange between Hans Neisser and Everett Hagen. Neisser's purpose was to demonstrate that no automatic mechanism of any kind existed to guarantee the reabsorption of technologically unemployed labor. In equilibrium analysis, Neisser found that the possibility of technological unemployment is denied "only as to a state of long-run general equilibrium proper, in which complete adjustment of all the variables of the economic system is attained (size of firm, input, output, prices of goods produced, prices of productive services, interest rate)." He also noted that the opinion was widely held that wage reductions of only a minor sort would be sufficient to absorb the technologically unemployed, and that any unemployment would only be of a short-run nature. Neisser claimed, however, that both of these beliefs were wrong and that long-run unemployment could exist. He gave a simple example assuming fixed coefficients of production to claim that there was no guarantee of a meaningful equilibrium solution under all conditions. Expanding this line of reasoning, he argued that even if coefficients of production were assumed to be variable, there was no guarantee of a meaningful solution. Thus "we are not entitled to expect from the marginal productivity mechanism the absorption of displaced workers beyond a certain, probably narrow limit." Neisser found that what had happened in the past to give an apparently satisfactory result was that "the reabsorption of displaced labor has been brought about, to by far the largest extent, by the accumulation and investment of capital; much more indeed, than by the processes analyzed in the preceding sections." He noted that no important theorist had denied that the accumulation of capital raises the demand for labor, but he found that claiming this as actually the key process at work had been considered unsatisfactory and that explanations had been sought elsewhere. In actual fact, however, Neisser found that "displacement and accumulation are two largely *independent* factors, and it is impossible to predict the outcome of the race between the two on purely theoretical grounds." As a result, Neisser found that "the conclusion is inevitable: there is no mechanism within the framework of rational economic analysis that, in any situation, would secure the full absorption of displaced workers and render 'permanent' technological unemployment in any sense impossible."[3]

In a comment on Neisser, E. E. Hagen noted that in the past eleven years there had been two major contributions to the theory of technological unemployment, the current work by Neisser and the two 1931 articles by Alvin Hansen.[4] Hagen's only criticism of Neisser was that Neisser ignored the Keynesian savings-investment problem. Hagen claimed that technological advance could lead to more money in fewer hands, thus possibly to more savings and a lower marginal propensity to consume. Thus even more investment would be needed to maintain even the new lower level of employment.

By the middle 1940s, then, the limitations of price flexibility as an automatic compensatory mechanism in the economy, which had been widely discussed since the appearance of Keynes' *General Theory*, had finally had an impact on the theory of technological unemployment. Claims that price flexibility was the key to stability and to proper adjustment could still be found in the literature as traces of the debates of the 1930s. The Brookings Institution, for example, continued to promote this theme.[5] But opinions that price flexibility had only a limited importance for full employment policy were being heard more and more. A final mid-1940s sample of economists' analyses of price flexibility and full employment supports this view.

In a 1945 book on *Price Flexibility and Employment*, for example, Oscar Lange expanded on several of his studies related to the issue of price flexibility. In this book, Lange turned to an explicit account of the impact of innovations. His major concern was with the mechanism of the effect of innovations on the demand for and employment of a factor. He found that reemployment, even under conditions of flexible prices, can occur automatically only under special conditions. Lange argued that there was good reason to believe that these conditions were approximately met in the period 1840 to 1914. However, he found that "in our present capitalistic economy, the forces that elicit oversaving, exhaustion of 'investment opportunities,' and 'technological unemployment' have greatly increased in strength. Simultaneously, the conditions which endowed price flexibility with a long-run stabilizing influence upon the economy (in particular the flexibility of prices of factors of production) have largely disappeared." As a result, Lange concluded that price flexibility as a policy had been rendered inapplicable under present conditions and that it may, in fact, even act as a destabilizing force.[6]

Two other late 1940s references also support the view that a new theoretical consensus had emerged. Two early postwar doctoral dissertations on employment and technological change examined in detail past theories of technological unemployment and reached conclusions in agreement with the Neisser-Hagan-Lange arguments. These dissertations, by Nathan Belfer in 1946 and Shou Shan Pu in 1949, both concluded that no economic mechanism existed to guarantee the automatic reabsorption of technologically displaced workers.[7] Both Belfer and Pu found that Keynesian analysis suggested a way of overcoming unemployment from technological change. But in the end, both found grounds for final pessimism, Belfer because of the possibility that the economy was reaching maturity, and Pu because of the apparent close connection between modern technological change and increasing industrial concentration.

In this mid to late 1940s theoretical literature, a third period of consensus was achieved to add to the consensus periods of 1927–29 (the Say-Douglas purchasing power argument) and 1933–40 (the neoclassical price-flexibility argument). As illustrated by the work of Neisser, Hagen, Lange, Belfer, and Pu, this consensus—built on Keynesian arguments—was that no mechanism existed in the economic system to guarantee the automatic reabsorption of technologically unemployed labor.

This is where the technological unemployment debates ended. With the full employment of World War II and the spread of Keynesian policy ideas about how to achieve full employment, the pessimism about unemployment and productivity trends that had motivated the debates of the 1920s and 1930s disappeared. The renewal of professional optimism about the unemployment effects of technological change was evident to the profession itself by the early 1950s. Jan Tinbergen, in 1952, for example, noted the new optimism in a comment on the "well-known old thesis that an *increase in labour productivity* leads to an increase in economic welfare. . . . Many times . . . doubt has risen concerning the validity of that thesis. There are the old nineteenth-century discussions on technological unemployment, and we all know their modern versions from the thirties. During the recent full-employment years the old optimism as to the consequences of increased productivity has been revived."[8]

In effect, by the early 1950s the state of aggregate professional opinion about technological unemployment had returned to the confident views of the late 1920s. The events of recent years, including the development of Keynesian analysis and the recent postwar near-full employment, provided a basis for confidence in this viewpoint which had been lacking for a quarter century. The professional debates had been put aside, but they were not to stay there. Within a decade a new professional debate again directly concerned with the impact of recent technological change on the level of unemployment had begun.

Before looking at these new disputes, a few additional comments on the technological unemployment debates are relevant. First of all, taking an aggregate point of view, it is evident that progress toward a consensus did occur. This movement, however, was almost exclusively on a theoretical level. In the empirical literature, progress toward a general professional agreement was not evident. The reasons for the divergent experience of these two kinds of discussions can be seen by considering each type of analysis in turn.

The theoretical question at issue in the 1930s disputes was whether there were automatic mechanisms in the economy that guaranteed the reemployment of technologically unemployed labor. If such mechanisms existed, then technological unemployment was no more than a short-run concern. If such mechanisms did not exist, then it was possible that technological change by itself could create a large and mounting unemployment problem.

In the professional exchanges over this issue, there were three periods of consensus, with transition periods in between. The first consensus centered around the classical Say-McCulloch purchasing power argument. This was the common view in the 1927–29 discussions and was the view supported by Paul Douglas in his 1930 theory paper. This view was soon challenged by other economists, however. Slichter, Tugwell, and Hansen explicitly attacked this approach soon after Douglas' analysis appeared. Haberler responded in partial defense. By the mid-1930s, however, it was clear that a new theory consensus was emerging. The classical analysis of technological displacement had been replaced by the neoclassical view. Slichter and Hansen had pointed in this direction, with Kaldor's 1932 article presenting the most careful defense of the ability of substitution and price changes to handle the automatic reabsorption of technologically unemployed labor. By the end of the 1930s, this neoclassical approach was the dominant one in the discussions. Theory comments by Slichter (1934) and Lonigan (1939), for example, strongly supported this view. Then, with the emergence of Keynesian arguments, a new approach appeared. As presented by Neisser, Hagen, Lange, Belfer, and Pu, the Keynesian pessimism about the ability of the economy automatically to achieve full employment was applied to the issue of technological unemployment.

That there was an evolution of the aggregate theoretical debates, then, is clear. This progress, however, was primarily due to updating the theoretical analysis of the issue in terms of rediscovered or newly discovered analytical concepts in economics. Progress in the theoretical literature was not due to discussions in concurrent empirical studies. In fact, there was little connection at all between the evolution of the theoretical and the empirical literature. The connections that did exist were in the direction of theory-to-empirical work. Paul Douglas, for example, proposed an ambitious research program in 1930 to collect data on the elasticity of demand in various industries based on his compensation theory analysis. The extensive 1930s empirical studies of price rigidities in the economy, notably by F. C. Mills and Gardner Means, also were based on the 1930s theoretical consensus that price flexibility was the key to resolving employment issues due to technological change. But there is no evidence that these empirical studies of price rigidities modified the mid-1930's professional consensus that, in Edna Lonigan's words, technological unemployment is really "price unemployment." Movement away from the neoclassical price-flexibility consensus only came after the introduction of the new Keynesian theoretical perspective, and not because of the negative empirical evidence of the price rigidity studies.

The reason for the division between the experience of the theoretical and empirical literatures had much to do with the fact that the central issue in the empirical contributions was different from that in the theory debates. It need not have been. The theory disputes, which were over the existence of a mechanism in the economic system, were susceptible to empirical study. For example, the flexibility of prices or the substitutability of factors in existing production functions could be studied, as in Means' and Mills' work. But little empirical work during the technological unemployment debates was tied in this way to the theoretical discussions. Rather, the major question attacked in the empirical literature was whether recent technological change had been responsible for a significant amount of recent or current aggregate unemployment. This question clearly was important, but it did not have a direct link to the theoretical analyses of the impact of technology on employment. Without this connection, the theory and empirical debates took on independent lives and evolved for reasons related to their own internal logic. The separate nature of the two literatures was also supported by the fact that economists who wrote theoretical and empirical studies were almost totally different groups.

Within the empirical discussions of the aggregate unemployment question there were a few areas of progress. The Clague-Couper, Myers, and Lubin type of displaced-worker studies were universally acknowledged as demonstrating that technological change did have a significant unemployment impact on some workers. These studies all focused on the prosperity years of the 1920s so that cyclical factors were effectively controlled. Other studies also seem to have had an impact on the aggregate empirical debates. Harry Jerome's study of mechanization in the 1920s was one of these. Mechanization, however, was only one of the important rationalization trends of the 1920s, and thus Jerome did not cover the entire range of technological-change effects. The many careful productivity and employment studies of individual industries had the same handicaps. These micro-level studies were valuable, but they did not settle the central empirical question of what the aggregate employment impact of recent technological change had been.

The problems in approaching this macro question through micro studies were well recognized. The 1931 methodological papers by Ewan Clague, Harry Jerome, and Boris Stern demonstrated this awareness clearly. The problem was the traditional one of making inferences about general cases from specific instances. But the technological unemployment question was particularly difficult to study due to problems of dispersed effects and agreeing on acceptable definitions for technological change and unemployment. The recognition of the difficulties of doing these studies, however, did not stop economists from making the effort. Because of severe data restrictions, most of the aggregate judgments economists made were for a few sectors, with manufacturing the area of particular concentration. In this aggregate work, however, taking an overview of all the published articles that appeared in the depression period, little change occurred that could be called movement toward a final consensus. The difficulty of making aggregate judgments on the basis of individual or industry studies explains much of this experience.

Leaving aggregate issues and turning to the individual level, a question of interest is how the views of individual economists evolved during the debates. During the 1930s discussions, there were only a few cases where individual economists made a significant number of contributions to the issue. Of ten economists who wrote often enough so that changes in opinion can be observed, four showed signs of change in their views.

The first economist whose work exhibited a notable change is Paul Douglas. Douglas was one of the first to comment on the new BLS-Commerce-Census productivity studies in 1927 and 1928. At that time he did not make any significant employment judgments. In 1930, however, Douglas entered the technological unemployment debates in a major way with several papers on the issues. Douglas' main point was clear. He felt that technological unemployment was only a short-run problem and that automatic mechanisms existed within the system to reemploy all displaced labor. Douglas' 1930 theory paper was the first major professional statement of this argument in the debates. The noticeable change in Douglas' views came in a 1933 article and a 1935 book. In each of these publications Douglas acknowledged the critiques that had been made of his views by Hansen and Haberler. Douglas accepted these critiques and modified his theoretical analysis accordingly.

A second economist whose work showed change is Sumner Slichter. Slichter changed his mind several times on the technological unemployment issue. Between 1927 and 1928 Slichter noticeably changed his emphasis on the seriousness of technological unemployment. In his last 1928 article Slichter criticized the view that technological change was the main cause of recent trends. Then, in a December 1931 paper, Slichter was sympathetic to the view that technological change was a major factor in recent unemployment. In a January 1934 article, Slichter was again critical of those claiming that technological change was a recent unemployment factor. The only acknowledgment Slichter gave of these shifts in view was in his January 1934 article, which had a footnote noting simply that his emphasis had changed since his 1931 article.

Another economist whose emphasis changed with respect to the issue is David Weintraub. In a 1932 article covering the railroad, manufacturing, and coal mining sectors, Weintraub reached an optimistic conclusion about the impact of technological change on unemployment during the 1920s. In his several late 1930s analyses as director of the National Research Project, however, Weintraub presented a distinctly different view. His "unrealized employment" study covering the 1920s and 1930s, for example, suggested that technological change had been a major factor in recent unemployment trends. All of Weintraub's NRP work supported this view.

A final economist whose views changed is Isador Lubin. In various 1929 analyses of his Brookings displaced-worker study, Lubin made first a positive, and then a negative interpretation of his results. In a 1930 paper Lubin again suggested that technological unemployment was a problem. In his 1940 TNEC testimony, however, Lubin took an optimistic view of the recent employment impact of technological change. It is difficult to compare Lubin's views between these contributions because his first discussions focused on the fate of individual workers, while his 1940 comments were directed to aggregate unemployment issues. But the suggestion is strong that Lubin's emphasis on the employment impact of technological change had changed.

These, then, are the instances where it appears that some significant modification of individual views took place during the 1930s debates. The list of economists whose work suggests no significant change in view is longer and includes Willford King, Rexford Tugwell, Alvin Hansen, Emil Lederer, Mordecai Ezekiel, and Frederick C. Mills. No other economists published often enough for a judgment to be made about the evolution of their work. Any judgment based on this small sample about the average tendency for change in individual thought must be a tentative one. But overall it appears that significant modifications in individuals' views were not a common occurrence. Adding these individual-level conclusions to those on the aggregate level, it is difficult to argue that data analysis played a dominant role in the progress of professional thought in the 1930s technological unemployment debates.

A final question about the 1930s debates is whether the failure of empirical analysis to contribute greatly to progress in the disputes lies mainly in problems with how the data was used or with the quality of the data itself. It is clear that methodological difficulties hindered the impact of empirical studies. F. C. Mills' 1932 conclusions were criticized by Wolman in 1933, for example, because Mills' choice of base years seriously influenced his results. The NRP construction of an "unrealized employment" data series was criticized in December 1938 *Journal of the American Statistical Association* articles as a meaningless concept. The Lubin, Myers, and Clague-Couper case studies were often noted as too restricted in coverage to support any aggregate conclusions. Slichter's (1930) major criticism of Douglas' (1930) ambitious empirical approach to the issue was based on the contention that Douglas' method was not justifiable. F. B. Garver (1932) criticized Willford King's (1932) analysis on similar grounds. Ezekiel's (1940) criticism of Bell (1940) was based on the fact that Bell's conclusions had little connection with his data.

There are thus many examples where the appropriate use of data was an issue. Overall, however, the balance of evidence favors the conclusion that the major factor restricting the impact of data analysis in the 1930s debates was the quality of available data sources. This fact was noted constantly and by almost every participant from the very beginnings of the debates. Comments about the limitations of available data from just the early 1930s include those by Baker (1930), Slichter (1930), Butler (1931), White (1931), Clague (1931), Jerome (1931), Garver (1932), and Stern (1932).

A fact reinforcing this view is that the major empirical studies that were done were extremely restricted in scope. Almost all of Mills' several studies focused only on manufacturing. Weintraub's major 1932 analysis was based on manufacturing, coal mining, and railroad data. Jerome's 1934 book ranged outside of manufacturing only to the extent of adding information on the experience of two dozen companies. Kahler and Woytinsky in 1935 used only manufacturing data. Other examples could be given, but the story is the same. Comprehensive output and employment data did not exist in the 1930s for most areas of the economy. Developments in the service sector in particular were not considered simply because no data existed. This problem of data availability was beginning to be solved by the late 1930s. The NRP analysis by Weintraub and Posner, for example, used a national income approach to make conclusions about aggregate trends, and national income and employment data were soon widely in use. By the end of the 1930s debates, however, these sources were still new and extremely rough.

The overall conclusion, then, is that the major factors limiting the impact of data analysis in the 1930s debates were the fact that the empirical literature addressed other questions than those at issue in the theoretical discussions, and the fact that relevant data were severely limited in quantity and quality. The first fact guaranteed that empirical investigations would have little impact on the evolution of the theory discussions. The second fact guaranteed that empirical conclusions about the aggregate employment effects of technological change could not be convincing. Given such fundamental problems, it is not surprising that the empirical work of the 1930s had little impact on progress in aggregate or individual thought.

7

Origin of the Structural Unemployment Debates

The structural unemployment debates of the 1960s evolved out of a series of events in the 1950s. A central factor in this development was the rise of automation as a popular issue. A second was recent trends in unemployment. A third was continuing professional interest in the nature and composition of unemployment. By 1959 all three factors had come together to motivate the first discussions among economists of the possibility of rising structural unemployment. It was not until early 1961, however, that a structural unemployment debate can be said to have begun.

The first important factor in this process was the rise of automation as a popular issue. The new technique of automatic control that was developed in World War II came to be known as "automation" by the late 1940s. At that time, many optimistic business articles appeared about the promise of the new methods. Through the Korean War, the general tenor of these popular remarks was one of optimism and relative unconcern. Some warnings about labor displacement problems appeared, but these were not numerous.[1]

After the Korean War, however, the economy entered a recession. The recent rise of business enthusiasm for automation was quickly linked in the popular literature to unemployment trends. As a result, during 1955 automation moved for the first time to center stage as an issue of concern. The popular debate became so intense in 1955 that the Baltimore *Sun* dubbed automation "The Cliche of the Year."[2]

The number of popular articles debating the consequences of automation soared during the mid to late 1950s. Congressional hearings on the issue were held in 1955, 1956, 1957, and 1960. There was a slackening in popular interest during the economic recovery of 1956–57, but interest picked up again with the downturn of 1957–58.[3] Automation then remained a major popular issue through the mid-1960s. Only after unemployment fell below 4 percent during the Vietnam War did automation begin to disappear as an everyday topic in popular publications.

These popular discussions were a critical background factor in the rise of the professional structural unemployment debates. An equally important factor was recent trends in unemployment rates. Since World War II, unemployment had cycled upward. By 1960 the length of the expansion in each postwar cycle had been shorter (1948–52, 45 months; 1953–57, 35 months; 1957–60, 25 months), and the average unemployment rate in each cycle had been higher (1948–49, 4.2%; 1953–57, 4.5%; 1957–60, 5.8%).[4] During the late 1950s, the major professional issue of concern was inflation. But recent unemployment trends became increasingly emphasized, and by the beginning of the 1960s the major economic issue of professional interest had shifted to unemployment.

The trends in unemployment and automation were closely connected in the popular press. In fact, the periods of the most intense popular automation debate coincided, with a slight lag, with the three post-Korean War recessions of the 1950s. As in the late 1920s, however, it took something more to involve professional economists in the technology and employment debates. Until the early 1960s, nothing that could be called a professional debate had begun as a result of the popular discussions. Many economists had written on the topic of recent unemployment trends during the 1950s. Many had written on automation. Some were optimists and some were pessimists. But a professional debate linking the automation and unemployment issues did not exist in the 1950s literature.

In the 1960s, however, such a debate existed. It was acknowledged within the profession that a debate existed, and the debate was reported as such in the popular press. The sequence of events leading to a renewal of professional debate over the relation between technological change and unemployment was the following.

The earliest response of economists to the popular automation debate was to claim that there was nothing to worry about. By the early 1950s the traditional confidence of economists in the positive effects of technological change had been restored.[5] The general belief was that careful Keynesian policy could handle all problems of technological unemployment. Thus, although it was admitted that individual short-run problems of adjustment could occur, the general professional view was that there was no cause for concern.[6]

At the same time that these optimistic analyses was being made, however, other economists interested in the nature and structure of unemployment began to identify specific trends that were worrisome. It was in these mid-1950s professional studies of recent unemployment that the foundations for the structural unemployment debates were laid.[7] In particular, the years 1955–57 saw the publication of a large professional body of literature on problems of chronic unemployment.[8] One aspect of this work involved case studies of automation-displaced workers. Several of these studies reported results that were remarkably close to those reported thirty years before in the late 1920s debates over technological unemployment, although no connection was made in the literature between the two groups of studies. A review of recent evidence in a 1957 *Monthly Labor Review* article found, for example, that "a good many recent studies have found that in practice workers are not so mobile as is commonly believed: that what mobility there is, is achieved only at a price of considerable sacrifice exacted from the worker and his family."[9]

The result of the mid-1950s professional studies tying recent automation concerns to unemployment was to identify possible problem areas. But in this work no critical difficulties were discovered. In particular, there was no debate over the extent of structural unemployment.[10] As employment levels deteriorated in the late 1950s, however, the concept of structural unemployment first became identified by economists as an issue.

During 1959 and 1960 structural unemployment became a commonly used term in professional policy discussions. Although no single professional paper can be identified as the first to use the concept, structural unemployment first appeared as a professional policy concern during late 1958 and early 1959. A review of a few late 1959 comments by economists illustrates the prevalence of the topic by that time.[11]

In November 1959 Joint Economic Committee hearings, for example, Neil Chamberlain found that "structural unemployment is easily differentiated from the seasonal, transitional and cyclical types. It and technological unemployment are often closely related, however, and sometimes not easily distinguished." Chamberlain found that he could "make no estimate of the present magnitude of the problem. Unemployment figures do not allow a ready sorting out of those whose jobless status is due to something we can define as structural change." Chamberlain did feel, however, that "regardless of this problem of estimating . . . and regardless of the number actually affected, I would contend that it is important that new policies be devised to provide greater protection to those affected."[12]

At the same November 1959 hearings, Philip Taft and Merton Stoltz addressed the same problem. Taft and Stoltz noted that "structural unemployment can be defined as involuntary idleness which arises from causes other than changes in aggregate demand. It is likely to be concentrated in an industry or a region or both. . . . It is a stubborn and persistent type of unemployment." In contrast to Chamberlain, however, they found that "[s]tructural is not distinguishable from cyclical and seasonal unemployment, nor are the various types of unemployment independent." But they claimed that "nevertheless, readily observable evidence indicates that structural unemployment is a problem of major importance."[13]

At separate late 1959 hearings, Herbert Parnes added his voice to those expressing structural concerns, as he found a significant tie between recent employment and technological trends. Parnes claimed that "if this so-called irreducible minimum is conceived necessarily to include the pockets of unemployment that develop in particular localities, and in particular industries and occupations as the result of structural changes in the economy, then we will probably have to reconcile ourselves to unemployment rates nationally of 4 to 5 percent, or perhaps even greater, as technological change accelerates." Parnes also noted the "paradox" that recent unemployment was apparently due, not to too few jobs, but to the wrong match between available jobs and workers. Parnes' solution was to study carefully other nations' experience with similar problems.[14]

Clarence Long in late 1959 Congressional testimony also found reason for structural concern. In his words,

I think most of the ways in which we have thought in terms of trying to get the unemployment rate down has been to operate on the demand side, through spending and other devices, but I think we are realizing the closer we get to this problem of unemployment, that most of the obstacles to reducing the rate of unemployment, getting a lower normal [are] on the supply side. They are in the nature of the unemployed person, where he is, what kind of a fellow he is, and if we can deal with the problem that way, I think we can achieve [a] much lower rate of unemployment.[15]

In a comment at the 1959 American Economic Association meetings, Jacob Kaufman stated the possible conflict between aggregate and structural policies even more strongly: "There must be a recognition of the fact that monetary and fiscal policy is concerned solely with levels of unemployment and can accomplish little in alleviating structural unemployment in our economy. Assuming this to be true, it is essential that various programs be developed to attack the problem of unemployment of particular groups—young persons, non-whites, women—and particular areas."[16]

By the end of 1959, then, structural unemployment as a concept and as a current policy problem was widely recognized among economists. From a few isolated remarks in 1958, the number of economists who were commenting on structural problems had risen to well over a dozen. Although all agreed that recent trends showed a significant problem of structural unemployment, there were notable differences of opinion among the various commentators. Some argued that recent technological change was an important contributing factor, while others did not. Some concluded that there was an important conflict between aggregate and structural unemployment policies, while others did not. But none of these differences were emphasized in the 1959 discussions. The dominant mood was one of agreement rather than conflict, with the common theme being that there was a significant unemployment problem that should be more widely recognized.

That the professional concerns of 1959 were having this impact was evidenced by the publication in the last months of 1959 of several major government studies on differential unemployment.[17] The most important of these studies was a Bureau of Labor Statistics study on "The Extent and Nature of Frictional Unemployment." This study reviewed previously unavailable data covering the period since 1945 with a focus on the period 1955–57. Frictional unemployment was defined in the analysis as "that level of joblessness that would not be reduced significantly in the short run by increased aggregate spending." The structural component of total unemployment was defined as

"unemployment of a longer duration associated with long-term declines in occupations, industries, and areas, reflecting the development of new products,
changing tastes, developing technology, etc."[18] The major conclusions were
that, of total unemployment in 1955–57, 10 percent was found to be due to
long-term structural changes, 10 percent to voluntary job changes, 20 percent to
seasonal unemployment, 20 percent to the entry of new workers, and 40 percent
to nonmeasured (mainly cyclical) factors.

The unemployment trends found in this study did not seem to support strong
structural unemployment concerns. However this study only covered the period
1955–57, and trends since 1957 seemed to imply a more serious current situation. The BLS results, then, did not stop structural unemployment concerns,
and comments about the structure of unemployment continued strongly into
1960. One publication of particular importance was a compilation of studies by
prominent economists issued by the Senate Special Committee on Unemployment Problems. In his introduction to the collection, John Dunlop supported
the recent emphasis on differential unemployment. Dunlop claimed that unemployment today "clusters and pockets in certain communities, occupations,
racial groups, age brackets, and short-time workers. It is less general but more
concentrated in certain classes of our citizens. Mass unemployment of the thirties gave way to class unemployment of the fifties. It is the balkanization of the
unemployed that is now of greater concern." Dunlop emphasized that economic growth was essential, but he felt that recent conditions of structural unemployment demanded special programs. In his words, "Public policies on
unemployment always need to be conceived in terms of twin related policies:
those designed to influence the level and others directed toward structure of
unemployment." Dunlop felt that

a great deal of mischief has been done in discussions of public policy concerning unemployment by allowing fiscal and monetary policies to preempt and dominate the field.
We need a much keener appreciation of the areas and limitations within which general
fiscal and monetary policy are the major appropriate tools to treat unemployment. . . .
General fiscal and monetary policies are blunt and crude tools to treat unemployment
within the range of 2 to 3 or 3.5 million in the light of the differential structure of class
unemployment.

In Dunlop's view, "public policies need to be tailormade to the diverse types of
class unemployment rather than geared exclusively to the largely obsolete issue
of mass unemployment."[19]

Dunlop's statement of the problem is an important one. In it, the difference
between the concerns of economists in the technological unemployment debates
of the 1930s and in the structural unemployment debates of the 1960s is made
clear. Concern in the 1930s was with Dunlop's mass unemployment. The fear
of those worried about technological unemployment was that unemployment
would be at permanently higher levels as a result of technological change. In
the new Keynesian world of the 1960s, mass unemployment was no longer an
issue. A decent level of aggregate unemployment could be guaranteed by ap-

propriate fiscal and monetary policies. Concern was now over Dunlop's class unemployment. The fear of those who worried about structural unemployment was that unemployment would be unevenly distributed and concentrated among certain vulnerable groups. Technological change was seen as one factor at work causing this clustering of the unemployed.

The Dunlop paper was only one of more than a dozen papers on recent structural unemployment developments in the Senate Special Committee on Unemployment collection.[20] Together they were a significant part of the accumulating evidence on the existence of a structural unemployment problem. All of these studies were concerned with demonstrating that a significant level of differential unemployment existed, and all of the authors were in favor of some type of special-aid (as opposed to general fiscal or monetary) policy to help alleviate the situation.

By early 1960, then, a significant amount of research had been conducted on the structure of recent unemployment, and many economists had expressed concern over these trends. During the rest of 1960 a considerable number of additional professional analyses of the effects of automation on employment appeared, as did several more analyses of recent unemployment trends.[21] Nothing that could be called a structural unemployment debate appeared in this literature, however. In these studies the existence of structural unemployment was clearly asserted. The possible conflict between aggregate unemployment and structural unemployment policy was noted. But in this era of Keynesian consensus about the fundamental forces at work in the macro economy, there was general agreement that the correct policy was one of growth with a complement of special-aid policies to help the structurally unemployed. There was no suggestion that current conditions argued strongly for one type of policy over the other. In particular, no cases could be found of economists emphatically denying that structural unemployment was a factor in recent unemployment trends. In effect, a period of consensus had emerged among those writing on recent unemployment trends. This consensus was that current unemployment was a serious problem, structural unemployment existed, and some special policies would be needed to combat the structural aspects of unemployment. This consensus among those writing on the issue at the time was based completely on recent empirical work. Formal data analysis appears here to have had a major impact on influencing professional thought.

This stage in the 1960s debates is analogous to the situation at the beginning of the technological unemployment debates in the late 1920s when several economists began to claim that recent data trends seemed to indicate a problem. The next stage in the structural debates also was much like that in the technological unemployment debates. Economists who did not agree with this view began to reply. The first responses to structural unemployment claims appeared in 1960. During 1961 a major response was made, and the structural unemployment debates were under way.

December 1960 Joint Economic Committee hearings on the *Current Economic Situation* previewed the debates to come. In his testimony Joseph Pechman claimed that "in my view the major impediment to economic growth during the past 5 years has been a combined monetary and fiscal policy which placed excessive restraints on the growth of aggregate demand."   Charles Schultz supported Pechman at the same hearings. After a review of relevant data for 1953–60, Schultz concluded that "the major reason for the failure of the economy to regain a full employment growth path after the 1958 recession, lies, I believe, in present Federal budget policies, and to a lesser extent in monetary policy." At the same hearings, Representative Thomas Curtis, who had become a strong structuralist, argued against Pechman and Schultz. The responses to Curtis anticipated the deficient demand positions that were soon to appear with increasing frequency. Schultz replied to Curtis that

the second and most important point I think you bring up is the difference between unemployment which is caused by too little overall demand and frictional or structural unemployment. . . . What you are saying is that currently technological advance, but more particularly, shifts in the pattern of the economy have become so rapid that full employment means 6 percent unemployed. This is the direction you are aiming at. This is what I don't agree with. . . . There is always imbalance. That is why we have the 4 percent [unemployment at full employment]. But is the extra unemployment we have had in the last cycle matched by an extra excess shortage of labor in other areas? . . . My own feeling would be . . . that this has not increased so substantially, that we can now say that we ought to be satisfied with 6 percent unemployment because really from an aggregate standpoint it is no worse than 6 percent.

Pechman supported Schultz's view in his reply that "if we convince ourselves that we are not suffering from a recession, that this is really a structural matter, we might try to go on having budget surpluses. . . . The present situation is one of economic contraction. It requires the usual fiscal and monetary measures to stimulate demand."[22]

In these remarks, the central point at issue was clearly defined. Was the full employment rate—the sum of frictional and structural unemployment—4 percent as normally claimed at the time, or now 6 percent due to technological and other changes in the economy? Although not mentioned in Schultz's or Pechman's comments, the existing Keynesian consensus acknowledged that unemployment could be driven as low as World War II levels of 1–2 percent, but only at a below-full employment cost of increasing inflation.

Another dimension to the soon-to-evolve structural unemployment debates was provided in a later 1960 paper by Clarence Long. Long presented a detailed argument that demand policy could not adequately solve current unemployment problems. According to Long, "only a small fraction of the average peacetime unemployment since 1947 has been directly traceable to the business cycle; five-sixths of it has been the kind that prevails even during the good years. . . . Unfortunately for the demand theory, it has not been able to explain why, in the face of very substantial increases in aggregate spending, unemployment can persist, and even increase." As an explanation for the upward

creep of prosperity unemployment, Long offered a neoclassical price malad-
justment argument very similar to those of the late 1930s.[23]

Long was a strong neoclassicist. Curtis was a strong structuralist. Pechman
and Schultz were strong aggregate demanders. In their analyses of late 1960,
the three major alternative positions were stated that were to be argued in the
structural debates of the 1960s. Looking at the history of professional discussions of unemployment up through 1960, however, there was little hint that
such a debate would evolve. However it did, beginning in 1961.

The first sign of an emerging debate occurred at Congressional hearings on
the 1961 *Economic Report of the President*. The 1961 report was the last by
the Eisenhower administration and was influenced by the differential unemployment studies of the past few years. In particular, the report proposed a distinctly structural-oriented policy program to deal with unemployment. According to the report, recent unemployment "is a problem that has structural as well
as cyclical aspects. The problem cannot be resolved only by the consideration
of the fluctuations in economic activity as a whole; a continued, more effective
watching of labor supply and demand in specific geographic areas, industries,
and occupations is also required."[24]

The structuralist conclusions about the nature of current unemployment by
the Eisenhower Council were reflected in continuing popular concern over the
impact of recent technological change. By early 1961 the relation of automation to unemployment had regained the level of popular attention it had
achieved in 1955–56. In the first months of 1961 the connection between recent unemployment and automation was widely discussed. A February 6, 1961
U.S. News and World Report article, for example, asked, "is the U.S. soon to
become a completely automated country? Do machines really rob workers of
jobs? Or do they, as some experts contend, create additional jobs over the long
run? Even the top authorities on automation agree that such questions are hard
to answer." These popular concerns were reflected in many other early 1961
statements. All of these articles contained detailed data on recent employment
and productivity trends.[25]

Unemployment, then, was a major issue by early 1961, and the particular
causes and nature of this unemployment were being widely discussed. The first
professional response to these concerns was made by economists who believed
in a deficient demand interpretation of current unemployment. In these discussions the final foundation for the structural unemployment debates was laid.

One of the first responses in early 1961 was in a report on current unemployment commissioned by President-elect Kennedy and written by Paul Samuelson. According to Samuelson's analysis, the American economy since 1956
had been suffering through a period of chronic weakness. Samuelson diag-
nosed the inflation of the late 1950s as cost-push, not demand-pull, and thus
judged there was no justification for keeping the economy slack.[26] The problem
was slow growth and the answer was fiscal stimulation.

At the annual February and March Joint Economic Committee hearings on
the *Economic Report of the President*, Samuelson's analysis was given full

support by the new Council of Economic Advisers (CEA), consisting of Walter Heller, Kermit Gordon, and James Tobin. The hearings hardly touched on the Eisenhower Council's report at all, but instead gave major attention to the policy proposed by Samuelson. In their testimony in support of this program, the CEA included a direct empirical attack on the notion that structural unemployment was a significant factor in recent unemployment. Because of later widespread reference, this paper deserves to be called the first entry in the structural unemployment-deficient demand debates.

The CEA's March 1961 testimony has become famous for its introduction of the concept of the full employment surplus, its claim that 4 percent unemployment should be the full employment target, and its explicit Keynesian argument that fiscal policy was the best way to achieve full employment. These arguments do not need to be reviewed. The important point here is that, because of this theoretical commitment to Keynesian analysis, the CEA added to its testimony a detailed attack on the notion that the structure of unemployment stood in the way of achieving full employment through aggregate policies. The CEA presented this argument in a special appendix to its prepared testimony. The CEA began its analysis by noting that

the question sometimes arises whether the obstinate refusal of the unemployment rate to decline below 5 percent since the end of 1957 is a consequence of long-term "structural" changes in the age, sex, and other composition of the labor force, and not of weakness in aggregate demand. If this were so, it would seem that measures to stimulate the general level of economic activity might fail to get the over-all unemployment rate down to tolerable levels. Indeed, as the cyclical component of unemployment vanished, leaving only the "hard core" the result might be inflationary wage increases. *But this argument can be shown to be false.*[27]

Using a tabular presentation of Current Population Survey data which compared percentage changes in various group unemployment rates over time, the CEA attempted to support this claim. The basic CEA argument was that if structural changes were responsible for the recent rise in unemployment, then unemployment should now be more concentrated in "hard core" unemployment groups. The data presented was claimed by the CEA to show that this had not occurred. The age-sex composition of unemployment in 1957 and 1960, for example, was very nearly the same despite the fact that unemployment had risen from 4.3 percent to 5.6 percent. The CEA then looked at occupational, industrial, marital, and educational categories, and claimed that the same results were true.

A close look at the CEA tables suggests that the CEA was reasonable in drawing these conclusions. There were no dramatic instances of particular groups showing large unemployment increases in the 1957 to 1960 data. Another empirical claim made by the CEA, however, was more controversial. The CEA calculated the effects of structural shifts on the aggregate unemployment rate by figuring what 1960 unemployment would be if the structure of the labor force had not changed since 1953. The same was done for 1957. The CEA found that age-sex shifts accounted for 20 to 22 percent of the 1957–60 rise in unemployment, and for 12 to 22 percent of the 1953–60 rise in unemployment. The CEA claimed that these figures were "an insignificant fraction" and thus reaffirmed its conclusion that the recent rise in unemployment was "over-whelmingly the result of increases in the category-by-category unemployment rates and only to a minor extent due to structural factors."[28] Whether these figures were "insignificant" or not was a central question raised later by other economists.

It is clear why the new CEA drew such strong conclusions in favor of a policy of aggregate demand stimulation. The political nature of its report guaranteed that emphasis would be placed on its policy conclusions. The fact that the CEA felt it necessary to add a special appendix specifically attacking the structural view, however, made it clear that the structural position had acquired a significant level of support by early 1961.

The major interest here in the CEA report is the effect it had on professional discussions of the issue. If the report was conclusive and convincing, it would be expected that the literature would reflect this impact. This, however, did not happen. Throughout 1961 the topic of structural unemployment continued to be debated at a steady level of intensity. There was no clear trend in these discussions. But there was one fact that had not been evident before 1961: there was now a distinct professional structural unemployment-deficient demand debate. The trade-off between structural and demand action had hardly been emphasized before 1961. It was now, however, a central topic of concern.[29]

During the year several economists commented on the developing structural unemployment-deficient demand issue. Some of these writings were aggregate demand in orientation.[30] Others were structural.[31] Still others took a balanced view of the need for both types of policy.[32] No one in this literature denied that both policies were needed. But the basic issue in the structural debates—where the emphasis in policy should lie—was clearly defined.[33] Although several of these 1961 contributions made interesting comments about the emerging debates, most only provided commentary on the current state of the dispute and did not make significant contributions to the discussions.[34] Late in the year, however, a series of specific professional attacks began to appear on the issue.

Harold Demsetz, in an October article, presented the most important professional analysis to appear on the question since the CEA's March analysis. Demsetz took a careful look at the issue in both its theoretical and empirical aspects. Demsetz's major hypothesis was that "there exists a hardcore of unemployables that prevent the unemployment rate from falling to frictional levels, grows secularly, and currently accounts for a significant percentage of the unemployed." To test the first part of this hypothesis—that structural unemployment exists—Demsetz used the same technique as the CEA did in its March analysis. Demsetz's results were very close to those of the CEA, but his interpretation of the results was just the opposite of the CEA's. Where the CEA claimed that the structural unemployment thesis was that hardcore unemployment rates should have risen since 1957, Demsetz argued that the structural unemployment thesis was that these rates should fall: "If there exist hardcore unemployed, the very fact that they remain unemployed when others find employment should make the hardcore unemployed a higher fraction of the unemployment in high employment years than in low employment years." In a footnote Demsetz specifically attacked the CEA reasoning on this point as "a serious logical error." Demsetz thus held that the CEA's own empirical findings confirmed that structural unemployment exists. As a test of the second part of his hypothesis—that structural unemployment was growing secularly—Demsetz compared hardcore group unemployment rates in months of comparable business cycle conditions and unemployment from 1949 to 1961. Here Demsetz found a strong tendency for secular structural increases. Demsetz's final test was of the last part of his hypothesis—that a significant percentage of the current unemployment was structural. Again using the CEA's own procedures, Demsetz found that "our estimate of the minimum numbers of structurally unemployed are about 10 percent in magnitude. . . . This percentage is certainly not insignificant." In a footnote Demsetz noted that the CEA in March had estimated that 22 percent of the rise in unemployment since 1957 was structural, and he criticized the CEA for concluding that this figure was "only an insignificant fraction" of the rise in unemployment. As a result of his evaluation of all three parts of his hypothesis, Demsetz concluded that the structural hypothesis "cannot be rejected and tends to be confirmed by available evidence." Demsetz thus claimed that "it may be wiser to concentrate efforts on retraining programs . . . [or] to increase the degree of downward flexibility in our wage structure, rather than to rely on aggregate techniques." In particular, Demsetz found that his "minimum estimate [of structural unemployment] is sufficient to prevent the unemployment rate from declining below five percent if frictional unemployment is between three percent and four percent."[35]

The Demsetz response to the CEA report presents the core of the structural unemployment argument. His criticism of the CEA's logical error in its analysis was well taken. In addition, his disagreement with the CEA over the significance of the very similar estimates that he and the CEA made of structural unemployment highlighted several important features of the debates. The first is that CEA economists in the structural debates tended to make strong policy-oriented statements. Although government economists contributed to the technological unemployment debates in the 1930s, their policy influence was restricted compared to that of the CEA. The political element added to the debates by the importance of the CEA in government policy decisions was new in the 1960s debates. A second feature is that direct confrontations like Demsetz's of the CEA came to characterize the debates. The lack of civility in exchanges over the issue soon was noted by observers and participants alike. A third feature is that Demsetz's approach is representative of the best approach taken by participants in the empirical debates. Demsetz's careful theory-based derivation of hypotheses for his data analysis was a model that was followed too infrequently in the months to come. Finally, the particular data used was not an issue. Demsetz and the CEA used the same sources, a feature that characterized the entire structural debates. As Edward Kalachek remarked in a review of the debates in 1973, "everyone agreed on the facts but differed in their interpretation."[36] The fact that disagreements in the debates could come down to whether or not a given number was "significant" was a prescription for frustration in reaching agreement in the disputes, a feature that the subsequent structural debates came to evidence in abundance.

The next major contributions to the debates also appeared in late 1961. The developing conflict over the question of structural unemployment was reflected dramatically in December 1961 Joint Economic Committee (JEC) hearings on *Employment and Unemployment*. Several economists testified at the hearings specifically on the issue. The most important contribution of the hearings, however, was not this testimony but the preparation of two background papers on recent unemployment, one by Edward Kalachek and James Knowles of the JEC staff, and the other by the Bureau of Labor Statistics (BLS). The Knowles-Kalachek and BLS papers analyzed almost exactly the same data, but the Knowles-Kalachek paper was much more sophisticated statistically and reached much more emphatic conclusions in support of the aggregate-demand position.

The BLS paper presented at the hearings was an update of the 1959 BLS study on the "Extent and Nature of Frictional Unemployment." In the earlier study the BLS had estimated that about 10 percent of the rise of unemployment from 1948 to 1956 was structural. The 1961 study carried results through 1960. In this work the BLS presented all the best available data on 1948–60 trends in unemployment, employment, labor force, the composition of employment, and the duration of unemployment. The 1959 results of 1948–56 trends were first reviewed and reaffirmed. Then, for the period 1957–60, the BLS concluded that of the 1.1 percentage points rise in unemployment, 0.2 percentage points were due to structural effects. As a result of this analysis, the study concluded that structural effects had not played a major role to date in raising unemployment. It did find, however, that there were indications that the structural component of unemployment was increasing.[37]

The JEC staff study by James Knowles and Edward Kalachek that accompanied the BLS paper reached much stronger conclusions from an analysis of nearly identical data. The Knowles-Kalachek paper was, like the March CEA and the October Demsetz papers, an explicit attempt to test empirically the opposing theories about the nature of recent unemployment. The major statistical comparisons of the Knowles-Kalachek paper were much like that of the CEA, Demsetz, and the companion BLS study. Previous studies had simply examined tables of these data. Knowles and Kalachek, however, were the first to present an econometric attack on the issue. Based on their results, Knowles and Kalachek concluded that there was no uptrend in structural unemployment.

Knowles and Kalachek began with a statement of the structural unemployment-aggregate demand controversy which tied the structural position to recent automation concerns. The structuralists maintained, according to Knowles-Kalachek, that recent unemployment was due "to technological changes which are currently reshaping the American economy at an unusually rapid pace."

Knowles-Kalachek then claimed that the structural argument was only concerned with unemployment trends since 1957. Knowles and Kalachek recognized that their definition of the structural position—as opposed to one that claimed deterioration in unemployment since 1948 or 1953, which was the one examined by the accompanying BLS paper—"has considerable significance." But Knowles and Kalachek cited the facts that unemployment was about the same in 1948 and 1955–57, that the lower unemployment of 1951–53 was due to the Korean War, and that only since 1957 had unemployment not fallen below 5 percent, as evidence in support of their view that the structural argument only applied to the period 1957–61. Knowles and Kalachek found, as had the BLS and all past professional studies, that direct counting of the structurally unemployed was impossible. They claimed, however, that "the accompanying symptoms [of a rise in structural unemployment] can be tested for empirically." It was their goal to define and test for these effects. The reason for their concern was that "the two theories differ sharply over where in fact this crucial zone [of full employment] is reached." The aggregate-demand position, according to Knowles-Kalachek, was that full employment was around 4 percent unemployment and that this level had not changed significantly since 1948 or 1955–57: "Advocates of the structural transformation theory, on the other hand, insist that full employment now occurs at a higher unemployment rate than it did earlier in the post-war period. They argue, therefore, that efforts to reduce the unemployment rate by expansionary fiscal and monetary policy will lead to inflation long before the unemployment rate approaches four percent."[38]

Knowles and Kalachek then defined the critical tests that they claimed would differentiate between the two theories. Knowles and Kalachek began by claiming that the structural hypothesis was "that unemployment has remained at relatively high levels in the period since mid-1957 in the face of adequate demand forces and despite the availability of a sufficient number of job opportunities." This statement of the structural position implied that all of the rise of unemployment since 1957 had been structural. Knowles and Kalachek claimed that this hypothesis was implicit in the work of past structuralists. (They did not name any structuralists who held these views, or acknowledge work such as that by Demsetz or the BLS which argued that structural unemployment was only a significant percentage of the primarily cyclical rise in unemployment since 1957.) It was on the basis of this strong structural statement that Knowles and Kalachek constructed all of their empirical tests. The tests conducted by Knowles and Kalachek included a statistical evaluation of the following questions for 1957–61. First, has productivity accelerated? Using BLS data and citing recent studies by Kendrick and Fabricant, Knowles and Kalachek found that postwar productivity trends had been above the long-run average, but not unusually so. Second, has productivity been associated with higher unemployment either in the aggregate or by industry? Here Knowles and Kalachek cited Solomon Fabricant's 1942 study of *Employment in Manufacturing* and John Kendrick's 1961 study of *Productivity Trends in the United States* to claim that in the short run no significant relation exists between productivity and employment and that in the long run a significant position correlation exists between the two variables. Third, has productivity change become more concentrated? Using manufacturing data, Knowles and Kalachek found no evidence for such a trend. Fourth, have occupational trends accelerated? An examination of decennial Census occupation data since 1900 showed that shifts since 1950 had not been unprecedented. Fifth, have the unemployed become less mobile? Citing Census studies, Knowles and Kalachek found that "the migration rate for unemployed males between March 1957 and April 1959, the last period for which data are available, was in line with the postwar average." Sixth, has the incidence of unemployment by groups changed significantly? This, according to Knowles and Kalachek, was the major question at issue, and here they provided their econometric comparison of predicted versus actual 1960 unemployment rates. The conclusions were clear: "Fluctuations in the unemployment rate in fact provide the major explanation for changes in the degree of concentration of unemployment. . . . The predictive model provides an exceptionally close approximation to reactional distribution of unemployment, taking into consideration the sampling error, the possibility of response error, and the fact that 1958 witnessed the sharpest recession of the postwar era."[39]

As their qualifications suggest, the regression results were not perfect, but Knowles and Kalachek were confident in their conclusions. (It is relevant to note that Knowles and Kalachek challenged the 1959 BLS study findings of a 10 percent rise in unemployment due to structural change between 1949 and 1956 precisely because the JEC results were "probably due to response error, sampling error, random occurrences, and the fact that the reconversion to peacetime patterns of consumption, production and labor force activity was not yet completed in 1948." They did not explain why they held that these errors should be a problem in pro-structuralist studies, but of little concern in their anti-structuralist study.) The last test Knowles and Kalachek considered was whether job vacancy data had gone up or the work week had lengthened. This was a direct test of the extreme structural statement that aggregate demand had actually been sufficient between 1957 and 1961, and that all unemployment was due to labor supply and demand maladjustments. Here, however, Knowles and Kalachek found that data did not exist for a careful test. Hours-worked data had gone down over the last three postwar cycles but the crucial aggregate vacancy data were nonexistent. The only closely relevant statistics did, however, support the Knowles-Kalachek conclusions. "The number of nonfarm job openings was 30 percent lower in 1959–60 than in 1955–57, while the value of the help-wanted index was 15 percent lower." The Knowles-Kalachek conclusions on the basis of these tests were emphatic.

A careful canvass of post-1957 developments produced little evidence for the structural transformation hypothesis. Those labor market symptoms which would indicate that higher unemployment has been due to structural causes are almost totally absent. . . . The evidence adverse to the structural transformation theory confirms the contentions of the aggregate demand theory. . . . If it is agreed that a four percent unemployment rate was readily attainable without inflation during the period prior to 1957, then it should have been possible during 1957–60, and should be possible during the current expansion.[40]

The Knowles-Kalachek paper had a major impact on the course of the structural debates. Their results were quickly disseminated throughout the profession and widely acclaimed by aggregate-demand analysts as the final word on the structural unemployment question. The result was that structuralist arguments were effectively reduced in significance in the literature.

This stage of the debates lasted through mid-1963. The Knowles-Kalachek analysis did not succeed, however, in finally resolving the debate. The form of the structuralist argument attacked by Knowles and Kalachek was extreme. No economist in 1960–61 argued for such an exaggerated version of the structural thesis. As a result, moderate structuralist remarks continued to appear regularly until, beginning in late 1963, the debates began again.

8

Evolution of the Structural
Unemployment Debates

The 1962–63 period was marked by a lower keyed debate over the structural issue. The number of contributions was reduced in number, and although differences of opinion remained common in the literature, the statement of these differences was made in reasonable tones. By mid-1963 it appeared that the debate was slowly fading away. A careful review of the entire issue at that time by Arthur Ross found that the differences expressed were now mainly "differences in shading."[1]

This status of the debates can be attributed in large part to the impact of the Knowles-Kalachek study. Knowles and Kalachek's work was referred to repeatedly in the following literature. Although the study had some major problems—especially its statement of an extreme structuralist hypothesis to attack—it provides a clear case where empirical work influenced the course of professional discussions.

The structural debates, however, did not disappear. In the fall of 1963 they began again at an unrivaled level of intensity. Continuing attention to the issue can be attributed to three factors. First, popular concerns about automation soared again in 1962–63. Dozens of popular articles kept the issue of the employment effects of new technology at the forefront of public awareness. Second, unemployment remained stuck at 5 to 5.5 percent. By the fall of 1963, the unemployment rate had been above 5 percent for six years. This experience gave little assurance that the commonly reported 4 percent level of full employment could still be reached without significant inflationary consequences—or even reached at all. Third, the Keynesian economic world of the late 1950s was now a Keynesian-Phillips Curve world. The Phillips Curve complemented the Keynesian analysis neatly by describing the unemployment-inflation trade-off that policymakers faced.[2] Criticisms of this trade-off—in particular the famous short-run versus long-run Phillips Curve analysis by Milton Friedman—were still a few years away.[3] In the early 1960s, the Phillips Curve was widely accepted, and it soon was used by economists as a foundation for making policy recommendations.

The importance of the Phillips Curve for the structural unemployment debates is that it could be used to claim a theoretical justification for policies proposed by structuralist economists. Training, retraining, and worker education—in the language of the time, "manpower" policies—were held to shift the Phillips Curve inward, thus allowing policymakers to break down the barrier of the unemployment-inflation trade-off. Given a theoretical justification, retraining programs quickly acquired support as policy prescriptions, and proposals for worker education policies soon were standard fare. The 1962 Manpower Development and Training Act (MDTA) was an important outcome of this movement, as was its mandate for a *Manpower Report of the President* to supplement the *Economic Report of the President*. The *Manpower Report* created an obvious forum for structuralist arguments, an opportunity that was pursued after the revival of the structuralist-aggregate demand debates in late 1963.

The professional contributions between the December 1961 Knowles-Kalachek paper and the resurgence of the structural unemployment debates in the fall of 1963 can be reviewed quickly. The impact of the Knowles-Kalachek analyses was almost immediately evident. At December 1961 JEC hearings, for example, John Kendrick, Lloyd Reynolds, and Paul Samuelson all voiced agreement with its results.[4] In a December Industrial Relations Research Association paper, Richard Wilcock and Walter Franke did the same in their own empirical analysis of the issue.[5] Relying primarily on CEA and Knowles-Kalachek data, they concluded that demand policy alone would reduce unemployment to 4 percent without inflation.

The debate-dampening effect of the empirical studies of late 1961 also was reflected in a January 1962 conference on The Labor Market and Social Security. Solomon Barkin, a labor representative, noted the course of the recent debate and found that "the present spokesmen of both positions are in agreement that aggregate demand will have to be raised to lower the current unemployment rate." He found that they only "differ in their emphasis, which fact is sometimes lost sight of in the heat of controversy and the sweep of enthusiastic rhetoric." William Miernyk found that

the debate over unemployment in this country is one of the most fruitless, if not potentially damaging controversies over an important economic issue in our time. . . . I think if economists and others continue to insist that it is a question of *either* faster growth *or* sounder labor market policy, we might end up with neither. . . . A much sounder policy, it seems to me, would be to recognize that we need both accelerated economic growth and an effective labor market policy.[6]

This closing of ranks behind a policy of joint aggregate and structural action and downplaying of debate was widely evident in early 1962. That there were still differences among economists about where to place the emphasis in structural and aggregate policies, however, was suggested by comments at the same conference by Richard Lester and Charles Killingsworth. Both Lester and

Killingsworth took note of recent studies demonstrating that structural changes in labor supply had been responsible for little of the increase in unemployment, and they both acknowledged the necessity of faster economic growth. Lester and Killingsworth, however, felt that there was still cause for concern about the structure of labor demand. Killingsworth in particular developed this point. From a review of recent studies, Killingsworth concluded that the major effect of recent changes has been "to decrease the number of low-skilled and unskilled jobs available and to increase very greatly the demand at the high-skill levels. Much of your factual information is consistent with the thesis that a good deal of unemployment is due not so much to changes in labor supply, or even changes in wage rates, but rather to a change in the nature of demand for labor, primarily as a result of technological change but contributed to by other factors."[7]

Killingsworth's and Lester's comments were a sign that the JEC studies had not closed off all areas of concern. These analyses, however, were developed only slightly in 1962. The impact of the contributions of late 1961 and the fact that output and unemployment levels improved soon led to a widespread optimistic professional outlook.

The professional optimism of early 1962 was nowhere more evident than in the 1962 *Economic Report of the President*. The CEA reported that 1961 had been a good year. Recovery, however, was not complete. Heller, Tobin, and Gordon thus proposed a list of policies that included both aggregate and structural measures. Along with the prevailing professional opinion, the CEA held that both types of programs were needed. The CEA firmly believed, however, that aggregate policy alone could reduce unemployment to 4 percent and that only then would structural measures be needed. The CEA referred to their early 1961 analysis and the Knowles-Kalachek paper to support this conviction.[8]

That the CEA analysis of the proper relative role and mix of structural versus aggregate policies was widely accepted by economists was evident in the following JEC hearings on the *Economic Report*. Of the dozen prominent economists who appeared, none disagreed in an important way with the CEA's unemployment analysis.[9]

Despite the diminishing of professional debate, it soon became clear that the general professional optimism was not to be matched by a popular one. Popular concern about the employment impact of automation took off in 1962, and this concern played a major role in keeping economists interested in the structural issue until the professional debate picked up again in 1963. The most prominent of the popular contributions made in early 1962 was a pamphlet by Donald Michael entitled *Cybernation: The Silent Conquest*. Michael's pamphlet became a classic in the automation alarmist literature and was soon widely quoted. Michael saw a future only twenty years hence where computers would do all the work and where jobs would exist only for the technicians needed to keep the computers running. The emergence of a new peak of popular concern over automation was reflected in almost all the popular periodicals. As a February *Business Week* article put it,

[t]he great automation scare is on. It came to a head last week when President Kennedy, at his press conference, said he regarded automation "as the major domestic challenge of the Sixties—to maintain full employment at a time when automation, of course, is replacing men." Public concern about automation has been building up for months— thanks to a television show called *Automation: The Awesome Servant*, a pamphlet called *Cybernation: The Silent Conquest*, and other grim prophecies by newspapermen, scientific experts, labor leaders.

The *Business Week* article summarized details of the recent debates, surveying all current data trends while quoting Donald Michael among others on the pessimistic side and the CEA and the Knowles-Kalachek paper on the optimistic side.[10]

Popular comments on automation-related unemployment issues became a flood in 1962.[11] The response of economists to the raging popular debate was to repeat analyses of the issue that they previously had made. Articles emphasizing the optimistic view of recent automation effects were published by Henry Hazlitt, Daniel Diamond, and John Diebold. Articles emphasizing automation-caused employment problems were published by Walter Buckingham, Hans Apel, Harold Sylvester, and Charles Killingsworth. Nothing in this work was new, but the continuing differences in published professional opinion over the role of automation in recent employment trends indicated that the conflicts that had led to the structural unemployment disputes of 1961 were still active.[12]

In the professional publications on the issue, pessimistic views on the adequacy of aggregate-demand policy for correcting current unemployment were in a distinct minority throughout 1962. One major empirical contribution in this period, however, was in the pessimistic category. This article, by Ewan Clague and Leon Greenberg, was first presented at the twenty-first meeting of the American Assembly in May 1962. The entire session was devoted to automation, with most of the papers discussing employment problems agreeing with the prevailing professional opinion that few problems existed. Clague and Greenberg, however, emphasized the displacement problems of recent technical change. Clague and Greenberg used BLS output, employment, and productivity data and John Kendrick's productivity data in order to examine the relationship of technical change and employment since World War II. They began by identifying two major questions of interest which were similar to those that had been approached in 1961 by Kendrick and by Knowles-Kalachek. In particular, Clague and Greenberg wanted to know if "industry by industry, have productivity gains been accompanied by employment declines or employment increases?" With respect to this question, a tabular examination of major sectoral trends since World War II found no statistically significant correlation between productivity and employment changes. Clague and Greenberg did find, however, that "it does seem as though there was a slight tendency for large gains in output per manhour to be associated with declines or small increases in employment, and for smaller gains in output per manhour to be associated with larger than average gains in employment." From this observation, which was very different from the conclusions that Kendrick or Knowles-Kalachek drew from the same data for the same period, Clague and Greenberg moved on to consider trends in individual manufacturing industries. They first found, as had Kendrick, Fabricant, and others before them, that "a detailed industry-by-industry analysis showed very little correlation between employment and output per manhour." Clague and Greenberg did not stop here, however. Within this context of low correlation, significant unemployment did occur, and Clague and Greenberg next attempted to estimate the magnitude of yearly technological displacement. Their final conclusion from an examination of both manufacturing and nonmanufacturing data was that "disemployment—decreases in employment associated with increased productivity—in nonagriculatural industries might amount to 200,000 workers or more per year during the next decade."[13]

The Clague-Greenberg analysis was a major empirical attempt to study the technological aspects of structural unemployment and was frequently quoted in later work. The impact of this study on the course of the debates, however, was insignificant at the time. The structural concerns raised by Clague and Greenberg were little reflected in other professional discussions of current trends which continued to emphasize the efficacy of Keynesian policies for handling unemployment problems. At August 1962 JEC hearings on the *State of the Economy*, for example, only one of the more than two dozen economists who testified voiced any structural concerns. The consensus of the other economists was for a faster rate of growth, to be realized most effectively, as almost every economist held, by a tax cut. Economists proposing this solution to the current economic malaise at the hearings included Daniel Suits, Otto Eckstein, Paul McCracken, Joseph Pechman, Leon Keyserling, and CEA members Walter Heller, Kermit Gordon, and Gardner Ackley.[14]

The leveling off of unemployment at around 5.5 percent in mid-1962 kept the issue of unemployment in the first rank of economic issues for the next year. The strength of the aggregate-demand view was demonstrated repeatedly in professional analyses during these months.[15] This general agreement held firm through mid-1963. Only a few professional structuralist remarks were heard in the period. This did not mean that the popular debates had disappeared, however. On the contrary, in the face of employment stagnation the popular debates over automation and unemployment continued at a high level of intensity.[16] Of particular importance was the fact that Congress tended to side more strongly with those raising structural concerns than with the aggregate demanders. No major aggregate-demand policies were passed in 1962, while on the structuralist side, in addition to the 1961 Area Development Assistance Act, Congress in 1962 passed the Public Works Acceleration Act, strengthened the United States Employment Service, extended unemployment insurance programs, and passed the Manpower Development and Training Act (MDTA).

By the beginning of 1963, then, the policy picture was still unsatisfactory from the point of view of the aggregate demanders. Unemployment had stabilized at 5.5 to 5.7 percent for the past year, but Congress had not been responsive to the call for demand stimulation. As a result, the 1963 *Economic Report of the President* was considerably more forceful than it had been a year before in demands for policy action. The CEA came down strongly for a tax cut to stimulate aggregate demand. Over and over again, in almost every section of the report, the CEA repeated the inadequate-demand thesis. If the tax cut was quickly passed as proposed, the CEA predicted that unemployment would be well on its way toward 4 percent.[17]

Witnesses at the January and February 1963 JEC hearings on the *Economic Report* focused their attention almost exclusively on the tax cut issue. The analysis of the *Economic Report* and by the economists at the JEC hearings was supported in the first *Manpower Report of the President*, published in early March 1963. Faster growth was listed as the number-one policy problem in the *Manpower Report*, and the tax-cut program was mentioned several times. As befitting a *Manpower Report* written under the provisions of the MDTA, a strong program of structural policies was advocated, but administration ranks held firm and these policies were only called for as a secondary policy to adequate growth.[18]

The state of the professional debates by mid-1963 was demonstrated well at a Conference on Unemployment at Berkeley in April 1963. Walter Heller in his conference paper reviewed the entire debate and reaffirmed the CEA position. Heller found that both sides of the structural debate acknowledged that both demand and structural policies were needed, but he found that "nevertheless, there does exist a difference of opinion concerning the weights to be attached to demand creation on the one hand and structural adjustments on the other." Heller found that the major dispute was over the point at which demand pressures would be dissipated by inflation and that a major reason for the current interest in the issue was "a new urgency related to the rise of 'automation' [which] is frequently given as a major explanation of the increase in unemployment that has occurred since 1957." Heller then reviewed data similar to those in the 1961 CEA report to conclude that "the facts as presented and interpreted above strongly suggest that an expansion of aggregate demand can produce a significant reduction in unemployment without encountering structural imbalance in labor markets."[19]

Otto Eckstein and Arthur Ross provided support for the CEA position in their conference papers. The most important paper was by Eckstein, who presented a new statistical attack on the problem. Eckstein reviewed data from the Knowles-Kalachek study and from the 1963 *Manpower Report of the President* to show that unemployment had risen nearly the same amount in all labor force groups, that the rate of productivity advance had not risen, and that no declines in worker mobility were evident. Eckstein then took a cue from two recent unpublished studies by Edward Denison that had shown that unemployment from 1950 to 1960 had become more equal across states and standard metropolitan statistical areas. Looking at 150 major urban areas from 1959 to 1962, Eckstein found that national unemployment had remained the same, but that fewer areas now had unemployment greater than 8 percent and that there was a significant rearranging in the unemployment rank of areas. From this analysis, he concluded that "the persistently high level of unemployment in the 1958–62 period is not due to structural peculiarities but is generally diffused into all broad sectors of the economy."[20]

Arthur Ross, in his paper, reviewed past discussions of the issue in reaching his conclusion that the weight of current opinion favored the demand side. His paper, however, had several important comments on the current state of the debates. In particular, Ross found that "in general Congress has been more sympathetic to the structural solutions up to the present time." He also noted that "Heller, Knowles, Kalachek, and others have reached their conclusions on the basis of rather meager factual data. . . . Thus inevitably the debate is rather inconclusive." Ross also noted that much of the recent concern over unemployment had been generated by concern over automation, and he devoted four pages of his twenty-seven-page article to debunking fears of aggregate unemployment from technological change.[21]

The fact that structural concerns were still alive, however, despite the dominance of recent aggregate demand statements was demonstrated at the conference in papers by Seymour Wolfbein and William Haber. Haber's emphasis was particularly strong on the structural side. Haber found that "it is not easy to determine whether this unemployment is due to a genuine weakening of demand or to structural factors," but his analysis suggested that recent studies had significantly shortchanged the structural aspects of the problem. Haber noted that "we might take the position that our unemployment problem would quickly melt under the warm sun of a more vigorous rate of economic growth." But he found that "recent observations of what has happened under improved economic conditions in many areas appear to suggest that this view is overly optimistic. A substantial amount of unemployment will continue even under a more vigorous prosperity than prevails at present. And to reduce it to acceptable levels requires more attention to the quality and direction of our manpower movement than we have normally provided."[22]

Haber ended his talk with the normal call for a fully-integrated aggregate-demand and manpower program. All participants at the conference, including Haber, Wolfbein, Eckstein, Heller, Bakke, Goldfinger, Rees, and McCracken, agreed on this general statement. For this reason Arthur Ross in his summary of the conference found "a surprising degree of agreement on the nature of the unemployment problem in the United States. . . . In addition to the conference's formal sessions there were several long, private discussion sessions among the 75 conferees; and in those sessions, too, the consistency of thinking was quite impressive." According to Ross, this consistency of thinking involved

basic agreement with differences in shading. One could not find a pure structuralist, nor a pure aggregative theorist. Perhaps there is still a residual controversy as to whether certain kinds of structural differentials have increased in recent years. Nevertheless, it is likely that most or all of the conferees would concur . . . [that], regardless of its etiology, the unemployment problem is both structural and aggregative from a practical standpoint.[23]

Ross' comments in the conference summary and in his other conference paper were accurate assessments of the state of the structural debates at the time. The influence of strong Keynesian statements by the CEA and the widely disseminated Knowles-Kalachek paper had created a near professional consensus on the issue. As Ross admitted, however, the empirical studies were "rather meager"; thus statements like those in Haber's conference paper were fairly common and "differences in shading" still characterized the discussions. Given that the empirical evidence was seen as inconclusive even by demand-siders like Ross, the dominant influence in creating the near consensus at the time must be accorded to the strength of professional belief in the efficacy of Keynesian ideas. The Knowles-Kalachek empirical results were important, but the Keynesian theoretical vision was what mattered most in determining the state of the debates in mid-1963.

This situation did not last. As unemployment remained steady at around 5.7 percent through the spring and summer of 1963, public and professional discussions of automation and unemployment continued.[24] Then, in the fall of 1963, a dramatic break occurred in Ross' "basic agreement with differences in shading."

The main forum where this new direction in the debate was revealed was in the Senate Committee on Labor and Public Welfare hearings on the *Nation's Manpower Revolution* that began in May. Running to ten parts and lasting through December, these 1963 hearings provide one of the most extensive collections of early 1960s views on the nature of unemployment problems. From the first day of testimony it was clear that the hearings were going to be dominated by discussions of structural unemployment and the impact of automation. It also quickly became clear that the dominant viewpoint on both subjects was going to be pessimistic.

Senator Clark set the theme for the hearings when he began by asserting that "we suspect that the changes now taking place in our national manpower needs are new, we are moving from a blue-collar to a white-collar economy, one which offers fewer and fewer opportunities for the unskilled and uneducated." The central questions that all the subsequent testimony revolved around were whether this assertion was true, and what difference it made for public policy. Secretary of Labor Willard Wirtz set the tone for the hearings by placing the blame for recent labor demand and occupational shifts on technological change, and by his emphasis on structural programs. Wirtz was followed by popular commentators Robert Theobald and Donald Michael who repeated their extreme alarmist views. In their opinion, automation marked a new era of economic organization, the only means of survival was to untie the traditional link between production and pay, and everyone should be given a guaranteed income. Academic economists testifying at the first May hearings denounced the extreme vision of Theobald and Michael, but their views also were slanted toward pessimism and a structuralist explanation. Eli Ginzberg, for example, emphasized the human side of unemployment problems and was plainly concerned about the present situation. To Senator Clark's inquiry, "I do not think we have had a witness yet who does not think that unemployment is going to get worse in the next few years, and I take it you agree with that?", Ginzberg answered "Yes." Ginzberg also expressed structural leanings by his reference to monetary and fiscal policies as "too gross" to solve current unemployment, and his comment that "we could have—and I think we are close to that in this country now—a real disparity between a series of jobs which want filling and a large number of people who want jobs, and the two just do not match." John Dunlop agreed with Ginzberg on this pessimistic outlook and expressed concern about the ability of the economy to adjust to recent occupational and employment changes by noting that "my personal estimate, even making generous allowances for the mobility of the American labor force, is that the degree of adjustment required is very large indeed: it is likely to tax our ingenuity and devotion." Herbert Striner also agreed with these judgments by claiming that "the rate of technological change is greater than ever before and our ability to adapt is given less time to perform than previously." Striner was well aware that "the work done by Denison, Salter, Kendrick, Knowles and Kalachek, among others, would seem to limit the culprit role which technological displacement plays in our unemployment picture." But he claimed that "to all of these studies, however, I would say that neither the available data, the state of the art, or the tools of analysis permit us to accept their findings with any degree of professional comfort." Striner ended by emphasizing the structural aspects of a national recovery policy.[25]

Ginzberg, Dunlop, and Striner all finished with an affirmation of the standard view that both demand and structural policies were needed, but their pessimism about the future course of unemployment and about the ability of labor markets to adjust to current changes set the tone for the entire course of the *Nation's Manpower Revolution* hearings. The common theme of all witnesses who approached the issue in the hearings through spring and summer 1963 was that while both demand and structural policies were needed, there was cause for concern about the structural aspects of the problem. In Part 2 of the hearings this theme was supported by administration officials representing the Department of Labor, the Bureau of Employment Security, and the United States Employment Service. At the third meetings in June, William Haber added a similar analysis, while William Miernyk opted for a centralist position.[26]

These "differences in shading" in the general agreement Ross found in April were stated more frequently in mid-1963. As Gerald Somers noted in an August article, "even though there appears to be some approach at a compromise on this issue in the last several months, a difference in emphasis is still quite noticeable." In particular, Somers found that

[m]any general university economists . . . and the Council of Economic Advisers . . . have been prone to play down the importance of structural change as an explanation of increases in unemployment since 1957. The economists with the Department of Labor, and to some extent the Federal Reserve System, on the other hand, have given much more emphasis to structural causes and, therefore, to labor market policies designed to combat structural deficiencies.[27]

Somers' identification of key groups in the debates is important. A central dimension of his sorting out of major groups is that structuralist problems tended to be emphasized by micro-oriented labor economists and demand problems by macroeconomists. A second important aspect of Somers' comment is his focus on the policy emphasis of most economists in the debates. This was not a debate about simply better understanding of an aspect of economic reality. It was a debate about how millions of dollars were to be spent by the government. The political nature of the dispute was never far below the surface in any of its discussions.

Despite the standard comment by all professional writers that both types of policy were needed, it was evident by mid-1963 that Ross' "differences in shading" were evolving to where "differences in kind" again characterized the professional discussions. The fact that so many structuralist statements were heard at the *Manpower* hearings suggests that those emphasizing a structuralist interpretation of recent trends had always been around, even during the relatively quiescent period of 1962 through early 1963. They had just been overshadowed by—and were not as vocal as—the aggregate demanders. As unemployment failed to improve as promised, however, the structuralists felt justified in emphasizing their differences from the deficient-demand view.

The fact that had to be accounted for was that, as the economy moved into the fall of 1963, unemployment was still above 5.5 percent. By this time it had been above 5 percent for seventy consecutive months. In addition, President Kennedy added to the gloom in his Labor Day 1963 speech when he said that even if a tax cut was passed immediately it would take two years for unemployment to fall below 5 percent. The addition of twenty-four months to the full-employment timetable was quickly compared by observers to CEA and administration predictions in 1961 and 1962 that unemployment would reach 4 percent by late 1963.

It was not long after Kennedy's Labor Day address that the first major structuralist argument was made by an economist since the early debates in 1961. As a result, the structural unemployment-deficient demand debates, which had simmered steadily since 1961, erupted into a heated professional confrontation.[28] The developments that marked this resurgence of professional debate over structural unemployment again were centered around Senate hearings on *The Nation's Manpower Revolution*.

The September 1963 hearings began with predictable analyses by Leon Keyserling and Otto Eckstein. Both took an aggregate demand view of current problems with Keyserling, as he had before, pushing for faster growth than planned in administration policy. Otto Eckstein's paper was also a standard exposition of the aggregate-demand view. Eckstein's claim that all group unemployment rates would move closely together to a "normal" level of 3.5 to 4 percent placed him squarely within the CEA aggregate-demand camp.[29]

The third speaker at the late September hearings, however, took a very different view of the situation. Charles Killingsworth had first suggested in January and March 1962 papers that automation was significantly affecting the structure of demand for labor in the United States. Killingsworth had been silent on the issue since then. In September 1963, however, with unemployment still at 5.5 precent and no signs of improvement in sight, Killingsworth ventured to express his earlier views in more detail. Killingsworth's claims were quickly challenged by Walter Heller of the CEA, an attack that Killingsworth felt compelled to rebut. It was soon clear that the issues debated by Heller and Killingsworth touched on basic foundations of modern professional beliefs about the workings of the economy, and other economists soon joined in the discussions. As a result, the structural unemployment-deficient demand debates were revived in full force, and the "basic agreement" noted by Ross in April 1963 quickly dissolved.

Killingsworth's argument centered around three points. First, Killingsworth claimed that automation was different from past technological change. Second, he claimed that the major effect of automation and its concomitant taste changes was to shift demand for labor rapidly away from low-level skills to higher levels of education and skill. And third, as a result of this "demand twist" effect of automation, Killingsworth claimed that public policy should emphasize structural measures over demand-stimulation policies. Killingsworth made these points in a long statement replete with examples and supported by an analysis of recent data trends.

Killingsworth supported his claim for automation marking a break from past technological trends on two grounds. First, he claimed that the economic environment was different from the past. In particular, Killingsworth felt that mass consumption had nearly reached its peak in a goods-saturated, industrially-mature United States economy. Killingsworth's second argument for automation marking a new era was that the characteristics of automation were different. In particular, Killingsworth argued for "the much broader applicability of automation," the fact "that automation appears to be spreading more rapidly than most major technological changes of the past," and that "automation has effects on the structure of demand for labor which are different from those of earlier technological developments." In answer to those who pointed out that productivity data had not shown any discontinuous change since World War II, Killingsworth noted that productivity advances were higher since World War II, that currently a large number of hours were being spent on producing and installing automated equipment so that the real increase would come later, and that many industries were currently operating at less than optimum capacity.[30]

From these arguments on the significance of automation, Killingsworth went on to defend his claim for a new labor demand effect due to technological change. According to Killingsworth, "the fundamental effect of automation on the labor market is to 'twist' the pattern of demand—that is, it pushes down the demand for workers with little training while pushing up the demand for workers with large amounts of training." The problem created by this twist in Killingsworth's view was that due to the speed and broad sweep of recent changes, labor supply could not adjust to the new structure of labor demand quickly enough. The result was the upward creep in unemployment that had been evident in the United States since 1948. Killingsworth backed his claims with a review of post-World War II unemployment trends. In this analysis, Killingsworth made a special use of data that was to be widely questioned by later analysts. For major unemployment trends by age and sex, Killingsworth used standard Current Population Survey data. For 1950 data on unemployment by education level, however, Killingsworth found it necessary to use decennial Census of Population data "adjusted" to fit contemporary Current Population Survey sources. From an analysis of these data, Killingsworth found that, although aggregate unemployment levels were near the same in 1950 and 1962, "the unemployment rates at the top of the education attainment ladder went down, while the rates at the middle and lower ranges of the ladder went up substantially." In particular, Killingsworth found that over the period 1950–62 all improvements in unemployment were concentrated in the 20 percent of the labor force with a college education, while for the other 80 percent unemployment rates were substantially higher in 1962 than in 1950. But Killingsworth found that even "these figures do not fully reveal the power of the labor market twist." In particular there was a reinforcing labor force participation effect so that "the participation rates at the lower end of the education scale, which were already relatively low in 1950, had gone much lower by 1962. At the other end of the scale, participation rates had gone up by 1962." Thus, "in all likelihood the official unemployment statistics substantially understate the size of the labor surplus of men with limited education." Killingsworth only used data for males in these calculations. He claimed that the same results existed for females, but he held that this was more difficult to discern due to the secular rise in female participation rates.[31]

Killingsworth then went on to consider the policy implications of his findings. The major implication of his results, according to Killingsworth, was that there was little likelihood of unemployment improvement in response to aggregate-demand policies either at high or low education levels. At high education levels, full employment already existed, while at low levels there was a "reserve army" of dropouts who could quickly step back into the labor force. Killingsworth's major conclusion thus was that

long before we could get down to an overall unemployment rate as low as 4 percent, we would have a severe shortage of workers at the top of the education ladder. This shortage would be a bottleneck to further expansion of employment. I cannot pinpoint the level at which this bottleneck would begin seriously to impede expansion; but . . . it seems reasonable to believe that we could not get very far below a 5-percent overall unemployment level without hitting that bottleneck.

Killingsworth thus took exception to the CEA position of emphasis on aggregate demand. He claimed that "the Council is the victim of a half truth," that "it is extremely unlikely that the proposed tax cut, desirable though it is as a part of a program, will prove to be sufficient to reduce unemployment to the 4-percent level," and that "the greatest shortcoming of the administration's program for reducing unemployment is the failure to recognize the crucial need to break the trained manpower bottleneck." As indicated by these comments, Killingsworth was not against the tax cut. His main contention was that "automation and the changing pattern of consumer wants have greatly increased the importance of investment in human beings as a factor in economic growth."[32]

It was not long before a specific response to Killingsworth was heard. In the meantime, the rest of the testimony at the September 1963 *Nation's Manpower Revolution* hearings indicated that the issues Killingsworth raised were a major concern of the time. Although often taking a pessimistic view of the problem, most of this testimony was within the bounds of the professional discussions that had taken place since 1961.[33] Killingsworth's paper also could be seen as simply a more explicit account of several of the arguments that had been made in the past two and a half years. The CEA, however, chose not to let the Killingsworth analysis pass without comment. In particular, Walter Heller attacked Killingsworth's position in an October 4 speech. Killingsworth replied with a defense of his views in speeches on October 7 and 26. The CEA countered with another attack on October 28 at the *Nation's Manpower Revolution* hearings. These exchanges received wide publicity. As a result, the professional debates over structural unemployment, which since late 1961 had been maintained at a reasonably impersonal level, soon developed into one of the most heated professional disputes of the postwar period.

The CEA's first reply to Killingsworth came in a speech by Walter Heller at an October 4 meeting of the American Council on Education. It was evident that Heller's main objection to the Killingsworth analysis was the bottleneck thesis. Heller had three main empirical points. First, Heller claimed that from 1957 to 1962 unemployment for those with eight or less years of education had risen 50 percent, while unemployment for college graduates had risen over 100 percent. Second, Heller found that the percentage of total unemployed with eight years of education had fallen from 1957 to 1962 from 47 to 36 percent, while the percentage for college graduates had risen. Third, Heller noted that in 1954 and 1962, both years with an average unemployment of 5.6 percent, that unemployment among professional and technical workers was at 1.7 percent. Heller held that all three points were in conflict with Killingsworth's increasing-educational-bottleneck thesis. As a result, Heller found that there was no reason why the 4 percent unemployment reached in 1957 could not be reached again.[34]

Killingsworth's first paper after the Heller critique was an October 7 speech at a meeting of the American Foundation on Automation and Employment. It was too soon after Heller's speech for Killingsworth to make a careful reply, so Killingsworth contented himself with contributing an edited version of his September 20 *Nation's Manpower Revolution* testimony. The only significant difference in Killingsworth's October 7 speech was that he added a section showing "real" versus actual unemployment rates by education groups for 1962. This calculation was made by taking into account changes in labor force participation rates by education groups over the period 1950 to 1962.[35]

Killingsworth's October 26 speech, however, was a direct reply to the Heller critique. Killingsworth responded to each of Heller's main arguments. With respect to Heller's point that unemployment for college graduates had risen over 100 percent over the period 1957 to 1962 while unemployment for those with eight years of education or less had risen by only 50 percent, Killingsworth replied that the lower unemployment rise for those with eight or less years of education was due entirely to labor force withdrawals by discouraged workers. To support this view, Killingsworth presented his analysis of "real" versus actual unemployment rates based on an adjustment for labor force participation rates. On Heller's point about the relative fall in total unemployment over 1957–62 of those with eight or less years of education and the relative rise in the percentage of unemployment of college graduates, Killingsworth replied that the relevant comparison was to see how group unemployment responded to declines in total unemployment. Making this comparison over 1950 to 1957, Killingsworth found that college level unemployment had fallen 73 percent, while unemployment of those with eight years of education and less had fallen only 25 percent. On Heller's third point about professional and technical unemployment being 1.7 percent in both 1954 and 1962, Killingsworth replied that the professional and technical group was too broadly defined and that a detailed analysis within the group showed the same "twist" of labor demand toward higher education levels. In particular, Killingsworth noted that within the professional and technical category in 1962, 24 percent of the workers did not have any college training and a few had as little as five years of education. As a result of these considerations, Killingsworth found no reason to change his earlier contentions, and again argued against administration policy. In Killingsworth's view, "the stimulus generated by the tax cut will quickly tighten existing shortages of certain kinds of highly educated manpower and create new ones while unemployment remains intolerably high among poorly educated workers." Killingsworth recalled that

in January 1962, the Council of Economic Advisers anticipated that the expansion then underway would reduce unemployment to 4 percent of the labor force by mid-1963. No recession intervened, but the official unemployment rate for July 1963 was 5.6 percent of the labor force. . . . The basic trouble is that the world of reality is much more complicated than the CEA models assume. The models and the policies based on them, have given too much attention to growth in the abstract . . . and too little attention to the changes in growth patterns that exploding technology and the maturing of our society demand.

Killingsworth ended by noting that aggregate-demand policies would be part of his policy program, but he asserted strongly that "the tax cut program is really like a one-legged ladder. The missing leg—or, more accurately, the dwarfed leg—is labor market policy."[36]

The second CEA response to Killingsworth came in testimony at the *Nation's Manpower Revolution* hearings of October 28. Walter Heller's lengthy statement attacked the entire range of structuralist and automation concerns. Heller found no reason to change the CEA analysis and finished with a strong restatement of the aggregate-demand view. Heller began by reassuring the Senate committee that a professional consensus existed that unemployment required both an aggregate demand and structural attack. In particular, Heller made it clear that the CEA recognized that structural unemployment is "a serious problem, which requires major policy actions to overcome its corrosive effects." After this nod toward the structuralist view, however, Heller went into a lengthly empirical attack on all the structural arguments that had been made. Heller repeated the Knowles-Kalachek comparison of the relation of group unemployment to total unemployment since 1957 to show that no great divergencies existed between predicted and actual results. Heller cited the April 1963 Conference on Unemployment paper by Otto Eckstein and early 1963 analyses of Edward Denison to further support these results. Heller then turned specifically to the Killingsworth bottleneck thesis. Heller first attacked Killingsworth's data by noting that

[t]here are problems of the noncomparability between decennial census data and information drawn from current population surveys; of the lack of appropriate annual series; of calculating appropriate current full-employment labor force participation rates for particular age and educational attainment groups instead of arbitrarily projecting the rates of a remote year; and of including not merely the male but the female components of our population.

Heller noted that the CEA had begun its own study of the bottleneck thesis. He did find, however, that a few facts already were evident. First, Heller claimed that the data showed that almost all educational requirements shifts had taken place before 1957. Since 1957 he noted that unemployment had risen twice as fast for college graduates as those with less than eight years of education. Second, Heller claimed that the data just were not good enough to make reliable claims about the trends of high education versus low education participation rates either before or after 1957. As proof of the difficulty of making these judgments, Heller cited the fact that "its recognition has caused Professor Killingsworth to reduce his estimate of the 'real' (aggregate) unemployment rate in 1962 by a full percentage point—from 8.8 percent in his speech of October 7, to 7.8 percent in a speech of October 26." The major convincing proof to Heller, however, was that to date no signs of bottleneck tension had developed and that the rise to full employment by demand policy would take two years or more. Heller also felt that a major point was "the failure of the bottleneck hypothesis to make any allowance for the proven capacity of a free labor market . . . to reconcile discrepancies between particular labor supplies and particular labor demand." Heller was confident that "if relative shortages of particular skills develop, the price system and the market will moderate them, as they always have done in the past." Based on all of these considerations, Heller concluded that "[t]he answer is clear: the evidence we have assembled and the tests we have made do not support the thesis that, overall, the incidence of structural unemployment has increased in importance since we last achieved high employment. . . . Expansion of the economy in response to a stepping up of the growth of demand will not be impeded by pockets of surplus labor existing in a number of categories."[37]

The Killingsworth and Heller arguments illustrate clearly the nature of the debates in 1963. They were almost pure data interpretation disputes. Killingsworth agreed with the CEA analysis of structural unemployment. The theory of structural unemployment, then, was not an issue. The question was simply, what do the data show about changes in differential unemployment? The discussions that were to develop in the next two years out of the Killingsworth-Heller exchange almost all had this same orientation. It was not until late in the debates that any significant change in the content of professional analyses appeared.

Another consequence of the Heller-Killingsworth exchange was the publicity the debates received. A November article in *Business Week*, for example, listed Killingsworth as the main proponent of the structuralist position and claimed that

the Michigan professor's skepticism about the magic powers of a tax cut finds several silent backers in the Labor Department. Some union people and liberal economists also think he's right, though they are willing to hold their fire to see if the tax cut works. He also has some noisy conservative supporters. . . . Killingsworth feels uncomfortable about such conservative support. He himself is not opposed to the Administration's proposed $11.1-billion tax cut. He merely says it won't do the complete job.

On the demand side, the article claimed that "Heller and the CEA argue that Killingsworth is simply playing into the hands of those who oppose the tax cut because of exaggerated fears of inflation." The article also found that

on the action front, supporters of both the structural-unemployment argument and the low-demand argument are starting to hedge their bets. . . . If the tax cut should be voted down, or if it should be enacted and still fail to improve unemployment, the Administration shows every indication of being prepared to move toward "structural" solutions. . . . On the other side, most structuralists today are getting behind the tax cut, even though they doubt it can do the whole job.[38]

As a result of the policy importance of the issue and the publicity it was receiving, signs of a renewed professional conflict over the structural unemployment-deficient demand issue quickly became evident during the last months of 1963. In the November *Challenge*, for example, a statement of the validity of structuralist views by Daniel Diamond was countered by a deficient-demand statement by Sidney Sufrin. At late year *Nations's Manpower Revolution* hearings Neil Chamberlain and Gunnar Myrdal both placed themselves on the structuralist side of center in the debates. At the same hearings Richard Nelson put himself on the demand side. At Senate hearings on public works, Leon Keyserling repeated his analysis suggesting that even more demand expansion was needed. In a December *Monthly Labor Review* article Robert Stein presented new data on the character of recent unemployment which to him made "it more difficult to cling to extreme positions" in the structuralist debates. And in a February 1964 article Richard Lester reaffirmed the structuralist leanings he had first expressed in January 1962.[39]

9

Peak Years of the Structural Unemployment Debates

The newly revived structural unemployment debates began 1964 with the most detailed discussion by the CEA to date in its January *Economic Report of the President*. Shortly thereafter, the economists at the Department of Labor challenged the CEA position—cautiously but clearly—in the March 1964 *Manpower Report of the President*. The political-policy dimension of the debates, which served to intensify rather than mollify differences of opinion, were explicit in this exchange.

The intensity of the structural unemployment-aggregate demand debates indicated by these statements continued at a high level for the next year and a half. Three notable developments took place in this evolution. First, the dispute now had been going on long enough for misreadings of the history of the debate to creep into the discussions. Second, the level of civility in exchanges between debate participants noticeably began to erode. And third, a few economists tried to provide comprehensive evaluations of the dispute. These attempts to identify the fundamental causes of the disagreements and to provide a solution were among the best of all of the professional contributions to the debates.

None of these developments was effective in resolving the debates. Rather, two other factors soon came to play a role in controlling the evolution of the discussions. In March 1964 the tax cut was finally passed. And, in mid-1965, the Vietnam War began to have a clear impact on the economy. As the unemployment rate quickly dropped toward the magic level of 4 percent under the influence of these events, the intensity of the structural unemployment debate fell with it.

This course of the debates began early in 1964 when the CEA used its January *Economic Report of the President* to give detailed attention to the issues of automation and structural unemployment. The CEA did not back off from its aggregate-demand position, and the message of the report thus was the urgent need for a tax cut. Because of the intensity of recent debates, however, the CEA felt it necessary to include in its report a chapter on the employment effects of technological change and a lengthy appendix that reprinted the October 28 Congressional testimony by Walter Heller reponding to the "twist" thesis of Charles Killingsworth. Testimony at the Joint Economic Committee hearings on the *Economic Report* showed that a wide range of opinion existed on the structural issue. Those siding with Killingsworth included Representative Thomas Curtis, economist Donald Webster of the JEC staff, the American Bankers Association, and the United States Chamber of Commerce. Those backing the CEA included economist Robert Nathan, business economist Walter Fackler, Walter Reuther of the AFL-CIO, and Leon Keyserling.

Another consequence of the fall 1963 Heller-Killingsworth papers was renewed professional attention to the role of technological change in recent trends. As suggested by the Heller-Killingsworth exchange, one of the factors behind the resurgence of the structural unemployment debates was continuing widespread concern over the effects of automation. This concern was reflected in 1964 by a tremendous outpouring of popular and professional literature debating the pros and cons of automation. Several empirical case studies of the effects of the new techniques were published during the year, but their results were inconclusive. The results supporting automation alarms were almost equally balanced by results claiming that there was nothing to worry about.[1] A mid-1964 review of this literature by Norman Pauling began with a long list of the various methodological obstacles in studying employment effects of technological change. His assessment of the automation literature was that it had failed miserably to meet this methodological challenge. Pauling found past studies vague, formal hypotheses rare, results generally descriptive and not analytical, no general models, a lack of imagination in identifying and quantifying significant variables, and no attention paid to comparability with past work. As a result, despite the vast amount of research, these studies did little to resolve the structural unemployment debates.[2]

As the Killingsworth and Heller papers indicated, the issue among economists in the revived structural debates was more general than whether technological change had been a factor in recent unemployment. The question was whether structural changes—whatever their cause—had created a differential unemployment problem that could not be resolved by aggregate-demand policy without creating significant inflation. It was on this broader issue that later major professional contributions concentrated.

In March 1964 the tax cut was passed as part of the Great Society program under Lyndon Johnson. In June and July unemployment was at 5.3 percent and 5 percent respectively, compared to 5.5 percent in January. This slow improvement did not stop, however, the revival of the structural debates begun by the Killingsworth-Heller exchanges of 1963. One of the first important developments in the resurgent professional discussions came in the 1964 *Manpower Report of the President*. It had been noted by several observers that many Department of Labor economists leaned toward a structuralist interpretation of recent unemployment. In a reflection of the intensity of current debates over the issue, the writers of the *Manpower Report* felt that a more outspoken statement of their differences from the CEA interpretation was permissible. Although the contrasts between the 1964 *Manpower Report* and the 1964 *Economic Report* were not made explicit, a reading of both documents reveals a sharp difference in opinion. The *Manpower Report*, as did the *Economic Report*, began with a general statement of the never-questioned professional consensus that both demand and structural policies were needed. The arguments presented however, in the *Manpower Report's* long sections on "Productivity, Changing Technology, and Employment," and "The Structure of Unemployment" made it clear that the *Manpower Report* authors felt that structural policies were an essential part of policy now, and not, as the CEA held, after unemployment reached a 4 percent level. In particular, the report presented data to support the Killingsworth view that "there have been some concrete indications that a decline in labor force participation for some groups represents a deterioration in their employment situation." This theme was developed in detail for nonwhites and the low-educated and used by the report to refute claims (made by Eckstein, Denison, and the CEA) that unemployment rates over the past few years had shown a distinct diffusion. (This diffusion had been held by Eckstein and Denison to prove that there had been a moderation of structural dislocations.) The *Manpower Report* argued that "the data on manpower utilization which were presented earlier . . . for Negroes and uneducated older workers suggest that part of the apparent decline in unemployment in contracting industries, occupations and areas may represent not an improvement in the employment situation, but a squeeze-out of workers from the labor force." Moreover, the report held that the data "suggests that the transfer of unemployment to other industrial sectors, rather than the improvement in employment, has been the significant factor in reducing unemployment in these specific sectors during the past several years." The report thus concluded that the relative employment position of the uneducated, unskilled, nonwhites, youth, and geographically isolated areas "has at best remained unchanged and in some cases deteriorated." In the sections on technological change and employment the *Manpower Report* again took a distinctly structural view of recent trends. There were no reassurances of the gradual nature of technological change or of the continuity of change. The report found instead (in direct opposition, for example, to 1963 assertions by A. J. Jaffe) that no sectoral division of the economy with productivity advances of 2.5 percent or more in the period 1957–62 had achieved output growth fast enough to avoid a reduction in employment. The positions the *Manpower Report* was attacking were never acknowledged explicitly. The names of Eckstein, Denison, Jaffe, or Heller did not appear. This was to be expected in a report supposedly demonstrating consensus in policy within an administration. But a close reading of the report in the context of the discussions that were taking place makes it clear that important differences did exist and that the circumspect statement of these differences was intentional.[3]

The structural-leaning *Manpower Report* was followed almost immediately by two of the strongest aggregate-demand papers to appear in the debates. The first paper, by Robert Solow, attacked the whole range of structural arguments, while the second, by R. A. Gordon, concentrated on unemployment dispersion arguments.

Robert Solow's paper was delivered as the April 1964 Wicksell Lectures in Stockholm. Solow was soon to join the CEA, and his analysis of the structural unemployment debate coincided with the CEA position. Solow's argument is of interest because it was a sign of the hardening of opposing positions. In particular, Solow argued that the possibility of inflation resulting from aggregate-demand policy was irrelevant to the debate, and that the real issue was whether demand action would reduce unemployment at all. Solow developed several empirical arguments to attack this exaggerated statement of the structuralist position. The arguments Solow used were primarily repetitions of those used before by Denison, Knowles-Kalachek, Heller, and others. Despite the strawman character of the structural hypothesis that Solow critiqued, his paper became widely referred to by anti-structuralists in future analyses.[4]

Shortly after Solow's address, another frequently quoted empirical paper taking an anti-structuralist view appeared. This paper, by R. A. Gordon, is of more interest because it made a new empirical contribution to the debates. Gordon began by noting that despite the empirical findings of Knowles-Kalachek, Heller, Eckstein, and others, "the debate continues, and those who have stressed the structural side of the worsened employment picture remain unconvinced that they are wrong." As a new test of the structural position, Gordon proposed a dispersion index where the percentage of unemployment in various groups was compared to average unemployment, while adjusting for the size of these groups compared to the total labor force. Using the years 1943, 1953, 1955, 1959, and 1962 for comparison, Gordon found that "the unemployment situation has not worsened *relatively* for any of the groups on which attention has been focused in the last few years." Gordon ended by voicing the standard support for both structural and demand policies. But he emphasized that the structural problem was not a new one, that it had not grown significantly worse recently, and that the major problem was the failure of aggregate demand to rise rapidly enough.[5]

During the spring and summer of 1964 the resurgence of professional debate was indicated by the appearance of several other contributions to the structural discussions. Several of these articles were interesting contributions and presented new arguments and new data. Few of them, however, can be considered as making a major contribution to the debates.[6] Two papers that are of particular interest, however, were presented at the second annual meeting of the Research Program on Unemployment in June 1964. These two studies, by Richard Lipsey and Barbara Berman, are important because they were the first significant attempts in the professional debates since Demsetz's paper in 1961 to provide a careful theoretical foundation for the analysis of structural unemployment.

Lipsey began by considering the consequences of failing to provide an adequate theoretical base for empirical studies. According to Lipsey, the pattern of past studies of structural unemployment had been to assert a list of implications of the structural unemployment argument and then proceed to show that these assertions were factually wrong. But, said Lipsey, these assertions were often themselves wrong and thus the structural unemployment argument was not defeated by past empirical attacks.

This argument by Lipsey is important because it became a frequent critique made by later evaluators of the debates. In effect Lipsey said that the empirical arguments in the debates did not resolve the issue because the questions they asked were irrelevant. In making this claim, Lipsey identified one of the major reasons for lack of progress in the empirical debates.

The first study to receive Lipsey's attention was the Knowles-Kalachek study. The first point Lipsey made was that the structuralist hypothesis Knowles and Kalachek set up to attack was the extreme one that all unemployment increases since 1957 had been structural. Lipsey found this version to be quite implausible. In particular, Lipsey found it "hard to believe that Professor Killingsworth holds to this [extreme] version." In attacking this hypothesis, Knowles and Kalachek asserted that it implied that unemployment would be more concentrated in certain labor force groups. Granting that this point of view was correct, Lipsey found that in fact Knowles and Kalachek had made no test of the structural hypothesis at all. The first Knowles-Kalachek test looked at productivity trends since 1909. Lipsey noted that 1909–45 data were completely irrelevant to the debate and that 1947–60 data did show an uptrend that was consistent with the structuralist view. The next Knowles-Kalachek argument was that there was only a low correlation between productivity and hours-worked data. Lipsey argued that the theory was more subtle than Knowles and Kalachek held, and that cyclical shifts along production functions might imply a nonlinear relation between productivity and hours worked, thus invalidating the Knowles-Kalachek analysis. The third major Knowles-Kalachek point was that no concentration of productivity gains had occurred recently. Lipsey found these data were acceptable, but he argued that there was no clear connection between this fact and the structuralist argument. A fourth Knowles-Kalachek result was that there had been no recent unusual concentration of unemployment in labor force groups. Lipsey had several points to make here. First, there was no theoretical reason to believe that structural changes would invariably concentrate unemployment in sectors with already high employment. Second, Lipsey found no reason to believe that the structure of unemployment should differ between the demand and structural cases. Third, Lipsey's visual inspection of the Knowles-Kalachek graphs led him to very different results from Knowles and Kalachek's formal statistical tests. Finally, Lipsey held that Knowles and Kalachek's analysis of predicted group unemployment rates compared to actual rates was of no value, again because there was no reason to expect any unusual behavior in this respect. After this attack on Knowles and Kalachek's major arguments, Lipsey pointed out that so little attention had been paid to the aggregate demand alternative in the paper that the Knowles-Kalachek analysis could not be accepted as a comparative study of the validity of the two hypotheses at all. Lipsey's conclusion was that "because a formal model is not developed, we do not have precisely formulated quantitative predictions following from the structural transformation hypothesis. Thus it is almost impossible to assess the relevance of some of the very interesting facts which are presented."[7]

After this analysis, Lipsey used essentially the same points to attack past papers by Heller, Eckstein, Gallaway, and Gordon. After this critique of the aggregate-demand side of the debate, Lipsey turned to a consideration of the pro-structuralist papers. Here again he found the same problems, only in a more extreme form. According to Lipsey, "again we find no precise, well-specified theory and thus no derivation of clear test statements."[8] Lipsey concluded that, given this experience, it was not surprising that the structural debates to date had hardly advanced at all.

Lipsey tried to move the debates away from this situation in the rest of his paper by providing an acceptable theoretical base for future empirical work. He did this by developing a structural unemployment theory based on a Phillips Curve analysis of the relation between inflation and unemployment. Thus defined, the key questions concerning structural unemployment centered on what was an acceptable rate of inflation and what was the level of unemployment where this rate of inflation would be reached. Based on this theory, Lipsey derived several testable hypotheses. His first hypothesis was that the unemployment rate where unacceptable inflation begins had shifted up suddenly in 1957–58. This was the extreme structural view that had been attacked most often in the past, and Lipsey agreed that "one of the few things about which we can be relatively certain in this whole debate is that this version is as close to being absolutely refuted as any probabilistic hypothesis could ever be." But Lipsey found that there was a much more plausible version of the structuralist hypothesis, and this was that the structural floor of unemployment had been slowly drifting up over time. Lipsey argued that a distinction between this case and a pure deficient-demand case could not be decided during a period of high unemployment simply by looking at the mix of the unemployed. The major difference between the two positions concerned what would happen as people are reemployed. Lipsey held that structuralists would argue that the demand mix for new workers as demand rose would be the same as the mix of those currently employed, so that there would be little improvement for high unemployment groups. The deficient demanders, Lipsey claimed, would argue that this is not the case. Thus "we find that we cannot distinguish between a rise in unemployment with technological causes and one with deficient demand causes until the upswing occurs." The only solution according to Lipsey was to try aggregate-demand policy until unacceptable inflation occurs, and then the debate would be resolved.[9]

Lipsey's careful attempt to move the debates forward was followed by a similar effort by Barbara Berman. Berman's stated aim also was to provide a definitional and theoretical approach to structural unemployment that had so far been lacking. Her major contribution was to point out the importance of distinguishing between the skill mix caused by growth in job demands and the skill mix caused by growth in labor supply. Berman did not apply her analysis to a critique of past studies or do any empirical work herself, but the implication was strong that past work had added little to knowledge about structural unemployment because of an inadequate theoretical base for the questions that were asked.[10]

With the completion of the Lipsey and Berman analyses it might be expected that the structural unemployment debates would move on to a more productive plane of analysis. The situation was analogous to the appearance in 1931 of several studies addressing the methodological issues of the technological unemployment debates. However, again similar to the technological unemployment experience, this did not happen. There is no evidence that the Lipsey and Berman efforts notably affected the content of the debates, and little sign that the structural debates were disappearing.

The dominant professional view in these continued debates remained by far the aggregate-demand view. The fact that the debates did not disappear, however, was evidence that structuralist views had an important following. Charles Killingsworth, for example, could be found expressing his structuralist views over and over again. A more important indication of the strength of structuralist sentiments, however, was the fact that a late 1964 survey of professional opinion by the Economic Research Division of Chase Manhattan Bank found that 37 percent of the economists interviewed held that inadequate demand and structural factors were equally important in recent unemployment, and 36 percent held that structural factors were the major cause of recent unemployment.[11] This indication that professional ranks were almost equally divided between those holding aggregate-demand, structuralist, and middle-ground positions explains much about why the intensity of the debates was sustained at a high level for so long.

A massive professional literature appeared on the structural issue from mid-1964 through 1965. However, little happened in this work that adds to the picture of the structural debates drawn so far. The primarily data interpretation nature of the debates continued unchanged. The Lipsey and Berman critiques had no effects on the evolution of the discussions. A recitation of the more important contributions suggests the extent of the debate.

At a July 1964 International Labour Organization conference on Employment Problems of Automation and Advanced Technology, relevant papers were presented by Otto Eckstein, George Hildebrand, and Charles Killingsworth. Eckstein and Hildebrand were both solid aggregate demanders. By this time Eckstein was a member of the CEA, and his empirical paper was in the tradition of past CEA analyses. Killingsworth disagreed sharply with the analyses by Eckstein and Hildebrand, and took this opportunity to defend his September 1963 analysis of structural unemployment and to reply to his critics. There was little, if any, backing off in Killingsworth's position, and all of his earlier structural unemployment arguments were repeated and defended.[12]

In late 1964 an October article by Richard Pasternak argued the structural side of the issue. A November article by Margaret Gordon took the aggregate demand side. A December Killingsworth article argued the structural side. A late 1964 Stanley Lebergott article argued the demand side. A December paper presented by Barbara Berman and David Kaun found that no serious bottlenecks existed for a demand expansion policy. A December article by N. J. Simler of the CEA staff argued the CEA case once again.[13] Among these late 1964 analyses, one is worth noting specifically. This November article by William Haber is of interest because by this time Haber had been participating in professional discussions of employment problems of technological change for forty years. In advocating a centralist position, Haber, however, only referred to the current debates.[14]

Through the first half of 1965, economists believed that unemployment would remain at around 5 percent for some time to come. No one expected the rapid fall in unemployment due to the Vietnam expansion that occurred at the end of the year. In this environment, the debates over structural unemployment continued to be intense. Early 1965 was notable for several major popular attacks on the structural position. Charles Silberman in a six-month series in *Fortune* attempted to attack every pessimistic automation and structural unemployment argument that had ever been made. Peter Drucker also added a critique of the structural position.[15]

The major early 1965 professional contribution was again the *Economic Report of the President*. By January 1965 the CEA (now comprising Gardner Ackley, Otto Eckstein, and Arthur Okun) was confident that the tax cut of 1964 had been the correct policy to pursue.[16] The entire 1965 report was optimistic and confident. The CEA did not foresee the impact that the Vietnam war was to have, however, as it predicted a gross national product (GNP) of $655–665 billion for the end of 1965, a real growth rate of 4 percent for the year, and a moderate fall in unemployment from the current 5 percent. The actual figures in January 1966 were a GNP of $675 billion, a real growth rate of 5.5 percent for the year, and unemployment at 4.1 percent. By late 1965 the entire economic picture had changed, and the year was a period of gradual realization of the powerful forces that were at work.

The early 1965 JEC hearings on the *Economic Report* contained only a few comments about the structural debates. Representative Thomas Curtis, who continued to be an ardent structuralist, criticized the CEA analysis. Seymour Harris and John Kenneth Galbraith also touched on the issue, with Harris taking the demand side of the argument and Galbraith taking a structural emphasis. Comments on the recent debate also were presented by William McChesney Martin of the Federal Reserve Board, Leon Keyserling, and Walter Reuther of the AFL-CIO. Martin's and Keyserling's testimonies were of interest because it was clear that neither of them had retreated at all from positions they had first presented early in the debates.[17]

The continued interest in the structural debate also was reflected in other early 1965 Congressional hearings. February House hearings on amendments to the Manpower Development and Training Act of 1962, for example, contained statements by many groups and several economists in favor of manpower programs. Economists supporting the manpower amendments included Eli Ginzberg, Richard Lester, and William Miernyk. Ginzberg and Lester said little of interest with respect to the structural unemployment debates, but Miernyk's statement was an important one. There were several features to Miernyk's statement worth noting. First, the debates had been going on long enough by 1965 that errors in reviews of the history of the debates had begun to appear. Two important points made by Miernyk were at variance with what had actually happened. First, Miernyk claimed that in 1960 everyone thought that the recent rise in unemployment had been due to inadequate demand. By 1960, however, structural arguments were common. Miernyk also claimed that almost all federal action had been taken in response to the consensus view that the problem was one of adequate demand. In 1963, however, the major complaint of the aggregate demanders was that almost all federal action had been structural. Basing his arguments on his distorted view of the history of the debates, Miernyk claimed that a major shift in professional opinion had occurred from a strict deficient-demand view toward a modified deficient demand and structuralist view. Miernyk noted recent popular attempts by Drucker and Silberman to "minimize the employment impact of automation and other forms of technological change" and claimed that among academic economists "these are now distinctly minor views. An increasing number of economists appear to be convinced that while adequate aggregate demand is a necessary condition for achieving full employment it is far from sufficient."[18]

Miernyk was right in pointing out that the majority of economists expressing their views in the literature in 1964–65 argued for both manpower and aggregate demand policies. The literature shows, however, that Miernyk got the history wrong, both by understating the strength of structuralist views prior to 1960 and overstating their strength in 1964–65. Similar inaccurate interpretations of what had gone on in the debates were to become a common feature in the rest of the discussions.

In February 1965 an NBER conference on collection of job vacancy data was held at which Charles Killingsworth again stated his views. This was a major statement by Killingsworth in that he replied to several critiques of the structuralist view and defended without change his September 1963 analysis.[19] Killingsworth's remarks suggested that by early 1965 the structural unemployment-deficient demand debates had not changed significantly. Both sides remained confident of the correctness of their data interpretations, and both sides predicted final vindication.

As a result, statements related to the debates continued to appear regularly.[20] One was the March 1965 *Manpower Report of the President* and the subsequent Congressional hearings on its contents. The report itself was important because of its continued adherence to the view asserted in the previous year's report that manpower policy was of equal importance to expanding demand. The annual Congressional hearings on the manpower report also demonstrated that the aggregate demand-structural unemployment debates were continuing. In his testimony at the hearings, for example, Harold Taylor claimed that "many" economists did not believe in the deficient demand interpretation about recent unemployment. He found that the CEA was the strongest holder of this view, and he noted rather carefully that "their own studies of unemployment data have seemed to them to support that conclusion." Taylor could not find anyone who held the extreme structuralist position that "factors of dislocation are, or will be, the sole cause of unemployment. In the debate between the structural people and the aggregate demand theorists, the structural people have simply insisted that a lot of our unemployment is structural and therefore that an all-out attempt to get these people to work by fiscal and monetary pumping would not dislodge the people and would lead to inflation." In his subsequent comments, it was clear that Taylor himself leaned toward a structuralist emphasis. In his testimony at the hearings, Eli Ginzberg also indicated that he was among the supporters of a structural emphasis concerning recent unemployment.[21]

The major testimony of interest at the hearings, however, was by Otto Eckstein of the CEA and by Charles Killingsworth. Eckstein's testimony was a further defense of familiar CEA policy arguments, but with a note of conciliation. Charles Killingsworth's paper, however, did not offer any compromises. Besides reasserting his structural beliefs, Killingsworth had one new point of interest to make. He felt that there were now going on "some rather startling efforts to rewrite history with regard to the positions that were taken and the predictions that were made in the debate that preceded the passage of the tax cut." In particular, Killingsworth found that advocates of the tax cut now said that it had done its promised job, but Killingsworth disagreed. Killingsworth in particular noted that unemployment after the tax cut had fallen only halfway to the promised 4 percent and that all informed experts, including the CEA, predicted a rise in unemployment in late 1965. Killingsworth also took exception to Eckstein's claim that in 1963 and 1964 the structuralist hypothesis was offered as an alternative to the aggregate demand view. Killingsworth argued that "I have never taken the position that stimuli to aggregate demand have no role whatever to play. My position simply was, and is, that sole reliance on tax cutting in particular is an inadequate remedy."[22]

Killingsworth was right in these comments. Misrepresentations of what had happened in the debates in the past had become common. But, more important, he was also right in his claim that misrepresentations of opposing views were a common ploy in the debates. Aggregate-demand policy advocates were particularly prone to this, with notable examples being the Knowles-Kalachek paper of 1961 and Robert Solow's analysis in 1964. But as Lipsey pointed out, structuralists were no better in testing carefully stated hypotheses.

As was clear from the April 1965 *Manpower Report* hearings, the structural unemployment debates were still at a point of irresolution. It is also evident that the fundamental nature of the dispute remained unchanged. The debates almost totally consisted of conflicting data interpretations.

Many contributions were made to the debates through the rest of 1965. One that deserves mention because of similar studies that were to follow was a *Monthy Labor Review* article by Denis Johnston of the BLS. Johnston analyzed the post–World War II trends in education and labor force participation which were a major part of the structural arguments proposed by Charles Killingsworth. Johnston's paper is an excellent example of an attempt to test directly a central hypothesis in the debate. His detailed analysis was not conclusive, however. The Killingsworth claims remained unsettled because the evidence available was not clearly in favor of either side of the debate.[23]

The most important contributions of mid-1965 were made at two conferences on unemployment in late spring 1965. One of the conferences included relevant papers by William Bowen, Arthur Okun of the CEA, Charles Killingsworth, and Richard Musgrave. Bowen's article presented a detailed statistical review of the incidence and trend of unemployment in the United States and settled for a middle ground in the debate. Charles Killingsworth's paper at the conference did not add or change anything in his views. Okun was a member of the CEA, and his paper supported the CEA view of the unemployment situation.[24] One point of interest in Okun's paper, however, illustrates the data-interpretation nature of the debate. In his analysis, Okun emphasized that recent occupational data showed a better unemployment improvement for worst-off groups. Killingsworth, however, argued in his *Manpower Report* hearings testimony (which was presented without change at the same conference as Okun's paper) that recent data showed just the opposite. Killingsworth used data broken down by race and age groups and did not consider occupations data, because he argued it was too broad to be of use. Okun did just the opposite. There was no way to bridge this gap in the debates. Either one accepted data series as "good enough" or one did not.

The final important paper at the conference was by Richard Musgrave.[25] Musgrave's analysis was a short theory paper that attempted to get a handle on the structural debate through an approach similar to that taken by Lipsey and Berman a year before. The details of Musgrave's analysis are not as important as his approach. Again there was the implication that past empirical studies were deficient because of a lack of careful justification for hypotheses that were tested. Similar critiques of past work were to appear during the next year. This type of analysis never became common in the debates, but the fact that they appeared clearly indicates that the discussions were not progressing toward a conclusion.

A second important unemployment conference in the middle of 1965 was the third meeting of the Research Program on Unemployment. A review of the individual analyses at this meeting shows that feelings about the structural unemployment-aggregate demand issue were still intense. This conference more than any other on the issue showed how far the debates had stretched professional politeness, as there was a notable lack of good humor in discussions of the issue. Almost all participants in the conference were aggregate demanders, but they found it necessary to reassert again and again the correctness of their position. The only structuralist at the conference was Charles Killingsworth, and he also argued strongly in favor of his views.

The first paper presented at the conference was by R. A. Gordon. Gordon's aggregate-demand position in the debates had not changed. One interesting point in Gordon's analysis, however, was his unemployment prediction for the immediate future. Gordon predicted a rise in unemployment in late 1965 and a decline to 4 percent unemployment in 1967. Gordon had no idea that unemployment would hit 4 percent only six months later. Thus as late as June 1965 the impact of the Vietnam War was still not foreseen. The discussions of the Gordon paper included comments by Otto Eckstein of the CEA, Joseph Pechman, and Martin Gainsbrugh of the NICB. Eckstein's views had not changed. Joseph Pechman's comments revealed that he was also an aggregate-demand defender. In Gainsbrugh's view, however, the unemployment remaining was primarily structural.[26]

The second paper at the conference was by Margaret Gordon. Gordon was clearly not a structuralist, and she noted with favor the fact that "the majority of American economists" agreed with the CEA that aggregate demand stimulation should be the primary instrument of policy. The comments on the Gordon paper by Solomon Fabricant and Stanley Lebergott touched only briefly on the structural debate, but neither took exception to Gordon's assumption that demand policy would be sufficient to reduce unemployment to 4 percent.[27]

The next two papers at the conference, by Gertrude Bancroft and by Edward Kalachek, carried on the aggregate-demand theme begun by the Gordons. The discussants of the Bancroft and Kalachek papers were Lester Thurow and Charles Killingsworth. Thurow agreed with their aggregate-demand analysis. Killingsworth, however, used his opportunity as a discussant to reassert his structuralist arguments. There was no evidence of any backing down by Killingsworth from his previous position. All of his original arguments were presented and defended in full. At the end of the paper, however, Killingsworth made an important comment. Killingsworth noted that the crucial aggregate-demand assumption was that "with a high level of demand the substitutability of various kinds and grades of labor is very high." Killingsworth did not believe that such substitutability could take place. In this remark, Killingsworth suggested the critical difference between a deficient-demand and a structuralist interpretation of policy needs. Substitutability and mobility of labor were necessary for Keynesian demand policy to work. A belief that it would take place was necessary for a belief in the deficient-demand view. This key point, however, was not pursued by any of the participants in the debates through 1965.[28]

The tenor of Killingsworth's remarks in this paper was also of interest. It was evident that he felt that his views had been misinterpreted by many economists. At one point he decried the "widespread and profound misunderstanding among professional economists" about structuralist views and rather bitterly noted that recent participants in the debates had implied that "talk about structural unemployment is the last refuge of reactionary scoundrels who are against significant action by government." Killingsworth claimed that structuralists held no such views, and that he himself merely emphasized a redirection and not a cessation of government efforts.[29]

The final conference paper, by Albert Rees, provided a fine example of many of the misinterpretations of the debates cited by Killingsworth. Rees claimed that the structuralists had held that the 1964 tax cut would not reduce unemployment at all. He held that the CEA never said the tax cut would reduce unemployment to 4 percent. (Rees cited the *Economic Report* of 1964 and 1965 and did not mention that in its 1963 *Report* the CEA did predict a fall to 4 percent unemployment from the tax cut.) Rees claimed that structuralism was an explanation of unemployment that had its "largest following among noneconomists," with milder views being held "by a few labor economists." (This was in stark contrast to the evidence of the 1964 Chase Manhatten survey.) He also claimed that almost no economist held that recent technological change had had employment effects different from those in the past. As is clear from these remarks, Rees was an aggregate demander. He held that the recent fall in unemployment had been "substantial." (Killingsworth called it "slight.") The only blemish Rees saw on the recent record was that there had been some change in the structure of the supply of labor. However, Rees held that more tax cuts would take care of all problems.[30]

At mid-1965, then, the structural debates were as intense as ever. If anything, positions had become more entrenched and confrontations more direct. At the time, almost all economists predicted a rise in unemployment during the rest of the year. Aggregate demanders called for more tax cuts to meet this challenge. Killingsworth, who had assumed the role as the primary structuralist spokesman, held that tax cuts would have no further effect and that a redirection of fiscal action to manpower spending was called for.

By December 1965, however, unemployment had fallen to 4.1 percent, having declined by a tenth of a percent per month from August. The continuing professional interest in the structural debate that was evident early in the year lasted during this period, but the future was clear. With full employment achieved, the central issue fueling the debates ceased to exist. As Lipsey pointed out in his 1964 analysis, however, the most plausible structuralist argument was that as unemployment fell, inflation would increase. There were thus good grounds for continuing discussions of the issue. These studies continued to appear long after the aggregate demand-structural uenemployment debates were over.

During the last half of 1965, however, debate continued. Among the contributions at the time were several books by economists.[31] All of these were interesting additions to the debates, with the most important being a thorough analysis of the issue by Eleanor Gilpatrick.[32] Gilpatrick's analysis was another sign of the fact that structural unemployment had risen to the status of a widely debated professional issue. As had occurred late in the technological unemployment debates of the 1930s, Gilpatrick was one of several economists who wrote their doctoral dissertations on the contemporary debate. An extended version of her thesis, her book was a long, empirical, theoretically-based evaluation of the entire issue which ended by occupying a centralist position in the discussions. Her conclusion was that recent unemployment was definitely a result of both deficient demand and structural change. This conclusion was not an unusual one. However, her method of attack was significant. Hers was again one of the few analyses to formulate a careful theoretical base for an empirical evaluation of the issue.

The details of Gilpatrick's tests are not as important as her method. Her empirical analysis was mainly descriptive. Only a few simple regressions were used because of what she felt were limitations in the data. However, Gilpatrick claimed—and rightly so—that her conclusions differed from so many of the studies that had been done before, not because of the statistical techniques she used but because of her theoretical analysis of structural unemployment. She argued that her interpretation was the correct one because of its foundation on the theory-based ideas of flexibility in the substitution of factors and skills.

Gilpatrick's book, as were Lipsey's, Berman's, and Musgrave's analyses, was a break in the typical pattern of the structural unemployment debates. Again, however, it was not to change the course of the debates significantly. These studies, which were motivated by a feeling that most work in the discussions was inadequate in terms of providing a convincing test of the issue, were inadequate themselves to produce a final resolution to the debates.

Gilpatrick's book was the major late 1965 contribution to the debates. It was not, however, the only one. The other contributions were similar to past analyses. The importance of these articles is that several of them added significant insights into the evolution of the views of individual economists. George Hildebrand, for example, contributed an August article that restated his belief that aggregate demand could reduce unemployment to 3 percent. Robert Solow added another article to his list of contributions that reaffirmed his faith in the deficient-demand view. Other demand-side articles were written by Robert Flanagan, Garth Mangum, Otto Eckstein, and Joseph Froomkin. On the structuralist side, analyses were made by Clyde Dankert, Robert Heilbroner, and William Gruber. Gruber's paper was the result of another mid-1960s doctoral dissertation on the issue.[33]

The continued appearance of these articles debating the issue showed that the structural debates had not disappeared by late 1965. A review of these late 1965 papers also indicates that the professional discussions had changed little in content or character. Gilpatrick's book was the only notable break from the norm. But behind these discussions, basic changes were taking place in the economy that soon would effectively eliminate the issue as a popular and professional economic concern. By October 1965 it was clear that the economy was beginning to expand rapidly. The October 9 *Business Week* reported that consumer confidence was at near-record levels and noted that forecasters just since mid-September had revised their average growth expectations for 1966 from 4.5 percent to 6 percent. In its October 16 issue, *Business Week* reported that unemployment was 4.4 percent, compared to 4.9 percent in April, and ac-knowledged that a major factor in the decline was the Vietnam buildup. *Time* on November 12 noted that economists were "surprised by how quickly the situation changed" with respect to unemployment since mid-year. It also re-ported that the stepped-up draft would reduce unemployment even further. The November 27 *Business Week* noted that the January 1965 CEA prediction of a December GNP of $655–665 billion had been revised to $670 billion. August 1965 CEA forecasts of an increase to $700 billion by December 1966 were re-vised to $715 billion. And forecasts of a stagnant economy and 5 percent un-employment in 1966 were changed to rapid growth and unemployment as low as 3.5 percent. The December 4 *Business Week* reported that the June 1965 estimated budget deficit of $4 billion now stood at $7 billion, that the draft had risen from 5,000 a month in spring 1965 to 40,000 a month in November, and that "during the past few weeks, the war in Vietnam has taken on a whole new dimension."[34]

10

Resolution and Interpretation of the Structural Unemployment Debates

A war effectively ended the structural unemployment debates in 1965 just as war had stopped the technological unemployment debates in 1940. The end of the structural debates also was similar to that of the technological unemployment discussions in another important way. Major contributions to the structural unemployment debates continued to appear long after the issue had lost its immediate importance. Major analyses appeared slowly but regularly all the way through the 1970s. These contributions are important for several reasons. For one, they illustrate the fundamental professional interest in the issue. Second, they show a movement toward a more careful theoretical justification of empirical work. And finally, they illustrate the fact that few individual opinions changed in the course of the debates.

A review of major contributions after 1965 illustrates the resolution phase of the debates. The 1966 *Economic Report of the President* set the tone for the economic concerns of the late 1960s. The CEA's main theme was that fiscal policy could hold back a too-rapid expansion. No longer was faster growth the issue. In this discussion, no mention was made of technological change or structural unemployment as a problem currently or in the past. The February 1966 JEC hearings on the *Economic Report* similarly contained no discussions of structural unemployment or technological change problems. The emphasis was all on the success of fiscal action in the past few years and on the likelihood of inflation in the future.[1]

The major relevant contributions of early 1966 came in the publication of the summary report and six thick supporting volumes of the National Commission on Technology, Automation and Economic Progress (NCT). Exactly like the creation of the National Research Project on Reemployment Opportunities and Recent Changes in Industrial Techniques (NRP) in the 1930s, the NCT was set up during the peak years of concern over technological change in the mid-1960s to study the issue in depth. The commission itself was comprised of a wide selection of business, labor, and government leaders. Only one econo-mist, Robert Solow, was on the commission. Garth Mangum was the director, however, and the staff included several other economists.

The summary report was optimistic about the impact of technological change on the economy. The report was empirical, detailed, and clearly not structuralist. The appendix volumes of the NCT were comprised in general of excellent scholarly studies, with the papers of most interest to the structural debates being written by Walter Buckingham and Clyde Dankert. Buckingham had been a worrier about the unemployment effect of automation since the 1950s, and the 1966 paper presented his current views. Contrary to the con-clusions in the official NCT report, Buckingham was as pessimistic, or even more so, than he had ever been about the impact of technological change on employment. Clyde Dankert's paper presented a review of the history of eco-nomic thought on technological change and employment similar to those that he had been providing since the mid-1930s. Dankert concluded that the history of past debates suggested that a balanced view was best, and that both extreme pessimism and extreme optimism should be avoided.[2]

The NCT work was a major contribution to the technology and employment discussions in terms of reviewing, updating, and adding to the relevant evi-dence. The NCT was a worthy successor in this regard to the work of the NRP in the 1930s. Coming when it did, however, the NCT's contribution essentially went unnoticed. The summary report was given wide publicity, but the exten-sive appendix studies were seldom mentioned. The issue the NCT attacked had been settled effectively by the course of current events before the report even appeared.

Another early 1966 contribution also signaled the demise of the issue. In February the JEC held a symposium reviewing the first twenty years of the Employment Act of 1946. The symposium as set up in October 1965 included a session on the structural unemployment-aggregate demand debate. By the time of the meeting, however, the issue was nearly dead. All of the economists present acknowledged that both manpower and aggregate policies were needed, but the dominant feeling was that fiscal action had been responsible for the recovery to date and for the current level of unemployment. The March 1966 *Manpower Report of the President* also added to the impression that the debate was over by explicitly acknowledging the preeminence of fiscal and monetary policy in bringing unemployment down to its current 3.7 percent level without the development of severe bottlenecks, distortions, or imbalances in the labor market. No longer was there any evidence in the report that its authors differed from the CEA in their assessment of the current situation.

Despite the fact that current concerns were now turning to inflation, the past debates over the nature of unemployment lingered on. Several relevant studies were published during the rest of 1966. In the April *Industrial and Labor Re-lations Review*, Vladimir Stoikov reexamined the whole structuralist debate and argued that "the structuralist hypothesis has been buried prematurely." In a May article, Robert Lekachman provided an analysis which concluded that the post-1963 expansion "provides as vivid a testimonial as one could wish to the efficacy of Keynesian public finance."   Another May paper by Barbara Bergmann and David Kaun also found little evidence through the early 1960s of an increase in the level of structural unemployment. They concluded that cyclical factors explained almost all recent trends.[3]

During 1966 a wave of doctoral theses also appeared on the subject. As during the technological unemployment debates, most of the theses came to nontraditional conclusions about the issue. George Iden analyzed the structure of unemployment in 141 major labor market areas over the period 1950–63 in his Harvard thesis and found evidence that he claimed limited simple aggregate-demand model prescriptions for reducing unemployment. Donald Wells' University of Southern California thesis made no original contributions to the debate, but analyzed and classified all of the important contributions from the late 1950s through 1964. Wells concluded that the amount of agreement in the discussions outweighed the disagreements, and that in effect the debates had been a waste of time and resources. Mamoru Ishikawa's thesis was concerned with testing whether structural factors were a basic cause of long-term unemployment regardless of the initial reason for the unemployment. He found that, indeed, the supply characteristics of the unemployed far overshadowed the importance of aggregate demand.[4]

Of the other relevant studies on both sides of the issue in 1966, one more is worth mentioning specifically. This study, by Murray Brown, was another careful theoretically based empirical study of the issue. Brown's main concern was with the theoretical underpinnings of the technological aspect of structural unemployment. After an analysis of the theory, Brown was led to conclude that "the implication is that when technological unemployment is present, only deliberate policy measures (or fortuitous events) are able to eradicate it." Brown singled out Neisser's 1942 analysis of the problem, which argued that there was no automatic mechanism of reabsorption, and claimed that this article "was an extremely lucid analysis of the problems of displacement and absorption of workers resulting from technological progress." Brown then did an empirical study of the periods 1919–37 and 1938–58 which showed that increases in output had "won the race" between technological progress and output growth. Thus he concluded that the aggregate employment effects of technological change had not been serious. In Brown's words, to date "technological change has not been sufficiently powerful to form a 'surplus population' or an 'industrial reserve army' in the Marxian sense."[5]

The Brown book was a rare example in the 1960s of a careful consideration of earlier theoretical contributions. Other economists had noted that previous debates had occurred, but few had analyzed these contributions seriously. This historical, theoretical, and empirical myopia was a dominant characteristic of the structural debates. Since the disputes made little progress, it might be hoped that a broader consideration of the issue would have been more successful. In fact, as Demsetz's 1961 paper and Lipsey's 1964 article showed, these approaches also had little effect in resolving the discussions. The fact that these broader analyses all concluded that both sides had elements of truth hindered their impact. These conclusions were right, but participants in the debates were looking for stronger results. They wanted a decision, not a compromise.

The decline in intensity of discussion of structural issues which was obvious during 1966 was completed in 1967. During the year almost nothing appeared on the debates in current policy discussions. The *Economic Report of the President* and the *Manpower Report of the President* did not approach the issue. Unemployment averaged 3.8 percent in 1966 and in 1967, and concerns were with over-full employment, not stagnation.

Although as a current issue the debates were effectively over, echoes of the past disputes continued to be heard for years. These echoes reflected many of the difficulties economists had in dealing with the issue in the early 1960s. Through 1967 and into 1968 all those who touched on the issue claimed the aggregate demanders had won the debates.[6] In mid-1968, however, signs began to appear that the Vietnam experience was not totally convincing to all structuralists as a vindication of the aggregate-demand view.

A 1968 collection of essays on retraining edited by Gerald Somers, for example, was enthusiastic about manpower policy. Somers noted that up until 1965 these programs did little to reduce unemployment. However, he did not attribute this to a lack of sufficient aggregate demand. Rather he felt that "the most obvious reason for this limited impact was the small scale of the retraining efforts relative to the size of the continuing unemployment problem." Similar views leaning toward a structural emphasis could be found in the work of other labor economists. Eli Ginzberg, for example, demonstrated his bias in favor of manpower policy in a 1968 collection of his essays. Ginzberg took a middle position on automation, technological change in general, and structural unemployment. He was not an alarmist by any means, but he was not overly optimistic either.[7]

The strongest evidence that structural ideas were still around, however, came in a May 1968 speech by Charles Killingsworth. Killingsworth looked back over the entire debates and provided a spirited defense of all of his original views. Since these remarks seemed so out of tune with the nature of almost all other professional analyses at the time, a review of Killingsworth's arguments is of interest. Killingsworth began by claiming that the structuralist position had never been properly tested. He dismissed all attacks on the position as being "less by direct confrontation of the pertinent data than by the elaboration of doctrine." In particular, he critiqued the Knowles-Kalachek 1961 study, as he had done before, as "an exercise in irrelevancy" due to its extreme statement of the structuralist position. Killingsworth also dismissed the subsequent body of empirical work on the issue as "a substantial body of literature which possibly equals the irrelevancy of the original" Knowles-Kalachek study. Killingsworth then turned to a defense of the structuralist view. He first claimed that "a structuralist is correctly defined as a Keynesian who believes that changes in the structure of the economy can have an independent effect on the levels of employment and unemployment." He found that the debates had been confusing on this point because of the existence of extreme structuralists, because of misinterpretations by those who wanted to discredit the structuralist view, and because a misleading desire for symmetry in the debates led to the statement of structuralist views as alternatives to the demand view. To Killingsworth, however, the main issue in the debates was whether "the labour market will automatically compensate or adjust for the differences in quality of labour. In short, the New Economics asserts that the labour market is a powerful automatic homogenizer of labour." Killingsworth, of course, disagreed. Killingsworth then repeated his education bottleneck thesis as he had consistently since late 1963. However, Killingsworth had to face a problem, and that was that unemployment in the United States had fallen to 3.8 percent by mid-1968. Killingsworth noted that "there is now a widespread belief among economists in the U.S. . . . that the course of events has passed a conclusive verdict on the structural-versus-aggregate demand controversy." But Killingsworth disagreed with what he called this current *post hoc ergo propter hoc* analysis and presented an empirical argument to show that his structuralist position had not been disproven. First, Killingsworth claimed that post-1965 manpower programs had—by official BLS estimate—reduced total unemployment by 0.4 percent. Second, he found that a recent redefinition of unemployment had reduced the aggregate figure by 0.2 percent (again by BLS estimate). Third, Killingsworth claimed that the Vietnam War buildup had drafted or forced into college to gain deferments enough people to reduce unemployment 0.5 percent. Taking into account recent early retirement programs, education fellowship programs, and so on, Killingsworth thus was able to claim that "it is an understatement to say that all kinds of structural programmes and related structural effects accounted for 1.1 percent points of the drop in the nation's unemployment rate from 1964 to 1967." Thus, according to Killingsworth, unemployment in the absence of these developments would be at 4.9 percent, or the exact point at which he claimed in 1963 that aggregate demand policies would cease to be effective. Killingsworth then reviewed recent group unemployment rates to claim that the best had gotten better-off and the worst worse-off in recent months. He also reviewed unemployment-by-education trends to show that the "twist" still existed. He finished by repeating that recent developments had not vindicated the aggregate demand view, and by claiming that "demand stimulation alone would not have reduced the unemployment rate much below 5 percent."[8]

Killingsworth's attempt to revive the structuralist position had little effect. His paper was presented in Glasgow and published in the *Scottish Journal of Political Economy*, not a mainstream forum. The fading structural debates, however, received a second jolt in the fall of 1968. In the September *Monthly Labor Review* two more articles directly considered the issue. Denis Johnston contributed one of the articles. Johnston had been writing on education and unemployment trends since 1963. In 1963 and 1965 *Monthly Labor Review* articles he had found indications of a shift in demand from lower- to higher-educated workers. But in neither case did Johnston make any conclusive remarks about the relevance of this information to the structural debates. In his September 1968 article, however, Johnston explicitly tied his analysis to this issue. Johnston began by stating that his purpose was to test the Killingsworth education-twist thesis for the periods 1950–60 and 1960–67. He stated Killingsworth's arguments carefully and claimed that often in the past Killingsworth (as Killingsworth himself asserted) had been misinterpreted. Johnson then analyzed 1950 and 1960 Census data and 1960–67 Current Population Survey data on unemployment, education, and labor force participation by age, sex, and race groups. According to Johnston, "[t]he 1950 decade was a period of declining labor force participation among less educated men at all age levels (both white and non-white) while the rates for the most educated were rising or, among older men, falling much more slowly. Thus the above evidence lends solid support to the Killingsworth thesis, at least for the 1950–60 period." Johnston also acknowledged that this had been the period that Killingsworth all along had emphasized. Johnston then turned to the post-1960 period. Here again he found that "on the whole, then, the 'twist' first observed by Professor Killingsworth for the period from the 1950 census to March 1962 appears to be still in operation despite the recovery since 1962, and has in fact acquired more torque among the older men."[9]

However, this left open the "big question" of to what extent these labor force withdrawals were due to reduced demand, and to what extent they were due to other factors. Johnston next turned his attention to this "interpretation" part of the facts. Looking in detail at the experience of different age groups in 1950–60 and 1960–67, Johnston found support for Killingsworth in the experience of those in the 55–64 age group. He also found that at all times the heaviest withdrawals were among the lowest educated. But for the over-65 age group, where most of the withdrawals had occurred since 1960, the evidence was not so clear. In the end Johnston was led to adopt a pro-Killingsworth interpretation of the 1950–60 period, but an anti-Killingsworth position for the period 1960–67. In Johnston's words,

labor force "disappearance" has continued to occur during both the 1950–60 and 1960–67 periods, despite the recent economic recovery. However, the heavy concentration of this "disappearance" among men 65 and over, and the somewhat weakened association between these withdrawals and levels of educational attainment, strongly suggest the operation of factors other than discouragement in the face of limited job opportunities.[10]

In the same journal, Charles Killingsworth added another article on the issue. Killingsworth's article was a reply to Johnston's analysis. As might be expected, Killingsworth agreed with Johnston's facts, but disagreed with Johnston's interpretations. Killingsworth began by restating his 1963–64 analyses of unemployment trends. Nothing new was added. He then reviewed Johnston's article and exclaimed that "surely I am the person least likely to challenge these conclusions!" He did find, however, that "some of Johnston's ensuing discussion, especially with regard to the 'discouraged worker' hypothesis, might provide some basis for debate; this portion of his discussion rests more on interpretation than on observed facts." Killingsworth then evaluated the 1962–67 period on his own to claim that his interpretation was indeed the correct one.[11]

The most important feature of these 1968 analyses is that they show that the data interpretation disagreements that had dominated the debates were still in evidence. Another important feature of these contributions, however, is that they suggest a reason for the strong reactions against Killingsworth's structural arguments besides the fact that they conflicted with the professional Keynesian consensus. Killingsworth had to rely on a significant number of data twists to support his demand-twist thesis. Killingsworth's use of "adjusted" Census data and his subsequent "real" unemployment rate in his 1963 analysis were open to criticism. Heller was quite justified in pointing out these problems. Killingsworth's "adjusted" unemployment argument in 1968 also must have been difficult to accept seriously in the face of the Vietnam boom. Killingsworth was right in claiming that statements about both his views and the actual course of the debates were often misinterpretations. Johnston's 1968 results also provided some vindication for Killingsworth's claims about trends in the early 1960s. However, given Killingsworth's data-twisting approach, given the political-policy nature of the dispute, and given the strong professional commitment to Keynesian analysis at the time, it is not surprising that his views received the response they did.

As it turned out, no one ever tried to test Killingsworth's explanation of the fall in unemployment from 4.7 percent in April 1965 to 3.7 percent in April 1966 by a study of the timing of the events Killingsworth emphasized. Killingsworth also did not acknowledge Denis Johnston's attempt to explain the fall in low-educated group participation rates by referring to the nature of the life-styles and occupations of low-educated individuals. It is also notable that Killingsworth never tried to defend his views by reference to the inflation that was becoming evident by 1968. The fact that these obvious paths to extend the discussions were never explored is more a sign that the issue simply did not occupy the position of importance it had before than of any lack of care in analysis.

By 1969 the structural debates had ceased to be a current professional debate. Relevant comments could be found from time to time, but only a few of these later studies are worth noting.[12] One such study was the result of a nationwide survey conducted by the University of Michigan in May and October 1967. This study was one of the best of all of the professional studies that had been done on the aggregate unemployment impact of technological change since the issue began to receive attention in the late 1920s. More than 2,500 workers were interviewed in the study. Conducted under the direction of Eva Mueller, the purpose of the survey was to analyze the impact of technological change on the labor force as a whole. As Mueller noted, the subject matter of this study is not new.   What *is* new is the scope of the study and the methodology employed. Previous investigations have been based on case studies. The results have often been of uncertain meaning, and even contradictory. . . . A survey of the entire labor force can lead to generalizations and statements about the relative frequency of various consequences which case studies do not permit the researcher to make.

The data collected were analyzed through the use of tables and simple regressions. The major questions were directed at whether workers used machinery and at whether they had experienced any changes in their jobs due to changes in machinery in the period 1962–67. All data results were based on worker recollections. A long series of conclusions were drawn, but the major theme was that overall the employment impact of technological change was not severe. For example, 10 percent of those interviewed experienced one or more machine changes in 1962–67 that significantly affected their job. An additional 12 percent experienced machine changes due to job changes, where the job change was not related to a machine change. Mueller thus concluded that "percentagewise, technological advance changed relatively few jobs to a significant degree—about 2 to 3 percent a year." Concentrating on the changes that did occur, Mueller also found that most new jobs were filled by workers from within the company. Overall, then, she found that

the impact of advance in machine technology on employment is largely indirect. The firm which introduces new labor-saving machinery often can rely on normal retirements or resignations plus an expanding market to bring its labor supply in balance with needs. Skilled and experienced people who have to be laid off tend to be re-employed quickly. Much of the unemployment resulting from labor-saving machinery "trickles down" to the most marginal groups in the labor force. Workers who might have been hired in the absence of technological change are not needed.

Mueller repeated this "silent firing" concept (as Walter Buckingham had been calling it since the early 1960s) several times in her analysis. She then expanded on this concept to conclude that "the survey findings *do* support the . . . statement which contends that aggregate demand is *the* key to the economy's ability to absorb technological unemployment. There is no need to defend or discuss the proposition that the answer to the job problem of the marginal worker is strong demand for labor throughout the economy plus job training, with the major emphasis on labor demand." Mueller later summed up these findings by remarking that "technological change has its major impact indirectly on the most marginal groups in the labor market: those at the end of the employment queue."[13]

The Mueller study is a landmark in the history of professional attempts to study the impact of technological change on employment. It was a laudable attempt to get around many of the shortcomings that had handicapped every past case study. In particular, the problem of generalization from specific results was handled effectively by the large scale of the study.

One major problem with the study is pertinent, however. Mueller's "silent firing" and "labor market queue" arguments had no direct factual foundation in the results of her survey. These arguments were supported by the reported survey fact that there was little direct unemployment due to technological change. However, these are only two of many possible inferences that could be made from her statistical results. The only clear fact she could claim from her study was that little direct unemployment was found. The tie between this fact and the idea of a "labor queue," which justified her policy prescription of aggregate demand action, was not evident in the data results.

Mueller was not alone in making a late major contribution to the issue. In 1969 another theoretical attack in the manner of Lipsey and Gilpatrick was provided by Richard Perlman.[14] Perlman made no empirical contributions because the data he found to be crucial were not available. But he did provide a theoretical review of the issue that included an attack on the methodology of almost every major past empirical contribution to the subject. Perlman argued that a proper definition of structural unemployment implied that changes in group unemployment rates and periods of rising unemployment shed no light on the extent of structural unemployment. As a result, he found, as had Lipsey and Gilpatrick, that almost all past empirical studies had been irrelevant. In particular, Perlman attacked in detail past studies by the CEA, Knowles-Kalachek, Gordon, Killingsworth, Simler, Berman, Denison, and Eckstein. Perlman's analysis came too late to affect the course of the structural debates. His critique of past work, however, is significant in its indication that the structural debates did not move readily toward a resolution because of a basic defect in the approach of most studies of the issue.

Although the 1960s structural debates had effectively disappeared by 1969, their echoes could be found through the 1970s. Three papers in 1970–71 by Charles Killingsworth, for example, reaffirmed his 1968 analysis. A late 1970 paper by MacRae and Schweitzer analyzed the 1960s and found little evidence in support of the structural argument. A 1971 book by Gallaway did the same. A 1971 paper by Denis Johnston claimed that the education-twist which he had found in the early 1960s had stopped in 1964–69. A 1972 analysis by Marshall and Perlman claimed that structural views were supported by the post-1965 inflation. A 1973 book by Kalachek claimed that 1960s evidence supported the aggregate-demand view. And a 1975 paper by Killingsworth confirmed that he had not changed his mind about the demand-twist position he had been defending for a dozen years.[15]

These post-mortem examinations of the 1960s debates add little to what previously has been said about how economists acted in the debates. Perhaps the most important fact about structural discussions in the 1970s is that they still were an issue. Debate over the experience of the early 1960s was no longer heard. The demand-side structuralism that was emphasized in the early 1960s received little attention. Supply-side structuralist arguments, however, were generally accepted by the 1970s. As a result, in the early 1970s the full employment level of unemployment was discussed as being around 4.5 percent.

By the late 1970s the figures were 5 to 5.5 percent. This result suggests that although the dominant opinion was that the aggregate-demand view was vindicated by the Vietnam experience, despite the weakness of many of their arguments the structuralists made a point that survived and had an important impact. Ultimately, neither side had a monopoly on truth in the debates. The aggregate demanders were right in their assertion that expanded demand could reduce unemployment below 4 percent. However, the structuralists were also correct in their claim that fundamental structural changes were shifting the level of noninflationary full employment.

Given this experience, what can be said about the structural unemployment debates with respect to questions about how economics works as a science? On a general level, a final professional consensus was never reached on the main question of whether structural changes or deficient demand were responsible for early 1960s unemployment trends. Conflicting views appeared throughout the debates, right up to their end during the Vietnam expansion. The majority of the published literature always supported the demand view, but structural opinions had wide support. The fact that much of the post-mortem literature on the issue found reason for supporting a structuralist view also suggests that the structuralist interpretation was never defeated.

This conclusion about the lack of progress toward a professional consensus requires qualification. There were times and areas of movement toward agreement. An enormous amount of information was collected on the fine structure of unemployment in the United States. These data were analyzed and reshuffled in a dozen different ways. It is undoubtedly the case that movement toward a consensus occurred on the experience of different groups in the labor force. It is also true that a major amount of work was done on the recent impact of automation in the economy. As was the case with the micro-level studies of the 1930s, several questions were effectively settled by this work. The conclusion that few workers were directly unemployed by automation was supported by almost all automation studies from the mid-1950s through the mid-1960s. That a large number of jobs were significantly changed in content was also a common finding. That workers who did become unemployed generally experienced significant hardships was another one. This work was clearly significant, and here the evidence points in the direction of a movement toward an aggregate consensus.

It is also the case that the late-1961 study by Knowles and Kalachek was a major factor in reducing the intensity of debate for over a year and a half. Everyone in the debates also agreed on the efficacy of Keynesian policy for stimulating labor demand. No one claimed that manpower policies were useless. Everyone felt that both structural and demand policies were needed.

It is also apparent that there were some changes in the nature of the major attacks on the issue. The first significant contributions were almost totally empirical. Later contributions, however, often adopted a more integrative theoretical-empirical approach. A comparison of early papers by Heller, Knowles-Kalachek, Clague-Greenberg, Killingsworth, and Gordon, with later contributions by Lipsey, Berman, Gilpatrick, Musgrave, and Perlman, illustrates this point.

There were areas of change in the debates, in other words, and some of this change was progress. It is also true that the debates did disappear. However, as to the question of whether the debates tended to disappear because of results generated within the profession itself, the balance of the evidence does not support a strong affirmative answer.

In those areas of progress that took place, data analysis played a central role. The structural unemployment-deficient demand debates were almost totally empirical in nature. The difference in this respect between the 1930s and 1960s debates is striking. The 1930s discussions had nearly equal theoretical and empirical components, and in each component a significant professional debate occurred. In contrast, the primarily theoretical work in the 1960s debates was minor compared to the empirical work, and no theory debates ever developed. This difference from the 1930s debates is not surprising, however. In the 1960s the participants, with few exceptions, were committed Keynesians. They believed that increased government spending would raise employment. The question in the 1960s debates, then, was what to emphasize in govenment spending. The basic theory was not an issue. Even those papers from 1964 on that attempted to provide a more solid theoretical justification for their empirical work did not engage in anything that could be called a theoretical debate. All the debates that took place relied primarily on data and its interpretation.

The main sources of data throughout the debates were decennial Census and Current Population Survey data from World War II to date. Other longer historical series also entered into the discussions, as in the Knowles-Kalachek (1961) or Fabricant (1962) surveys of long-run productivity data. Case study information on the impact of automation was also used, but Census and population survey sources were by far the major elements in the debates. The many analyses that were made of these data, however, apparently were not effective in stopping the structural debates. Killingsworth and Demsetz used the same data to argue for significant structural unemployment that Heller, Knowles-Kalachek, Solow, Eckstein, and others used to argue against a significant rise in structural unemployment. It was this inability of a simple examination of the data to settle the issue that led to the more careful theoretical justifications of structural unemployment conclusions by Berman, Lipsey, Musgrave, Gilpatrick, and others after 1963.

The impact of this more theory-based work, however, was also mixed. Lipsey found that all past work on both sides of the issue was irrelevant. Berman implied the same thing. Musgrave, however, found support for the aggregate-demand view in a similar review of the question. Gilpatrick again found that past work was irrelevant, but her theory-based empirical studies came down right in the middle between structural unemployment and deficient demand polar positions.

There was also little evidence that this more theoretically based work had a significant impact on the contributions of other economists. Later writers did not pick out the theoretical contributions as the highlights of the debates. Rather, the discussions continued much as they had before, but with an added element of more careful theory-based papers being published at the same time.

Taking an overall view of the course of the aggregate debates, it appears that formal data analysis did not move the debates in a clear way to a final consensus. The debates ceased only when the sharp drop in unemployment due to the Vietnam buildup simply stopped all interest in the subject. One could view the Vietnam expansion as a controlled experiment whose outcome ended the debate. A sharp increase in aggregate demand certainly did produce full employment. Detailed analysis of past data was suddenly irrelevant. But even this experience, however, turned out to be insufficient to totally convince the structuralists. The resulting inflation, for example, was later taken as structuralist evidence. The 1960s debates ended with Vietnam, but structural views survived. This overall experience implies that the contribution of formal data analysis was significantly modified by other factors with respect to its impact on progress in the structural unemployment debates. In this case, the main modifying factors were an inadequate theoretical statement of the issue and the onset of the Vietnam War.

Turning to the individual aspect of the debates, there is a firmer basis for making judgments about the disputes of the 1960s than for those of the 1930s. Several publications were found by each of several individuals. Some economists had also been writing on related issues since the 1950s or even the 1930s. As a result, it can be said with greater confidence for the 1960s debates that there were few cases where significant changes were made in the views of individual economists. A review of the contributions of several economists will illustrate this point.

Those economists who had written in the area for some time before the 1960s debates included William Haber, Ewan Clague, Alvin Hansen, Clyde Dankert, Solomon Fabricant, and Yale Brozen. A review of the work of these economists suggests that few significant changes in emphasis took place in their analyses, even over extended periods of time. This is true with respect to both the evolution over the long run of approaches to employment problems and to specific views about the structural unemployment debates themselves.

A review of the work of economists whose contributions were more closely restricted to the structural debates leads to the same general conclusion. Walter Buckingham, William Miernyk, and Richard Wilcock are three economists whose relevant work dates over a period intermediate between those whose work dates back to the 1940s and those who just participated in the structural controversy. Buckingham's emphasis was always on the impact of technological change, and he always expressed concern about the employment effects of these changes. Miernyk shifted from a centralist position in the debates toward a stronger structuralist view over time. Wilcock also showed a slight shift, but this time in the aggregate demand direction. The main impression, however, is more of consistency than of change in their views.

The list of economists who made a significant series of contributions only during the period of the structural debates includes Walter Heller, Neil Chamberlain, Clarence Long, Otto Eckstein, Edward Kalachek, Charles Killingsworth, Leon Keyserling, Leon Greenberg, Robert Solow, Eli Ginzberg, A. J. Jaffe, Robert Aaron Gordon, George Hildebrand, Vladimir Stoikov, Garner Ackley, Lowell Gallaway, and Richard Perlman. The one major feature that characterizes all of these contributions is that few economists changed their views with respect to the issues debated. This would not be surprising if all the economists involved agreed with one another so that there was nothing to be debated. However, this is not the case. At least four major positions are represented in this list. The first is the dominant aggregate-demand position in the debates. As represented by Heller, Eckstein, Kalachek, and Solow, this view held that demand policy alone was sufficient to reduce unemployment to 4 percent, and that structural change had not been responsible for the rise of unemployment since 1957. The second position is an even stronger aggregate-demand position. As represented by Keyserling, this view held that the CEA-proposed demand expansion policy was not nearly strong enough to reduce unemployment to 4 percent and that a much stronger policy was needed. The third position is the neoclassical view. As represented by Yale Brozen and Clarence Long, this view was that high minimum wages and a rapidly rising average wage rate were responsible for recent unemployment. Neither the structuralist nor the aggregate-demand position was seen as adequate for reducing unemployment in this view. The fourth position is the structural unemployment case. As represented by Killingsworth, and less strongly by Chamberlain, Ginzberg, Stoikov, and Perlman, this view held that recent demand-side structural changes in the economy had been responsible for a significant amount of the post-Korean rise in unemployment, and that demand policy alone would not be sufficient to reduce unemployment to 4 percent without major inflation.

In all of this list of contributors, only a few significant changes in opinion are evident. One economist whose work suggests some change is Clarence Long. In 1959 Long was among the first to emphasize that labor force supply policies would be needed to reduce current unemployment. In 1960 Long repeated this analysis, but with a neoclassical emphasis that minimum wage increases had been responsible for the unemployment rise. In early 1961 Long repeated this opinion without change. In late 1961 and early 1962, however, Long shifted his emphasis to the position that both structuralist and aggregate-demand policies were necessary to reduce unemployment to 4 percent.

Another economist who exhibited some change in view is George Hildebrand. In a 1964 paper Hildebrand found that deficient demand had been the primary cause of unemployment in the United States since the late 1950s. In a 1965 paper, Hildebrand reaffirmed this opinion, but he now emphasized more than before that inflationary pressures resulting from an expansion of demand necessary to achieve full employment would be unacceptable. Hildebrand thus came out in support of a more balanced structuralist-aggregate demand policy.

Another economist whose work showed signs of change is Leon Greenberg. Greenberg was a BLS economist. In his 1962 and 1963 work, Greenberg leaned in the direction of taking a pessimistic view of recent technological change trends. In 1964 and 1965, however, Greenberg found that the trends evident through 1963 had turned around, and he was much more optimistic in his evaluations. Greenberg was primarily an empirical economist, and it is reasonable to assume that his shift in emphasis was closely tied to the facts of recent data trends.

These few shifts in emphasis exhaust the list of noticeable changes in views evident in the professional contributions to the 1960s debates. Heller was consistent in his view that, although both types of policy were needed, demand action alone was sufficient to reduce unemployment to 4 percent. Neil Chamberlain consistently emphasized a mild structuralist view. Otto Eckstein was consistent in his support of the Heller position. Edward Kalachek never had sympathy for the structuralist view. Charles Killingsworth first stated his structuralist ideas in 1962 and first presented them strongly in 1963. In all the rest of the debates there was no sign of any significant change in his views.

The same story holds for work by Keyserling, Solow, Ginzberg, Jaffe, Gordon, Stoikov, Ackley, Gallaway, and Perlman. Both aggregate demand and structuralist views are represented by this group, but no one showed any sign of a major shift in emphasis with respect to the structural unemployment issue.

Part of this experience can be attributed to the political-policy dimension of the structural debates. This factor helped make individual statements stronger than they might otherwise have been. However, this was not the whole story. The same experience had occurred in the 1930s, when the direct political-policy aspect of the debates was less important. Thus the tendency of economists to remain committed to a view once it had appeared in print transcended the intense political focus of the structural debates.

Adding this individual-level evidence to the aggregate-level conclusions reached before, the evidence of the 1960s debates suggests that data analysis did not play a dominating role in motivating progress in professional thought. There are two reasons for this conclusion. First, progress on both the aggregate and the individual level was limited in the debates. Although there was significant progress in some areas—and some individuals did modify their views over time—these developments did not dominate the discussions. Second, in those areas where progress in thought did take place, the evidence suggests that factors other than data analysis played a significant role. The evolution of the aggregate debates seems to have been influenced by theoretical considerations and by current events as much as by quantitative studies. Evidence that individuals changed their opinions as the result of quantitative studies is rare.

It is also apparent that the common approach in the debates was one of confrontation. The 1961 CEA analysis began this pattern by providing an empirical attack on the structural hypothesis. No other economists were mentioned by name in this paper, but the issue itself was confronted directly. The immediately following Martin critique of the Heller view, and the subsequent early 1961 attempts at resolution by Samuelson, Hansen, Chamberlain, and others, added the dimension of referring specifically to other economists' work. Demsetz's late 1961 article continued this approach with a detailed critique of the Heller-CEA analysis. The late 1961 Knowles-Kalachek paper again did not refer to other economists by name, but it did attack the structural view explicitly and in detail in order to support the aggregate-demand view.

Confrontations of opinions then became common throughout the debates. The most dramatic episode was the Killingsworth-Heller exchange of 1963–64. However, the approach of a critique of others' views can be found elsewhere as well. Borus (1965), for example, specifically criticized Gordon (1964) who was in turn attacking the structuralist view. Stoikov (1965) critiqued Gallaway (1963) who was attacking the structuralists. Butler (1967) critiqued Stoikov (1966) who had critiqued Gordon (1964) who was attacking the structuralist view. The general approach seems to have been to defend one's position, with this defense typically taking the form in large part of a critique of others' views.

Overall, it appears that it was the questions asked of the data that gave rise to many of the problems in the 1960s discussions and not the data itself. This conclusion, however, requires qualification. There were many comments in 1960s papers about the inadequacy of available data. One unavailable data source that was held to be crucial by some debaters was job vacancy data. Richard Perlman, for example, held that these data were essential in making a decision between structural and cost-push factors in the post-1965 Vietnam inflation. Other examples of problems with available data sources also could be found. Killingsworth, for instance, always complained that occupations data were too broad to be used in looking for structural change effects and that official unemployment data did not adequately account for labor force participation rates.

There is no doubt, then, that the quality of available data was a factor hindering progress in the debates. It was differences over data interpretations, however, that gave rise to the greatest problems. The 1963 Killingsworth-Heller exchanges are particularly clear examples of this problem. An overview of the entire course of the debates supports this view strongly. Everyone used the same data sources. But because there was a lack of clarity about just exactly what structural unemployment was and what evidence of its existence would look like, these data were of little help in settling the dispute.

This claim is supported by two other features of the debates. First, after the debates had gone on for some time, a more careful theoretical view of the issue began to be developed. As evidenced by the work of Lipsey, Berman, Gilpatrick, and Brown, this approach suggested that almost all past empirical work was irrelevant to a proper test of the issue. Second, it was obvious in many cases that the questions being attacked by different contributors were different. Knowles and Kalachek, for example, directed the bulk of their energy to attacking the assertion that structural unemployment had risen suddenly in 1957–60 and that this was responsible for all of the unemployment rise since 1957. Robert Solow attacked essentially the same issue. Killingsworth in his work argued that since 1950 structural unemployment had gradually worsened, so that by 1963 the full-employment unemployment rate was now closer to 5 percent than to 4 percent. Killingsworth did not deny the efficacy of aggregate-demand policy for reducing unemployment below 6 percent, nor did he ever claim that demand policy was not needed. Other structuralist-leaning economists, including Chamberlain, Ginzberg, Gilpatrick, or Miernyk, took a more balanced structural-demand policy view than did Killingsworth. No economist held the strong structuralist views attacked by Knowles-Kalachek or Solow. This problem of attacking different questions was evident throughout the entire debates. Killingsworth's major complaint in 1965, for example, was that the structuralist position was being misrepresented by its detractors.

Overall, then, the balance of evidence suggests it was the questions asked as much as the data available that hindered the impact of quantitative data analysis in the 1960s debates. If this is true, then it is not clear that better data would have resolved the disputes. If the debates had continued, the best hope would have been that participants would have started to follow the lead suggested by Lipsey, Hildebrand, Gilpatrick, and others late in the debates, and begun to carefully define the issue before attempting any further empirical tests.

Conclusion

In the early 1980s, a new series of debates began among economists about the employment impact of technological change. The dispute was centered this time, however, not in the United States but in Europe.[1] As unemployment rates rose in most European nations from the 2–3 percent levels of the 1950s and 1960s to the 8–10 percent levels of the 1980s, reasons for this experience became a central topic of concern. One factor receiving blame for these changes was the impact of new computer technologies, and as a result economists were led once again to address in detail the technological change and unemployment issue.

Interest in the topic in the United States, however, remained at a low level. A steady stream of contributions appeared, much as in the periods before the technological unemployment debates of the 1930s and during the 1940s and 1950s. Topics were pursued which had their origins in the structural unemployment debates, such as the application of vacancy data to the issue, and new developments were identified such as the implication of the latest stages of computerization.[2] Nothing that could be called a professional debate, however, recurred in the United States. As the 1930s and 1960s debates demonstrated, economists have a fundamental optimism about the ability of the economic system to adjust to technological change. It takes something more to get them concerned about the issue. In particular, the technological unemployment and structural unemployment debates suggest—as do the 1980s European discussions—that widespread popular concern plus the appearance of anomalous empirical trends are necessary requirements.

All such conclusions based on the technological unemployment and structural unemployment debates must be evaluated with care. These debates, after all, are only two of dozens of twentieth-century disputes among economists. Any generalizations from specific cases are questionable, and none more so than those derived from a very small sample of a large population. Nonetheless, a few general conclusions seem appropriate based on the experiences of these debates.

Beginning broadly, it is not surprising that economists have become involved repeatedly in debates over the employment impact of technological advance. Ceaseless and substantive change is the very essence of market economies. As long as economic systems are open to changes in tastes, resource availability, and technology, the adjustments required to accommodate these changes will be a topic of interest. Since there are invariably winners and losers in these adjustments, there always will be debate over what might be done to reduce the costs. The fact that the resulting discussions inevitably have a policy component adds an important political dimension to the discussion. As shown in the structural debates, tying analysis to policy prescriptions tends to harden positions and makes resolving differences of opinion more difficult.

The inevitability of debate over issues related to economic change is exacerbated by the fact that economists' analytical tools have limits. Economists are model-builders, and models by definition are simplifications of reality. Although economists have been quite good at building models that help in understanding the gist of what is going on and pointing out the direction of adjustments, many debates about economic issues are about details. Because of the limits of their analytical techniques and the limits of data sources, economists are bound to disagree about the fine points.

Within this context of fundamental interest in change and limited tools to study its consequences, economists face a particularly difficult problem in evaluating the impact of technological change on employment. The question is just a very complex one. There are short-, medium-, and long-run effects, all of which can be quite different. The multidimensionality of technological change—process versus product, firm-level versus industry-level, shop-floor versus managerial-suite change—makes even the phenomenon of interest difficult to define. The central forces at work and issues of concern are fundamentally micro, yet the major questions of public and professional interest are about macro results. All of these problems created conflicts in the technological unemployment and structural unemployment debates, and they will continue to do so whenever the issue is discussed.

Debate caused by the complexity of the issue was made worse in the 1930s and 1960s by the fact that a strongly held professional belief was challenged. In both periods there was a fundamental professional optimism about how the world worked. In the 1930s, recent history and neoclassical analysis created a strong faith in the ability of the economic system to adjust to technological changes. In the 1960s, recent history and Keynesian analysis created an equally strong faith that any employment difficulties due to technological change could be taken care of by appropriate policy. Economists who were concerned about the details of the adjustment process because of the time involved or the extent of displacement effects had a difficult time convincing their colleagues that there was an issue worth worrying about.

Once the debates began, they developed the patterns reviewed in the preceding chapters. Dogmatism was common. There was little careful reading of past work. Opposing claims often were set up as strawmen. Authority and strongly stated claims were influential. Conflict and criticism were a standard approach. A key data source always was found to be missing. In the 1960s, political-policy statements tended to harden positions. In the 1930s, the empirical and theoretical debates had separate histories because they addressed different questions.

Offset ing these debate-enhancing features, however, were a set of characteristics that are ultimately encouraging about how economics works as a social science. Economists were reacting to real concerns; the issue is an important one and worth attending to. New techniques were applied to the issue soon after they were available. New data sources were sought, created, and then used, some with substantial and lasting effects, such as the founding of modern federal productivity series by the NRP in the late 1930s. Insightful and productive uses were made of limited existing sources. Several careful, balanced studies were eventually published which summed up what could be known given contemporary techniques and sources; these thoughtful contributions were convincing in their efforts to identify problems in the debates and to try to resolve them.

Given this history, a final question is whether similar periods of debate can be expected to recur among economists in the future. The answer is an almost certain yes—in the right circumstances. The general issue behind all past discussions about technological change and employment has been the ability of the economic system to respond to change. As long as change occurs, and as long as lags and imperfections exist in the ability of markets to adjust to change, questions about the employment consequences of technological change will be an issue. Given a period again when technology surges and employment lags, the impact of technological change on employment can be expected to return as an issue of popular and professional concern.

Notes

INTRODUCTION

1. David Ricardo, *On the Principles of Political Economy and Taxation*, Vol. I of Piero Sraffa, ed., *The Works and Correspondence of David Ricardo* (Cambridge: Cambridge University Press, 1951–52), 392.

2. See, for example, Maxine Berg, *The Machinery Question and the Making of Political Economy, 1815–1848* (Cambridge: Cambridge University Press, 1980), or Alexander Gourvitch, *Survey of Economic Theory on Technological Change and Employment*, Work Projects Administration, National Research Project, May 1940.

3. Karl Popper, *Conjectures and Refutations: The Growth of Scientific Knowledge*, 4th ed. (London: Routledge & Kegan Paul, 1972); Imre Lakatos and A. Musgrave, eds., *Criticism and the Growth of Knowledge* (Cambridge: Cambridge University Press, 1970); Thomas Kuhn, *The Structure of Scientific Revolutions* (Chicago: University of Chicago Press, 1962); and Paul Feyerabend, *Against Method: Outline of an Anarchistic Theory of Knowledge* (London: New Left Books, 1975).

4. Bruce Caldwell, *Beyond Positivism: Economic Methodology in the Twentieth Century* (London: Allen and Unwin, 1982); J. C. Glass and W. Johnson, *Economics: Progression, Stagnation or Degeneration?* (Ames: Iowa State University Press, 1989); Mark Blaug, *The Methodology of Economics: Or How Economists Explain*, 2nd ed. (Cambridge: Cambridge University Press, 1992); Donald N. McCloskey, *The Rhetoric of Economics* (Madison: University of Wisconsin Press, 1985); Daniel Hausman, *The Inexact and Separate Science of Economics* (Cambridge: Cambridge University Press, 1992). For a survey of recent contributions to the discussion of economic methodology, see Roger E. Backhouse, ed., *New Directions in Economic Methodology* (London: Routledge, 1994).

5. For a recent example, see "Where Are the Jobs?" *The Economist*, May 22, 1993, 17–18; or "A World without Jobs?" *The Economist*, February 11, 1995, 21–23.

6. John Kenneth Galbraith, *The Age of Uncertainty* (Boston: Houghton Mifflin Co., 1977), 218.

7. Y. S. Katsoulacos, *The Employment Effect of Technical Change* (Lincoln: University of Nebraska Press, 1986), 150.
8. Katsoulacos xiv.
9. Katsoulacos 145.
10. Katsoulacos 146.
11. Both quotations are from Marco Vivarelli, *The Economics of Technology and Employment* (Aldershot, England: Edward Elgar, 1995), 168.
12. Eleanor G. Gilpatrick, *Structural Unemployment and Aggregate Demand: A Study of Employment and Unemployment in the United States, 1948–1964* (Baltimore: Johns Hopkins University Press, 1966), 4.
13. Gilpatrick 7.
14. Gilpatrick 215–16.
15. Vivarelli 168, 169.
16. Hans Neisser, "'Permanent' Technological Unemployment: 'Demand for Commodities Is Not Demand for Labor,'" *American Economic Review*, March 1942, 70–71.
17. Hausman, *Inexact*; and David Colander, *Why Aren't Economists as Important as Garbagemen?* (Armonk, N.Y.: M. E. Sharpe, Inc., 1991). Also see Donald N. McCloskey, "Other Things Equal: Why Don't Economists Believe Empirical Findings?" *Eastern Economic Journal*, Summer 1994, 357–60.
18. In Donald McCloskey's terms, their rhetoric is right.
19. An attempt was made to interview a selection of participants through an exchange of letters. It quickly became obvious, however, that memories of what happened were too inaccurate to be of use, and this approach was not pursued.
20. Hausman, *Inexact*, 265–66. Also see Donald McCloskey, "Economics: Art or Science or Who Cares?" *Eastern Economic Journal*, Winter 1994, 118–19; and Harry Landreth and David Colander, *History of Economic Thought* (Boston: Houghton Mifflin Co., 1994), 16.

CHAPTER 1

1. See, for example, James Steuart, *An Inquiry into the Principles of Political Oeconomy* (1967), Andrew S. Skinner, ed. (Edinburgh: Oliver and Boyd, 1966), Vol. I, 122; or Josiah Tucker, *Instructions for Travellers* (1758), in R. L. Schuyler, ed., *Josiah Tucker, A Selection from His Economic and Political Writings* (New York: Columbia University Press, 1931), 241.
2. The views of the well-known classical economists are presented in their major works. The views of Chalmers, Babbage, Barton, and Marcet are found in Thomas Chalmers, *On Political Economy*, 2nd ed. (Glasgow: William Collins and Co., 1832), 474–75; Charles Babbage, *On the Economy of Machinery and Manufactures*, 2nd ed. (London: Charles Knight, 1832), 330–33; John Barton, *Observations on the Circumstances Which Influence the Condition of the Labouring Classes of Society* (London: John and Arthur Arch, 1817); and Jane Marcet, *Conversations on Political Economy*, 4th ed. (London: Longman, Rees, Orme, Brown and Green, 1821), 114.
3. Jean-Baptiste Say, *Treatise on Political Economy: Or the Production, Distribution, and Consumption of Wealth*, 2nd American ed. (Boston: Wells and Lilly, 1924), Vol. I, 30.
4. John Ramsey McCulloch, "The Opinions of Messrs. Say, Sismondi and Malthus, on the Effects of Machinery and Accumulation, Stated and Examined," *The Edinburgh*

Review, March 1821.

5.   Ricardo, *Principles*.

6.   See Ricardo 390, 392, 395; Say 31; John Stuart Mill, *Principles of Political Economy with Some of Their Applications to Social Philosophy*, W. J. Ashley, ed. (London: Longmans, Green and Co., 1909), 97; and Nassau W. Senior, *Political Economy*, 2nd ed. (London: John Joseph Griffen and Co., 1850), 163.

7.   See the letter from McCulloch to Ricardo in *Letters 1819–June 1821*, Vol. VIII of Sraffa, *Works*, 382.   Paul Samuelson has recently examined the issues raised by Ricardo in detail.   See Paul A. Samuelson, "Mathematical Vindication of Ricardo on Machinery," *Journal of Political Economy*, April 1988, 274–82; or "The Classical Classical Fallacy," *Journal of Economic Literature*, June 1994, 620–39.

8.   See, for example, Thomas Robert Malthus, *Principles of Political Economy Considered with a View to Their Practical Application* (Boston: Wells and Lilly, 1821), 312–13.

9.   Mill 94–99.

10.   Karl Marx, *Capital: A Critique of Political Economy* (Chicago: Charles H. Kerr and Co., 1906), Vol. I, 480–87, 690–94.

11.   Mill 79.

12.   Babbage 332–33.

13.   Say 31; Mill 97; and Ricardo 395.

14.   Malthus 404; or Say 31.   Also John Ramsey McCulloch, *Principles of Political Economy* (London: Ward, Lock and Co., 1886), 97.   For a contrasting view, see Mill 79, 96.

15.   McCulloch 115.

16.   Babbage 331.

17.   Arthur T. Hadley, *Economics* (New York: Putnam's Sons, 1896), 337.

18.   Arthur L. Perry, *Elements of Political Economy* (New York: Scribner's Sons, 1873), 276.

19.   David A. Wells, *Recent Economic Changes* (New York: Appleton and Co., 1889), 374.

20.   John Shield Nicholson, *The Effects of Machinery on Wages*, 1st ed. (Cambridge: Deighton, Bell and Co., 1878); 2nd ed. (London: Swan Sonnenschein and Co., 1892).

21.   Sidney Webb, *Socialism*, Fabian Tract no. 51, 1894, 8.

22.   Sidney Webb, preface to F. Isabel Taylor, *A Bibliography of Unemployment and the Unemployed* (London: P. S. King, 1909), vii.

23.   William H. Beveridge, *Unemployment: A Problem of Industry (1909 and 1930)* (London: Longmans, Green and Co., 1930).

24.   See, for example, Alfred Marshall, *Principles of Economics*, 6th ed. (London: MacMillan and Co., 1910), 462–76; John Bates Clark, *Essentials of Economic Theory* (New York: MacMillan and Co., 1909), 301–20; or Knut Wicksell, "Marginal Productivity as the Basis of Distribution in Economics" (1900), in Erik Lindahl, ed., *Knut Wicksell: Selected Papers on Economic Theory* (Cambridge, Mass.: Harvard University Press, 1958).

25.   Joseph A. Schumpeter, *History of Economic Analysis* (New York: Oxford University Press, 1954), 684.

CHAPTER 2

1. Professional work relevant to the issue in the early 1920s includes William Haber, "Workers' Rights and the Introduction of Machinery in the Men's Clothing Industry," *Journal of Political Economy*, August 1925; and a series of articles by George E. Barnett in the *Quarterly Journal of Economics*, May, August, November 1925 and February 1926, as summarized in his book *Chapters on Machinery and Labor* (Cambridge, Mass.: Harvard University Press, 1926). Examples of related professional work in the decades just before the 1920s includes two editions of John Shield Nicholson's *The Effects of Machinery on Wages* (Cambridge: Deighton, Bell and Co., 1878; London: Swan Sonnenschein and Co., 1892); several analyses by John A. Hobson including "The Influence of Machinery upon Employment," *Political Science Quarterly*, March 1893; *The Evolution of Modern Capitalism: A Study of Machine Production* (London: W. Scott, 1894); and *The Economics of Unemployment* (London: G. Allen and Unwin, 1922); Alvin Johnson, "The Effect of Labor-Saving Devices upon Wages," *Quarterly Journal of Economics*, November 1905; and Thomas Nixon Carver, "Machinery and the Laborers," *Quarterly Journal of Economics*, February 1908.

2. The studies are E. Dana Durand, "Progress in National Efficiency," in *The Fifteenth Annual Report of the Secretary of Commerce*, 1927 (also see a similar revised report in the annual report for 1928); E. E. Day and Woodlief Thomas, *The Growth of Manufacturers 1899–1923*, United States Bureau of the Census, Monograph VIII, 1928 (a preliminary report was released May 4, 1927); and a series of articles in the July, October, November, and December 1926 *Monthly Labor Review* (these were revised and summarized in "Productivity of Labor in Eleven Industries," *Monthly Labor Review*, January 1927). The Bureau of Labor Statistics published its own total manufacturing index in the May 1927 *Monthly Labor Review*, but the nearly simultaneous publication of the Day-Thomas Census data immediately outdated the study.

3. The Bureau of Labor Statistics *Handbook of Labor Statistics 1924–26*, BLS Bulletin 439, June 1927, 527, in describing the recent widespread interest in productivity, claimed that "of particular importance" in this development is the fact that unions "have committed themselves to the principle of basing wages, in part at least, upon the productivity of workers." Beginning in the early 1920s this concern gave rise to the first BLS studies specifically aimed at measuring productivity.

4. "Labor Efficiency and Production," *Monthly Labor Review*, August 1922, 109.

5. One reason these studies appeared when they did is that only by the mid-1920s could such data be developed. The BLS noted in one of its first productivity studies that the development of productivity data "would hardly have been feasible before the war; it has become feasible only because of the enormous expansion in the gathering of all kinds of production and employment statistics during and after the war." "Index of Productivity of Labor in the Steel, Automobile, Shoe and Paper Industries," *Monthly Labor Review*, July 1926, 1–2.

6. "Index of Productivity of Labor in the Steel, Automobile, Shoe and Paper Industries," *Monthly Labor Review*, July 1926, 1. Also see the comment by E. Dana Durand, "Progress in National Efficiency," *Fifteenth Annual Report of the Secretary of Commerce*, 1927, xxix.

7. Secretary Davis was quoted in James L. Wright, "Need We Be Afraid of a Job Famine?" *Nation's Business*, January 1927.

8.   The September *Nation's Business* article was James L. Wright, "Is the Machine Replacing Man?" For a report on Davis' speech, see the *Monthly Labor Review*, September 1927, 32–33.

9.   The quotes are from "Victims of the Machine," *New Republic*, October 26, 1927, 249; Lewis Corey, "An Estimate of Unemployment: Cyclical Idleness Added to Technological," *The Annalist*, March 9, 1928, 444; *Railroad Trainman*, January 1928, 65; and Corey 443.

10.   During late 1928, labor in particular developed the theme that growing technological unemployment was an endemic factor in current industrial organization. Chester M. Wright, for example, in a September 1928 article claimed that the United States faces a "desperate and rapidly enlarging problem of chronic unemployment." Wright acknowledged that "acute unemployment has diminished materially since those spring days [of 1928] when figures and charges flew back and forth across Washington," but he claimed that "permanent, or 'technical' unemployment, as it is called in American Federation of Labor headquarters, is still with us." C. M. Wright, "A Nation of Men—Or Machines?" *Nation's Business*, September 1928, 39–40. Similar labor, business, and popular discussions on both sides of the issue were published throughout 1928 and 1929, with a widely known contribution being a Stuart Chase book entitled *Men and Machines*.

11.   For the nonalarmist view see, for example, Magnus Alexander, "Unemployment Not Machine-Made," *Iron Age*, March 15, 1928; E. S. Gregg, "What Puts Men out of Work?" *Nation's Business*, April 1928; Magnus Alexander, "Unemployment Exaggerated—Not Due to Mechanization," *Iron Age*, May 3, 1928; Charles Norton, "Labor-Saving Machines Lead to Prosperity, Experience Shows," *Iron Trade Review*, May 17, 1928; Henry Dennison, "Would 5 Day Week Decrease Unemployment?" *Magazine of Business*, November 1928; T. H. Grammach, "Miracles of Re-employment," in *Trade Unions Study Unemployment* (Washington, D.C.: American Federation of Labor, 1929); and Edward S. Cowdrick, "Labor Explores New Fields," *Nation's Business*, March 1929. That the issue had become a prominent one is also indicated by the discussion of productivity in the Bureau of Labor Statistics *Handbook of Labor Statistics 1929 Edition*, BLS Bulletin 491, August 1929, 619. In contrast to the 1924–26 edition, the 1929 edition stated that interest in productivity was due mainly to rapid technological advances and widespread worker displacements. The issue also was placed on the Democratic platform in the presidential election of 1928. See *Current History*, August 1928, 802.

12.   The papers were Paul Douglas, "The Modern Technique of Mass Production and Its Relation to Wages," *Proceedings of the Academy of Political Science*, 1927; E. Dana Durand, "Progress in National Efficiency," *Fifteenth Annual Report of the Secretary of Commerce*, 1927; Rexford Tugwell, *Industry's Coming of Age* (New York: Harcourt, Brace and Co., 1927); Woodlief Thomas, "The Economic Significance of the Increased Efficiency of American Industry," *American Economic Review, Supplement*, March 1928; John D. Black, "Discussion" of papers on unemployment by Thomas and Paul Douglas and Charles Cobb, *American Economic Review, Supplement*, March 1928; and Sumner Slichter, "Some Ways in Which Trade Unions Can Help Reduce Unemployment," a speech at the July 30–31 American Federation of Labor Unemployment Conference, published in the *American Federationist*, October 1927.

13.   Douglas, "Modern Technique," 17.

14.   Tugwell, *Industry's*, 26.

15.   Paul Douglas in a July article, for example, raised the question of labor reaction to the recent trends, but dismissed it by saying "fortunately there are many straws in the

wind to indicate that the American labor movement will be more anxious to promote technical improvements in the future than it has been in the past." Douglas, "Modern Technique," 23.

16. Black, "Discussion," 171. For a similar comment see Durand, "Progress," xxix.

17. Reported in the *Journal of the American Statistical Association*, June 1928, 180–81.

18. Sumner Slichter, "The Price of Industrial Progress," *New Republic*, February 8, 1928, 316–17.

19. Irving Fisher, "Full Employment: Prosperity's Problem," *Magazine of Wall Street*, April 7, 1928, 1024–25.

20. Ewan Clague, "Productivity and Unemployment," in *Trade Unions Study Unemployment*, 1929, 39.

21. William Leiserson, "Unemployment, 1929," *Survey*, April 1, 1929, 9–10.

22. W. Jett Lauck, *The New Industrial Revolution and Wages* (New York: Funk and Wagnalls Co., 1929), 235–36.

23. Wesley C. Mitchell, "Machines Make Jobs," *Nation's Business*, September 1929, 43, 112. For a similar popular presentation of Mitchell's views, see "Americans All," *Survey*, June 1, 1929.

24. Leiserson, "Unemployment, 1929," 78.

25. Ewan Clague, "Productivity and Wages," *American Federationist*, March 1927, 295; and "Productivity and Unemployment," 40.

26. Slichter, "Industrial Progress," 317.

27. The first Bureau of Labor Statistics employment indexes on other industries began to appear in October 1928. In the following year current indexes on wholesale and retail trade, public utilities, coal mining, hotels, quarries and nonmetallic mining, metalliferous mining, and canning and preserving all appeared for the first time. All data were current, however, and were not carried back in time. Some states reported similar wider data before 1928, but only on a very limited scale.

28. For an example of an argument opposing this analysis, see "Victims of the Machine," *New Republic*, October 26, 1927, 249.

29. Lawrence B. Mann, "Occupational Shifts since 1920," *Journal of the American Statistical Association, Supplement*, March 1929, 47.

30. For a reference using the argument that occupation flows absorbed all the technologically displaced, see Magnus Alexander, *Mechanization of Industry and Economic and Social Progress* (New York: National Industrial Conference Board, 1928).

31. Lawrence B. Mann, "Occupational Shifts in the United States, 1920 to 1927," in *Trade Unions Study Unemployment*, 1929, 56.

32. Isador Lubin, "Measuring the Labor Absorbing Power of American Industry," *Journal of the American Statistical Association, Supplement*, March 1929, 27.

33. The first publication of the Lubin results was in Lubin, "Measuring." Final publication was in Isador Lubin, *The Absorption of the Unemployed by American Industry* (Washington, D.C.: Brookings Institution, July 1, 1929). The Myers study was published as Robert J. Myers, "Occupational Readjustment of Displaced Skilled Workers," *Journal of Political Economy*, August 1929. The first presentation of the Myers data, however, was in December 1928 by B. M. Squires in an address before the American Association of Labor Legislation.

34. Lubin, "Measuring" and *Absorption*. For another negative presentation of his results, see "Let Out," *Survey*, April 1, 1929.

35. Related to the same topic but of less significance were two articles in the March 1930 *American Economic Review, Supplement* by E. G. Nourse, "Some Economic and

Social Accompaniments of the Mechanization of Agriculture," and Henry Dennison, "Some Economic and Social Accompaniments of the Mechanization of Industry."

36.   The Conference committee sponsoring the research was a mixed group of labor, management, political, and academic appointees, and as such, its report on the results of the survey was decidedly middle-of-the-road. The fact that recent debates over the impact of technological change were of first importance to the committee, however, was clear from its report. The first words in the committee's final report were aimed at assuaging popular concern over this very issue. According to the committee, "acceleration rather than structural change is the key to an understanding of our recent economic developments." In order to emphasize that there was nothing to fear in current developments, the committee repeated this theme several times: the United States is not "on the verge of a new economic era, an era of fundamental change"; "The changes have not been in structure but in speed and spread." "Report of the Committee on Recent Economic Changes of the President's Conference on Unemployment," *Recent Economic Changes*, Vol. I (New York: McGraw-Hill, 1929), ix.

37.   Dexter Kimball, "Changes in New and Old Industries," 93; Henry Dennison, "Management," 516; and Wesley C. Mitchell, "A Review," 877, 879; all in *Recent Economic Changes*, 1929.

38.   Sumner Slichter, "Market Shifts, Price Movements, and Employment," *American Economic Review, Supplement*, March 1929, 7, 13, 17. For a popular presentation of Slichter's argument, see Sumner Slichter, "Recent Employment Movements," *Survey*, April 1, 1929.

39.   These arguments appeared in Slichter, "Market Shifts"; Mitchell, "A Review"; and Dennison, "Some Economic."

CHAPTER 3

1.   The direct impact of the onset of the depression on this development is not clear. No economist said that the slide of 1929–30 was the reason for their interest in the topic of technological unemployment. It also took time for people to become aware of the magnitude of the disaster that was to come. Through the first half of 1930, for example, the general opinion was that the downturn was like those of the past and that recovery would soon be under way. See, for example, the optimistic articles by W. R. Smith, "Has Business Reached the Turning Point?" *Magazine of Wall Street*, June 14, 1930; and T. M. Knappen, "Is the Business Cycle Scraping Bottom?" *Magazine of Wall Street*, July 12, 1930. It was not until late 1930 that it was clear that an unemployment emergency was at hand. But it is reasonable to assume that the onset of the depression was a factor in prolonging the technological unemployment discussions. The popular debates were certainly kept alive by the depression, and it is likely that rising unemployment was a major reason in maintaining interest in the topic among professional economists.

2.   The quotes in the preceding paragraph are from Michael Scheler, "Technological Unemployment," *The Annals of the American Academy of Political Unemployment and Its Remedies* (New York: League for Industrial Democracy, 1931), 17; U.S. Congress, House, Committee on the Judiciary, *Unemployment in the United States*, Hearings, 71st Congress, 2nd Session, 1930, 41; L. E. Keller, "Efficiency and Unemployment," *American Federationist*, June 1930, 676; Theodore M. Knappen, "The Machine Turns On Its Master," *Magazine of Wall Street*, May 3, 1930, 68; and U.S. Senate, Select Committee on Unemployment Insurance, *Unemployment Insurance*, Part 2, "Report of the Commit-

tee on Technological Employment to the Secretary of Labor," November 1931, 72nd Congress, 1st Session, 1931, 560.

3. The chairman of the House Committee on the Judiciary brought up the possibility of a moratorium on patents in *Unemployment in the United States*, Hearings, 36. For some views on the machine-taxing movement, see Max Daniels, "Taxing Machines to Relieve Joblessness," *American Federationist*, October 1932; "Taxing the Machine," *The Survey*, December 1933, 418; C. N. Edge, "Measurements of Technocracy: Taxation of the Machine," *Living Age*, January 1933; an article by Representative John Lesinski in the *Washington Times*, February 28, 1934; and, in particular, the testimony and exhibits in U.S. Congress, House, Committee on Labor, Hearings, *Investigation of Unemployment Caused by Labor-Saving Devices in Industry*, 1936.

4. See, for example, Magnus Alexander, "Unemployment Problems— Technological Unemployment," *National Industrial Conference Board Bulletin*, August 20, 1931.

5. Machinery and Allied Products Institute, *Ten Facts on Technology and Employment*, 1936; *Machine Made Jobs*, 1936; *Technology and the American Consumer*, 1937; and *Machines and Working Hours*, 1937.

6. Paul Douglas, "Technological Unemployment," *American Federationist*, August 1930. Willford I. King, "The Effects of the New Industrial Revolution upon Our Economic Welfare," *Annals of the American Academy of Political and Social Science*, May 1930.

7. Douglas, 925, 923, 928, 930, 938.

8. The Douglas argument was a demand approach that solved the problem of reabsorption by claiming that aggregate demand was increased by technological change. Other economists approached the problem from a different direction. The Ricardian argument, for example, that the sudden introduction of new machinery could have harmful employment effects was reflected in papers by Ewan Clague and Rexford Tugwell. See Clague, "Productivity and Unemployment," *Trade Unions Study Unemployment*, 1929; and Tugwell, "Occupational Obsolescence," in Morse A. Cartwright, ed., *Unemployment and Adult Education: A Symposium* (New York: American Association for Adult Education, 1931). A second alternative approach took the neoclassical point of view that recent unemployment was primarily due to maladjustments of the pricing system. See Slichter, "Market Shifts." A third approach considered technological change as a critical factor in causing business cycles. Of particular note were John A. Hobson, *Rationalisation and Unemployment: An Economic Dilemma* (London: Allen and Unwin, 1930); Joseph Schumpeter, "The Explanation of the Business Cycle," *Economica*, December 1927; and Arthur B. Adams, "Discussion," *American Economic Review, Supplement*, March 1931. For other early 1930s arguments that the causes of the depression can be traced to maldistribution of income and the gains from productivity advances, see Fred Henderson, *The Economic Consequences of Power Production* (London: Allen and Unwin, 1931); and Morris P. Taylor, *Common Sense about Machines and Unemployment* (Philadelphia: John C. Winston Co., 1933).

9. Rexford G. Tugwell, "Occupational Obsolescence," in Cartwright, *Unemployment*, 20–21.

10. Sumner Slichter, "The Problem of Technological Unemployment," in Cartwright 33, 35.

11. Rexford Tugwell, "The Theory of Occupational Obsolescence," *Political Science Quarterly*, June 1931, 213–214.

12. Alvin Hansen, "Institutional Frictions and Technological Unemployment," *Quarterly Journal of Economics*, August 1931, 688, 692.

13. Alvin Hansen, "The Theory of Technological Progress and the Dislocation of Employment," *American Economic Review, Supplement*, March 1932, 26–27, 29, 31.

14. Sumner Slichter, "Technological Unemployment: Lines of Action, Adaptation and Control," *American Economic Review, Supplement*, March 1932, 42, 44.

15. Gottfried Haberler, "Some Remarks on Professor Hansen's View on Technological Unemployment," *Quarterly Journal of Economics*, May 1932, 558, 559, 560.

16. Alvin Hansen, "A Rejoinder," to Haberler, *Quarterly Journal of Economics*, May 1932, 562–63.

17. Emil Lederer, *Technischer Fortschritt und Arbeitslosigkeit* (Tübingen, 1931).

18. Nicholas Kaldor, "A Case against Technical Progress?" *Economica*, May 1932, 190, 195–96.

19. Mentor Bouniatian, "Technical Progress and Unemployment," *International Labour Review*, March 1933, 343.

20. Emil Lederer, "Technical Progress and Unemployment," *International Labour Review*, July 1933.

21. Paul Douglas, "Technocracy," *The World Tomorrow*, January 18, 1933, 60–61. Douglas published a very similar analysis of the problem in 1933 in "Technological Aspects of Unemployment," *Bulletin of the University of Georgia*, August 1933.

22. See, in particular, Frederick C. Mills, "Industrial Change and Unemployment," in *Essays in Social Economics in Honor of Jessica Blanche Peixotto* (Berkeley: University of California Press, 1935), 240–41; and Sumner Slichter, "Implications of the Shorter Hour Movement," *Proceedings of the Academy of Political Science*, January 1934, 70. Also see Slichter, "Selling More Labor," *Atlantic Monthly*, September 1936.

23. Gardiner Means' early administered price work included "Price Inflexibility and the Requirements of a Stabilizing Monetary Policy," *Journal of the American Statistical Association*, June 1935; "Industrial Prices and Their Relative Inflexibility," Senate Document 13, 74th Congress, 1st Session, 2–8; and "Notes on Inflexible Prices," *American Economic Review, Supplement*, March 1936. Early commentary on this work included Frederick C. Mills in *Prices in Recession and Recovery* (New York: National Bureau of Economic Research, 1936); and John Kenneth Galbraith, "Monopoly Power and Price Rigidities," *Quarterly Journal of Economics*, May 1936.

24. The works debating this point are John R. Hicks, *The Theory of Wages* (New York: MacMillan, 1932); A. C. Pigou, *The Economics of Welfare*, 4th ed. (London: MacMillan, 1938), 674; and Joan Robinson, "The Classification of Inventions," *Review of Economic Studies*, February 1938.

25. For a survey of the prevalence of Keynesian ideas before the publication of the *General Theory*, see J. Ronnie Davis, *The New Economics and the Old Economists* (Ames: Iowa State University Press, 1971).

26. See, for example, Arthur B. Adams, *The Trend of Business 1922–1932* (New York: Harper and Brothers, 1932); *Our Economic Revolution* (Norman: University of Oklahoma Press, 1933); and *National Economic Security* (Norman: University of Oklahoma Press, 1936); Emil Lederer, "The Problem of Development and Growth in the Economic System," *Social Research*, February 1935; Joseph Schumpeter, "The Analysis of Economic Change," *Review of Economic Statistics*, May 1935; and *Business Cycles* (New York: McGraw-Hill, 1939); John Maurice Clark, *Strategic Factors in Business Cycles* (New York: National Bureau of Economic Research, 1934); and *Economics of Planning Public Works* (Washington, D.C.: National Planning Board of the Federal Emergency Administration of Public Works, 1935); Irving Flamm, "The Problem of Technological Unemployment in the United States," *International Labour Review*,

March 1935; Paul Douglas, *Controlling Depressions* (New York: Norton, 1935); and "Purchasing Power of the Masses and Business Depressions," in *Economic Essays in Honor of Wesley Clair Mitchell* (New York: Columbia University Press, 1935); and Frederick C. Mills, "Industrial Change and Unemployment," in *Essays in Social Economics*, 1935.

27.   Edna Lonigan, "The Effect of Modern Technological Conditions on the Employment of Labor," *American Economic Review*, June 1939, 248, 250–52, 256.   For another late-Depression statement of the thesis that flexibile prices were the key to technological unemployment, see Clyde E. Dankert, "Views on Machinery and Unemployment," *Scientific Monthly*, February 1940.

28.   Alvin Hansen, "Economic Progress and Declining Population Growth," *American Economic Review, Supplement*, March 1939, 14.   For another comment on the issue from the same time, see Glenn McLaughlin and Ralph Watkins, "The Problem of Industrial Growth in a Mature Economy," *American Economic Review, Supplement*, March 1939.

29.   William Fellner, "The Technological Argument of the Stagnation Thesis," *Quarterly Journal of Economics*, August 1941.   For another detailed critique of the stagnationist theory, see George Terborgh, *The Bogey of Economic Maturity* (Chicago: Machinery and Allied Products Institute, 1945).

CHAPTER 4

1.   Paul Douglas, "Technological Unemployment: Measurement of the Elasticity of Demand as a Basis for Prediction of Labor Displacement," *Bulletin of the Taylor Society*, December 1930, 254.

2.   Elizabeth Baker, "Discussion" of Douglas paper, and Sumner Slichter, "Discussion" of Douglas paper, 265, both in *Bulletin of the Taylor Society*, December 1930.

3.   Results were first reported by Ewan Clague at a May 1930 meeting in New York of the American Statistical Association.   Results were later published as Ewan Clague and W. J. Couper, "The Readjustment of Workers Displaced by Plant Shutdowns," *Quarterly Journal of Economics*, February 1931.   Elizabeth Baker's work was first reported in "Unemployment and Technical Progress in Commercial Printing," *American Economic Review*, September 1930.

4.   Isador Lubin, "Finding the New Job," in Cartwright, *Unemployment*, 24–25.

5.   Elizabeth Baker, "Machinery versus Trade Skills," in Cartwright 27–28.

6.   *The Social Aspects of Rationalisation* (Geneva: International Labour Office, 1931), 265.

7.   Harold Butler, *Unemployment Problems in the United States* (Geneva: International Labour Office, 1931), 56, 52, 59.

8.   R. C. White, "Technological Unemployment," *Social Forces*, June 1931, 576.

9.   Ewan Clague, "Memorandum on Technological Unemployment," in *Report of the Advisory Committee on Employment Statistics*, Bureau of Labor Statistics, Bulletin 542, May 1931, 20.

10.   Boris Stern, "Discussion" of papers on technological unemployment by Hansen, Jerome, and Slichter, *American Economic Review, Supplement*, March 1932, 58.

11.   Harry Jerome, "The Measurement of Productivity Changes and the Displacement of Labor," *American Economic Review, Supplement*, March 1932.

12. One area of expanded empirical work during these years was the further development of case studies of displaced workers. See Caroline Manning and Harriet A.
Byrne, *The Effects on Women of Changing Conditions in the Cigar and Cigarette Industries*, United States Women's Bureau, Bulletin 100, 1932; and Otis E. Young,
"Technological Change and Retraining," *Personnel Journal*, June 1934. In addition to
these studies, the work of several large-scale unemployment projects begun in 1930–31
was published. The University of Minnesota Employment Stabilization Research Institute published twenty-five bulletins and more than thirty articles, books and pamphlets
between 1932 and 1935. A sample of relevant studies includes Alvin Hansen, Nelle
Petrowski, and Richard Graves, *An Analysis of Three Unemployment Surveys in Minneapolis, St. Paul and Duluth*, Bulletins, Vol. I, No. 6, August 1932; Jessie Bloodworth,
Social Consequences of Prolonged Unemployment, Bulletins, Vol. 2, No. 5, August
1933; M. R. Trabue and Beatrice Dvorak, *A Study of the Needs of Adults for Further
Training*, Bulletins, Vol. 3, July 1934; and John Darley and Donald Paterson, *Employed
and Unemployed Workers: Differential Factors in Employment Status*, Bulletins, Vol.
3, No. 6, September 1933. All publications were by the University of Minnesota Employment Stabilization Research Institute. The Institute of Human Relations at Yale
University, which had sponsored the Clague-Couper study, expanded in 1932 to carry
its analysis of unemployment into all aspects of the readjustment problem. One of the
most profitable collaborations of the depression also began to be realized in the publication of several works by the state of Pennsylvania, the University of Pennsylvania, and
the city of Philadelphia. The relevant studies included Ewan Clague and Webster
Powell, *Ten Thousand out of Work* (Philadephia: University of Pennsylvania, 1933);
Gladys Palmer, *Thirty Thousand in Search of Work*, Pennsylvania Department of Labor
and Industry, 1933; and Gladys Palmer, *Union Tactics and Economic Change*
(Philadelphia: University of Pennsylvania Press, 1932). Elizabeth Baker also continued
her work on commercial printing in a 1933 book on *Displacement of Men by Machines*.

13. Frederick C. Mills, *Economic Tendencies in the United States* (New York: National Bureau of Economic Research, 1932), 481, 531–33.

14. David Weintraub, "The Displacement of Workers through Increases in Efficiency and Their Absorption by Industry," *Journal of the American Statistical Association*, December 1932, 399.

15. Willford I. King, "The Relative Volume of Technological Unemployment,"
Journal of the American Statistical Association, Supplement, March 1933, 33, 38–39.

16. F. B. Garver, "Discussion" of King paper, *Journal of the American Statistical
Association, Supplement*, March 1933, 41.

17. Boris Stern, "Technological Displacement of Labor and Technological Unemployment," *Journal of the American Statistical Association, Supplement*, March 1933,
43, 47.

18. Also see the papers at the March 7, 1933 JASA meeting summarized by W. I.
King as "Are We Menaced by Machines?" *Journal of the American Statistical Asso-
ciation*, June 1933. Also "A Review of Findings by the President's Research Commit-
tee on Social Trends," *Recent Social Trends in the United States* (New York: McGraw-
Hill, 1933); and William G. Roylance, "Significance of Nonmechanical Factors in Labor
Productivity and Displacement," *Monthly Labor Review*, November 1933.

19. Leo Wolman, "Machinery and Unemployment," *The Nation*, February 1933,
202–4.

CHAPTER 5

1.   Harry Jerome, *Mechanization in Industry* (New York: National Bureau of Economic Research, 1934), 21–22, 387.

2.   Frederick C. Mills, *Aspects of Manufacturing Operations during Recovery*, National Bureau of Economic Research Bulletin 56, May 10, 1935, 17.   Also see F. C. Mills, *Changes in Prices, Manufacturing Costs and Industrial Productivity*, NBER Bulletin 53, December 22, 1934.

3.   Alfred Kahler, "The Problem of Verifying the Theory of Technological Unemployment," *Social Research*, November 1935, 452–54, 456, 460.

4.   Wladimir Woytinski, *Three Sources of Unemployment*, Studies and Reports, Series C, No. 20 (Geneva: International Labour Office, 1935); Frederick C. Mills, *Prices in Recession and Recovery* (New York: National Bureau of Economic Research, 1936).   Also see F. C. Mills, "Man and the Machine," *Today*, November 28, 1936.

5.   *The Recovery Problem in the United States* (Washington, D.C.: Brookings Institution, 1936).   For another mid-1930s optimistic view, see   Mordecai Ezekiel, "Population and Unemployment," *Annals of the American Academy of Political and Social Science*, Vol. 188, November 1936.

6.   With respect to unemployment, the revitalization of the United States Employment Service and the beginning of a nationwide unemployment insurance program under the Social Security Act provided detailed periodic information on the number and characteristics of the unemployed.   Near the end of the period the beginning of the Works Projects Administration (WPA) monthly national unemployment survey marked the first collection of a series of current unemployment data.   As to employment data, the continuing improvement of BLS data and the start of the Social Security and WPA surveys again marked the beginning of all the best series that are used today.   With respect to historical employment trends, the National Research Project collected, revised, and made consistent all of the best historical employment series to date for manufacturing, agriculture, and mining.   The story of developments for output figures was even more impressive.   Regular current national product figures began to be published for the first time, and the continuing national income work sponsored by the NBER, notably by Simon Kuznets, produced several revisions of past and current series.   The effect of these basic data developments on productivity data was equally dramatic.   The national income data made feasible the first formation of relatively accurate estimates of productivity for all sectors.   In addition, the work of the National Research Project provided independent productivity estimates for several sectors, as well as adding many specific case study records to the existing evidence.

7.   With respect to agriculture, see Paul Taylor, "Power Farming and Labor Displacement in the Cotton Belt, 1937," *Monthly Labor Review*, March and April 1938; and Eugen Altschul and Frederick Strauss, *Technical Progress and Agricultural Depression*, NBER Bulletin 67, November 29, 1937.

8.   Frederick C. Mills, "Industrial Productivity and Prices," *Journal of the American Statistical Association,* June 1937.

9.   Frederick C. Mills, *Employment Opportunities in Manufacturing Industries in the United States*, NBER Bulletin 70, September 25, 1938, 5, 8, 11.

10.   The nine sectors for which technological histories were written were agriculture, minerals, transportation, power, communications, chemicals, electrical goods, metallurgy, and construction.   See Part 3 of U.S. National Resources Committee, *Technological Trends and National Policy*, June 1937.

11.   David Weintraub and Harold Posner, *Unemployment and Increasing Productivity*, NRP Report G-1, March 1937, 2, 55–56, 75. This was also published in the National Resources Committee final report as "Technological Trends and Their Social Implications," 1937.

12.   A May 1937 article by Weintraub and Lewis Hine, for example, found that due to the rise in the importance of capital and durable goods as a result of technological progress, "we are heading toward greater instability of employment." David Weintraub and Lewis Hine, *Technological Change*, NRP unnumbered report, September 1937, 5. *A Summary of Findings to Date, March 1938*, by Weintraub and Irving Kaplan, found that since the late 1920s the primary cause of productivity advance had been in auxiliary instruments that improve existing techniques. The result was a large jump in productivity that had occurred with little capital investment. As a consequence, they concluded that recent productivity advances had done much to displace labor and little to reemploy it. David Weintraub and Irving Kaplan, *Summary of Findings to Date, March 1938*, NRP Report G-3, March 1938. Also see David Weintraub, "Effects of Current and Prospective Technological Developments upon Capital Formation," *American Economic Review, Supplement*, March 1939.

13.   The papers referred to are Harry Magdoff, "The Purpose and Methods of Measuring Productivity"; Arthur Wubnig, "The Measurement of the Technological Factor in Labor Productivity"; Elmer Bratt, "Did Productivity Increase in the Twenties?" and David Weintraub, "A Rejoinder" to Bratt; all in the *Journal of the American Statistical Association*, June 1939. For another explanation of NRP methods, see David Weintraub, "Statistical Problems Confronted in the Analysis of the Relationship between Production, Productivity and Employment," *Journal of the American Statistical Association, Supplement*, March 1937.

14.   D. I. Vinogradoff, "Effects of a Technological Improvement on Employment," *Econometrica*, October 1933.

15.   J. J. J. Dalmulder, *On Econometrics: Some Suggestions Concerning the Method of Econometrics and Its Application to Studies Regarding the Influence of Rationalisation on Employment in the U.S.A.* (Haarlem: De Erven F. Bohn N.V., 1937).

16.   Jan Tinbergen and Paul de Wolff, "A Simplified Model of the Causation of Technological Unemployment," *Econometrica*, July 1939, 193, 203–4. Near the same time, Oscar Lange presented a similar model, but no data, in "The Theory of Technological Unemployment," *Report of the Sixth Annual Conference* (Chicago: Cowles Commission for Research in Economics, 1940).

17.   U.S. Senate, Temporary National Economic Committee, *Technology and Concentration of Economic Power*, Hearings, Part 30, 76th Congress, 3rd Session, 1940. For another optimistic evaluation, see Hans Staehle, "Employment in Relation to Technical Progess," *Review of Economic Statistics*, May 1940.

18.   Solomon Fabricant, *The Relation between Factory Employment and Output since 1899*, NBER Occasional Paper 4, December 1941, 30–31.

19.   Spurgeon Bell, *Productivity, Wages and National Income* (Washington, D.C.: Brookings Institution, 1940).

20.   Mordecai Ezekiel, "Productivity, Wage Rates and Employment," *American Economic Review*, September 1940, 508, 521.

21.   John M. Blair and Ruth Aull, "Technology and Economic Balance," in *Technology in Our Economy*, TNEC Monograph No. 22, 76th Congress, 3rd Session, 1941, 136, 219–20. Also see John M. Blair, *Labor Productivity and Industrial Prices* (Unpublished doctoral dissertation, The American University, 1941).

CHAPTER 6

1. See, for example, Solomon Fabricant, *Employment in Manufacturing, 1899–1939*, 1942; *Labor Savings in American Industry, 1899–1939*, NBER Occasional Paper 23, November 1945; and Yale Brozen, *Some Economic Aspects of Technological Change* (Unpublished doctoral dissertation, University of Chicago, 1942).

2. The literature on the relationship of price flexibility to full employment was extensive in the late 1930s. An excellent summation of the state of the debates by 1940 was included as Part II of *The Structure of the American Economy*, National Resources Planning Board, "Toward Full Use of Resources," June 1940. Papers included were by Gardiner Means, D. E. Montgomery, J. M. Clark, Alvin Hansen, and Mordecai Ezekiel.

3. Hans Neisser, "'Permanent' Technological Unemployment: 'Demand for Commodities Is Not Demand for Labor,'" *American Economic Review*, March 1942, 51, 65, 70–71.

4. E. E. Hagen, "Savings, Investment and Technological Unemployment," *American Economic Review*, September 1942.

5. Edwin G. Nourse, *Price Making in a Democracy* (Washington, D.C.: Brookings Institution, 1944). For a critique of this Brookings argument, see Abram Bergson, "Price Flexibility and the Level of Income," *Review of Economic Statistics*, February 1943.

6. Oscar Lange, *Price Flexibility and Employment* (Bloomington: Principia Press, 1945), 83. Lange's work leading up to this book included "The Theory of Technological Unemployment," *Report of the Sixth Annual Conference* of the Cowles Commission for Research in Economics, 1940; "Say's Law: A Restatement and Criticism," in *Studies in Mathematical Economics and Econometrics in Memory of Henry Schultz*, O. Lange, F. McIntyre, and T. Yntema, eds. (Chicago: University of Chicago Press, 1942); and "A Note on Innovation," *Review of Economic Statistics*, February 1943. Also see the similar analysis by Don Patinkin, "Price Flexibility and Full Employment," *American Economic Review*, September 1948.

7. Nathan Belfer, *Technical Change and Technological Unemployment* (Unpublished doctoral dissertation, Harvard University, 1946); Shou Shan Pu, *Technological Progress and Employment* (Unpublished doctoral dissertation, Harvard University, 1949). Also see Nathan Belfer, "The Theory of the Automatic Reabsorption of Technologically Displaced Labor," *Southern Economic Journal*, July 1949.

8. Jan Tinbergen, "The Influence of Productivity on Economic Welfare," *Economic Journal*, March 1952, 68.

CHAPTER 7

1. This first use of the term was apparently by the Ford Motor Company. For an announcement of the formation of the Automation Department at Ford, see "Mechanical Muscles Release Manual Labor," *Business Week*, October 23, 1948. A list of optimistic discussions of the new techniques through the Korean War would include *Factory Management and Maintenance*, January 1948, 65–70; Thomas Carskadorn, "Do Machines Destroy Jobs?" *NEA Journal*, March 1946; Lazare Teper, "This Thing Called Productivity," *American Federationist*, November 1948; "The Automatic Factory: The Threat-and-Promise of Laborless Machines Is Closer Than Ever," *Fortune*, November 1946; E. W. Leaver and J. J. Brown, "Machines without Men," *Fortune*, November

1946; "Automation: A Factory Runs Itself," *Business Week*, March 29, 1952; "Coming Industrial Era: The Wholly Automatic Factory," *Business Week*, April 5, 1952; "Automation: Road to the Robot Plant," *Business Week*, November 22, 1952; John Diebold, "Automation and Jobs," *The Nation*, October 3, 1953; John Diebold, *Automation: The Advent of the Automatic Factory* (New York: Van Nostrand, 1952); *Calling All Jobs: An Introduction to the Automatic Machine Age* (New York: National Association of Manufacturers, 1954); Erick Schiff, *The Primary Employment Effects of Productivity Gains* (Chicago: Council for Technological Advancement, 1954); and *Trends in Technology and Employment* (Chicago: Council for Technological Advancement, 1954). A list of pessimistic discussions during the same period would include Benjamin Graham, "National Productivity: Its Relationship to Unemployment-In-Prosperity," *American Economic Review*, May 1947; Justin McCarthy, "Introduction of Labor-Saving Devices Poses Serious Problems, Survey Urged," *The Baker's and Confectioner's Journal*, April 1949; "Why Output Rises, Jobs Shrink," *U.S. News and World Report*, April 14, 1950; Norbert Weiner, *Cybernetics* (New York: Wiley, 1947); Norbert Weiner, *The Human Use of Human Beings* (Boston: Houghton-Mifflin, 1954); articles in *Steel Labor*, February 1952, and *The Trainman News*, April 7, 1952; and Warner Bloomberg, "The Monstrous Machine and the Worried Workers," *The Reporter*, September 29, 1953.

2.   Quoted in *Business Week*, October 1, 1955, 78. A sample of optimistic views on the issue during the mid-1950s popular debate includes Peter Drucker, "The Promise of Automation," *Harper's Magazine*, April 1955; "Technological Alarms," *Fortune*, May 1955; "Did Reuther Speak for All Labor?" *Control Engineering*, February 1955; Carl Huhndorff, "Labor Can Handle Automation," *Machinist's Monthly Journal*, April 1955; "Man Is Not Outmoded," *Steel Labor*, May 1955; Cledo Brunetti, *The Meaning of Automation* (Minneapolis: General Mills Inc., 1955); *Automation—Friend or Foe?* General Electric Employee Relations Newsletter, April 8, 1955; John Snyder, "The Automatic Factory and Automation," *Washington Post and Times-Herald*, Outlook Section, January 23, 1955; "Automation and Jobs," *Industry's View*, National Association of Manufacturers, December 1955; "Automation," *Economic Intelligence*, United States Chamber of Commerce, November 1955; "Automation and the Labor Force," *First National City Monthly Letter*, February 1956; "Are New Machines Cutting Down Jobs?" *U.S. News and World Report*, February 18, 1955; "Machines at Work," *Newsweek*, December 12, 1955; "Automation—Friend or Foe?" *Colliers*, May 13, 1955; and "Automation—The Facts behind the Word," *Business Week*, October 1, 1955. A sample of pessimistic views includes Gabriel Kolko, "Nobody Wants to Sound Defeatist—Publically," *New Republic*, July 11, 1955; Nat Weinberg, "Labor on the Hook," *Saturday Review*, January 22, 1955; Frederick Pollock, *Automation: A Study of Its Economic and Social Consequences* (New York: Praeger, 1957); *Robot Revolution: The Implications of Automation* (Philadelphia: Socialist Party USA, 1955); Walter Reuther, "The Automation Revolution," CIO Presidential Address, December 1954; Walter Reuther, "What Will Automation Do to the Worker?" *Washington Post and Times-Herald*, Outlook Section, January 23, 1955; Jack Conway, "Labor Looks at Automation," *Business Topics*, June 1955; Warner Bloomberg, *The Age of Automation*, League for Industrial Democracy, Pamphlet Series, 1955; Robert Bendiner, "The Age of the Thinking Robot," *The Reporter*, April 7, 1955; J. G. Cross, "Automation and Labor," *The Baker's and Confectioner's Journal*, April 1955; and statements on individual industry effects at the Joint Committee on the Economic Report hearings, *Automation and Technological Change*, October 1955, by labor representatives Howard Coughlin, James B. Carey, Joseph Beirne, Otto Pragen, and Walter Kennedy.

3. The Congressional hearings were all by the Joint Economic Committee and included *Automation and Technological Change*, 84th Congress, 1st Session, 1955; *Instrumentation and Automation*, 84th Congress, 2nd Session, 1956; *Automation and Recent Trends*, 85th Congress, 1st Session, 1957; and *New Views on Automation*, 86th Congress, 2nd Session, 1960. For evidence of the slackening of popular interest in the automation issue in 1956–57, see George Meany, statement before the Joint Economic Committee, *Instrumentation and Automation*, Hearings, 1956, 188–91; Nat Goldfinger, "Labor Looks at Automation," Conference on Automation, Changing Technology and Related Problems, San Francisco, January 9, 1957; and "Increased Output Becomes a Bone of Contention," *Business Week*, August 11, 1956. In "The Automation Depression," *The Nation*, November 29, 1958, 339, it was noted that "we don't hear much of automation these days. There was a flurry of interest a few years ago, many articles and several books were written and forgotten, and everybody got bored with the subject." For a sample of articles on both sides of the issue indicating the resurgence of interest in the late 1950s, see "The Jobs That Are Gone Forever," *Business Week*, December 20, 1959; "The Automation Depression," *The Nation*, November 29, 1958; Ben B. Seligman, statement, Joint Economic Committee, *Relationship of Prices to Economic Stability and Growth*, Hearings, 85th Congress, 2nd Session, 1959; Everett M. Kassalow, "Automation and Technological Change," speech before the Professional, Technical and Salary Conference Board of the International Union of Electrical, Radio and Machine Workers, Boston, Massachusetts, June 27, 1958; "More Jobs and a Sounder Dollar," *Fortune*, November 1958; James Stern, "Fact, Fallacy and Fantasy of Automation," *Proceedings of the Eleventh Annual Meeting*, Industrial Relations Research Association (IRRA), Chicago, December 1958; Herbert Northrup, "Automation: Effects on Labor Force, Skills and Employment," *Proceedings of the Eleventh Annual Meeting*, IRRA, Chicago, December 1958; "Jobs Go Begging Despite Unemployment," *Nation's Business*, May 1959; "Why Jobs Are Slow to Come Back," *U.S. News and World Report*, February 13, 1959; Cledo Brunetti, "Meeting Automation Full-On," in Howard Jacobsen and Joseph Roucek, eds., *Automation and Society* (New York: Philosophical Library, 1959); Stanley Ruttenberg, "Economic and Social Implications," *Monthly Labor Review*, February 1959; "Growing Pains of Automation," *America*, October 17, 1959; John Diebold, "Automation Needs a Human Policy," *Challenge*, May 1959; statements by Andrew Biemiller, Nat Goldfinger, Joseph Moody, Solomon Barkin, and Walter Fackler before the Senate, Special Committee on Unemployment Problems, *Unemployment Problems*, Hearings, 86th Congress, 1st Session, 1959; "Specks on the Crystal Ball," *IUD Digest*, Winter 1960; "Automation: Good or Bad?" *The Advance*, January 15, 1960; "Automation, Productivity and Jobs," *IUD Digest*, Fall 1960; "The Big Question," *IUD Digest*, Summer 1960; "New Processes, New Machines, Prove Need for Unemployment, Job and Rate Protection," *UE News*, June 20, 1960; "Union Meetings Air Job Security Issue," *Business Week*, September 17, 1960; *Automation: A Prime Source of More and Better Jobs* (New York: National Association of Manufacturers, September 1960); *Productivity: A Measure of Economic Progress* (New York: NAM, November 1960); Milton O. Cross, "Automation: The New Technology," *Business Topics*, Summer 1960; William G. Caples, "Automation in Theory and Practice," *Business Topics*, Autumn 1960; "Unemployment—A Headache That Prosperity Hasn't Cured," *U.S. News and World Report*, June 13, 1960; Robert W. Smith, "Sweeping Personnel Changes Foreseen as Result of New Automation Revolution," *Office Management and American Business*, August 1960; and "More out, for Longer, in More Industries," *Business Week*, December 17, 1960.

4. These figures were quoted by Joseph Pechman in his statement before the Joint Economic Committee, *Current Economic Situation and Short-Run Outlook*, Hearings, 86th Congress, 2nd Session, 1961, 114.

5. Explicit reference to the return of an optimistic consensus was made by Jan Tinbergen, "The Influence of Productivity on Economic Welfare," *Economic Journal*, March 1952, 68. For a sample of late 1940s to early 1950s optimistic professional comments, see Sumner Slichter, *The American Economy: Its Problems and Prospects* (New York: Knopf, 1948); William Haber, "Quieting the Unemployment Ghost," *The Survey*, October 1949; Ewan Clague, *Productivity, Employment and Living Standards*, statement by the Commissioner of Labor Statistics, Conference on Productivity, University of Wisconsin, Industrial Relations Center, Milwaukee, Wisconsin, June 4, 1949; Abraham Gitlow, "An Economic Evaluation of the Gains and Costs of Technological Change," in L. Reed Tripp, ed., *Industrial Productivity* (Chicago: IRRA, 1951); Yale Brozen, "Studies of Technological Change," *Southern Economic Journal*, April 1951; and Sumner Slichter, "Productivity: Still Going Up," *The Atlantic*, July 1952. For a more guarded analysis, see Wassily Leontieff, "Machines and Men," *Scientific American*, September 1952. This optimism, however, applied only to industrialized countries. During this same period a theoretical literature appeared which showed that a problem of technological unemployment was possible in capital-short economies. John R. Hicks, "World Recovery after the War," *Economic Journal*, June 1947; and E. S. Simpson, "Inflation, Deflation and Employment in Italy," *Review of Economic Studies*, 1949–50, developed this argument for war-ravaged European countries. The literature concerning lesser developed countries included Jan Tinbergen, "The Influence of Productivity on Economic Welfare," *Economic Journal*, March 1952; *Measures of the Economic Development of Underdeveloped Countries* (New York: United Nations, 1951); Ragnar Nurkse, *The Problem of Capital in Underdeveloped Countries* (New York: Oxford University Press, 1953); D. Hamberg, "Full Capacity versus Full Employment Growth," *Quarterly Journal of Economics*, August 1952; Evsey Domar, "Further Comment," *Quarterly Journal of Economics*, November 1953; R. S. Eckaus, "The Factor Proportions Problem in Underdeveloped Areas," *American Economic Review*, September 1955; W. A. Lewis, "Economic Development with Unlimited Supplies of Labor," *The Manchester School of Economics and Social Studies*, May 1954; Henry J. Bruton, "Growth Models and Underdeveloped Economies," *Journal of Political Economy*, August 1955; Masao Fukuoka, "Full Employment and Constant Coefficients of Production," *Quarterly Journal of Economics*, February 1955; and Yale Brozen, "Technological Change, Ideology and Productivity," *Political Science Quarterly*, December 1955. James Tobin, "A Dynamic Aggregative Model," *Journal of Political Economy*, April 1955, and Robert Solow, "A Contribution to the Theory of Economic Growth," *Quarterly Journal of Economics*, February 1956, advanced the theory to show again that technological change created no unemployment threat to an advanced industrialized country.

6. For early to mid-1950s professional comments that illustrate this view, see George P. Schultz and George B. Baldwin, *Automation: A New Dimension to Old Problems*, Annals of American Economics (Washington D.C.: Public Affairs Press, 1955); Peter Drucker, "The Promise of Automation," *Harper's Magazine*, April 1955; Henri deBivort, "Automation—Some Social Aspects," *International Labour Review*, December 1955; Yale Brozen, "Automation: Creator or Destroyer of Jobs?" *Iowa Business Digest*, February 1956; Almarin Phillips, *Automation: Its Impact on Economic Growth and Stability* (Washington, D.C.: American Enterprise Association, 1957);

George Shultz, "The Importance of Economic and Technological Change in the Econo-
mies of Canada and the United States Today," in H. Woods, ed., *Industrial Relations
and Technological Change* (McGill University: Industrial Relations Centre, 1957);
James G. Witte, *Automatic Production and Unemployment: A Theoretical Analysis*
(Unpublished doctoral dissertation, Indiana University, 1956); Adolph Lowe,
"Technological Unemployment Reexamined," in Gottfried Eisermann, *Wirtschaft und
Kultursystem* (Stuttgart: Eugen Rentsch Verlag, 1955); and Clyde Dankert, *Sharing the
Gains of Technological Change* (Hanover, N.H.: Amos Tuck School of Business Ad-
ministration, Dartmouth College, 1955). For an empirical study reaching substantially
the same conclusions as Dankert, see Mordecai Ezekiel, "Distribution of Gains from
Rising Technical Efficiency in Progressing Economies," *American Economic Review*,
May 1957.

7. One response to automation concerns was the beginning of a series of case studies by the Bureau of Labor Statistics. BLS plant-level studies in this period included
studies of a radio plant (*Monthly Labor Review*, January 1956), an insurance company
(*Monthly Labor Review*, January 1956), and a bakery (*Monthly Labor Review*, September 1956). An extensive bibliography on *Automatic Technology and Its Implications*
was published as BLS Bulletin 1198 in August 1956. The Occupations Outlook program was expanded in response to automation concerns, and promotion of local programs to forecast retraining needs was begun. Attention was particularly directed to
problems of older workers. For a review of automation-related BLS programs through
1956, see the testimony by Rocco Sicilian before the Joint Economic Committee, *Instrumentation and Automation*, Hearings, 1956. Worker mobility studies completed by
researchers in this period included William Miernyk, *Inter-Industry Labor Mobility:
The Case of the Displaced Textile Workers* (Boston: Northeastern University Press,
1955); William Haber, John Carroll, Mark Kahn, and Merton Peck, *Maintenance of
Way Employment on U.S. Railroads* (Detroit: Brotherhood of Maintenance of Way Employees, 1957); Harold Sheppard and James Stern, "Impact of Automation on Workers
in Supplier Plants," *Labor Law Journal*, October 1957; Richard Wilcock, "Impact on
Workers and Community of a Plant Shutdown in a Depressed Area," *Monthly Labor
Review*, September 1957; and Leonard Adams and Robert Aronson, *Workers and Industry Change—A Case Study in Industrial Mobility* (Ithaca, N.Y.: Cornell University
Press, 1957). A small sample of case studies of the employment effects of automation
includes J. R. Bright, "Thinking Ahead," *Harvard Business Review*, November–
December 1955; John Robert Summerfield, *Some Economic Effects of the Development
of Automatic Process Controls in American Industry* (Unpublished doctoral dissertation, University of California, Berkeley, 1956); Jack Stieber, "Automation and the
White-Collar Worker," *Personnel*, November–December 1957; and the half dozen case
studies in *Man and Automation*, Society of Applied Anthropology, Yale University,
December 1955. For other case studies see the many listed in the bibliographies: *Automatic Technology and Its Implications*, BLS Bulletin 1198, August 1958; and Gloria
Cheek, *Economic and Social Implications of Automation* (East Lansing: Labor and Industrial Relations Center, Michigan State University, 1958).

8. For a sample of optimistic evaluations of current evidence, see James Bright,
"Thinking Ahead," *Harvard Business Review*, November–December 1955; Richard
Lewis, *Effects of Automation on the Occupational Structure*, address before the Ameri-
can Statistical Association, New York City, December 29, 1955; Yale Brozen,
"Automation," *Iowa Business Digest*, February 1956; and Yale Brozen, "The Economics
of Automation," *American Economic Review*, May 1957. On the negative side of cur-

rent case study evaluations, see Walter Buckingham, "Industrial Significance," in *The Challenge of Automation* (Washington, D.C.: Public Affairs Press, 1955), and Buckingham's testimony before the Joint Committee on the Economic Report, *Automation and Technological Change*, Hearings, 1955, 34. For another important cautionary view, this time with respect to increasing lags between output and employment recovery in recent business cycles, see Richard Wilcock, "Jobs, Productivity and Full Employment," *Illinois Business Review*, August 1955, 6, 7. For comments suggesting that automation was creating a serious problem in terms of a gap between the demand and the supply of highly skilled workers, see Drucker, "Promise," *Harper's*, April 1955, 45; and Shultz, "Importance," in Woods, *Industrial Relations*, 1957, 20–21. For similar comments see Edgar Weinberg, "A Review of Automatic Technology," *Monthly Labor Review*, June 1955, reprinted in BLS Bulletin 1287, *The Impact of Automation*, November 1960, 10; Ewan Clague, *How Necessary Is Automation to America?* address by the Commissioner of Labor Statistics, University of Chicago, Chicago, November 14, 1955, 13; and Edwin Nourse, statement before the Joint Committee on the Economic Report, *Automation and Technological Change*, Hearings, 1955, 621. For comments about the developing problems of chronic unemployment in distressed areas, see Herman Travis, "The Structure of Unemployment in Recent Years," *Monthly Labor Review*, October 1956; Richard Wilcock, "Employment Effects of a Plant Shutdown in a Depressed Labor Area," *Monthly Labor Review*, September 1957, 1047; and Vincent Gegan and Samuel Thompson, "Worker Mobility in a Labor Surplus Area," *Monthly Labor Review*, December 1957, 1451. Also see U.S. President, *Economic Report of the President*, January 1956, 61, and comments by Naomi Riches, "Education and Work of Young People in a Labor Surplus Area," *Monthly Labor Review*, December 1957; Sar Levitan, *Federal Assistance to Labor Surplus Areas*, a report to the House Committee on Banking and Currency, 85th Congress, 1st Session, April 15, 1957; William Miernyk, *Depressed Industrial Areas—A National Problem* (Washington, D.C.: National Planning Association, January 1957); Howard D. Marshall, "The Problem of Depressed Areas," *Labor Law Journal*, July 1957; Guy Waterman, "Adjustment to Localized Unemployment," *American Economic Security*, November–December 1956; and the many statements at the various Congressional hearings on area aid programs, including House, Committee on Banking and Currency, *Area Assistance Act of 1956*, Hearings, 84th Congress, 2nd Session, 1956; Senate, Committee on Labor and Public Welfare, *Area Redevelopment*, Hearings, 84th Congress, 2nd Session, 1956; and Senate, Committee on Banking and Currency, *Area Redevelopment*, Hearings, 85th Congress, 1st Session, 1957.

9. "Report of the Director-General to the 40th Session, International Labour Conference, 1957," *Monthly Labor Review*, July 1957, reprinted in BLS Bulletin 1287, *The Impact of Automation*, November 1960, 18–19.

10. For evidence of a shift in professional interest in 1957–58 from unemployment to inflation, see James Dusenberry and John Meyer, "Brief Comments on the Recession," *Review of Economics and Statistics*, November 1958, and the evolution of concern from unemployment and tax cuts to inflation in testimony before the Joint Economic Committee in *January 1958 Economic Report of the President*, Hearings, 85th Congress, 2nd Session, January–February 1958; *Fiscal Policy Implications of the Current Economic Outlook*, Hearings, 85th Congress, 2nd Session, April 1958; and *Relationship of Prices to Economic Stability and Growth*, Hearings, 85th Congress, 2nd Session, May 1958. For evidence of a lack of professional concern about unemployment problems due to automation, see Julius Rezler, "The Impact of Automation on the Stability of Manufacturing Employment," *Current Economic Comment*, May 1958; George

Wilson, "Technological Change and Unemployment," *Current Economic Comment*, May 1958; Julius Backman, "Here's How to Make Jobs," *Nation's Business*, May 1958; articles by P. Naville, J. R. Gas, and Paul Einzig in the *International Social Science Bulletin*, No. 1, 1958; and Jack Rogers, *Automation: Technology's New Face* (Berkeley: Institute of Industrial Relations, 1958). For evidence of the carryover into 1959 of inflation as the major policy issue, see the January 1959 *Economic Report of the President*; the Joint Economic Committee hearings on *Employment, Growth and Price Levels*, 86th Congress, 1st Session, especially Part 1 (March 1959), Part 4 (May 1959), Part 7 (September 1959), and Part 8 (September–October 1959).

11.   For other 1958–59 references to structural unemployment problems not referred to below, see, for example, Charles Killingsworth, "Automation in Manufacturing," George Shultz, "Discussion," and Bernard Karsh, "Discussion," all in *Proceedings of the Eleventh Annual Meeting*, IRRA, December 1958; Floyd Mann and Lawrence Williams, "Organizational Impact of White-Collar Automation," at the same meetings; Seymour Harris, statement, House, Committee on Banking and Currency, *Area Redevelopment Act*, Hearings, 86th Congress, 1st Session, 1959, 585; William Miernyk, statement, Senate, Committee on Banking and Currency, *Area Redevelopment Act*, Hearings, 86th Congress, 1st Session, 1959, 291–94; William Haber, statement, House, Committee on Banking and Currency, *Area Redevelopment Act*, Hearings, 1959, 885–86; William Haber, "The Persistence of Unemployment," *Labor Law Journal*, July 1959; Clyde Dankert, "Technological Change and Unemployment," *Labor Law Journal*, June 1959; Joint Economic Committee, *Staff Report on Employment, Growth and Price Levels*, 1959, 170, 173, 183; Myron Silbert, "Discussion" of paper by William Miernyk, *Proceedings of the Twelfth Annual Meeting*, IRRA, December 1959, 53; Solomon Fabricant, statement, Senate, Special Committee on Unemployment Problems, *Unemployment Problems*, Hearings, 86th Congress, 1st Session, 1959, 155; Walter Fackler, statement, Senate, Special Committee on Unemployment Problems, *Unemployment Problems*, Hearings, 1959, 52; John Turnbull, statement, Senate, Special Committee on Unemployment Problems, *Unemployment Problems*, Hearings, 1959, 184; Richard Wilcock, "Fast-Changing Technology—Its Impact on Labor Problems," *Pennsylvania Business Survey*, December 1959; William Miernyk, "The Incidence of Persistent Unemployment," *Proceedings of the Twelfth Annual Meeting*, IRRA, 1959; Robert Aronson and Jacob Kaufman, "Discussion" of Miernyk paper, *Proceedings of the Twelfth Annual Meeting*, IRRA, 1959; Robert Aaron Gordon, statement, Joint Economic Committee, *Employment, Growth and Price Levels*, Hearings, Part 9a, 1959; Richard Wilcock, statement, Senate, Special Committee on Unemployment Problems, *Unemployment Problems*, Hearings, 1959; William Haber, statement, Senate, Special Committee on Unemployment Problems, *Unemployment Problems*, Hearings, 1959; Clarence Long, "Prosperity Unemployment and Its Relation to Economic Growth and Inflation," *American Economic Review*, May 1960; Thor Hultgren, "Productivity and Unemployment," *Challenge*, March 1959; and Kenneth Kurihara, "Beyond Keynes," *Challenge*, December 1958.

12.   Neil Chamberlain, statement, Joint Economic Committee, *Employment, Growth and Price Levels*, Hearings, Part 8, 1959, 2703–4. For other relevant testimony at the same hearings, see the statements by Leon Keyserling in Part 1 and Stanley Lebergott in Part 3.

13.   Philip Taft and Merton Stoltz, statement, Joint Economic Committee, *Employment, Growth and Price Levels*, Hearings, Part 8, 1959, 2707–8.

14.   Herbert Parnes, statement, Senate, Special Committee on Unemployment Problems, *Unemployment Problems*, Hearings, 1959, 179.

15.   Clarence Long, statement, Senate, Special Committee on Unemployment Problems, *Unemployment Problems*, Hearings, 1959, 182.

16.   Jacob Kaufman, "Discussion" of paper by Clarence Long, *American Economic Review*, May 1960, 173.

17.   These government studies included *Who Are the Unemployed?* BLS, June 1958; *The Unemployed, Spring 1959*, BLS, May 1959; *Chronic Labor Surplus Areas: Experience and Outlook*, Bureau of Employment Security, Report No. R-192, July 1959; *A Case Study of an Automatic Airline Reservation System*, BLS Report 137, 1959; *Trends in Output Per Man-Hour in the Private Economy, 1909–58*, BLS Bulletin 137, 1959; "The Structure of Unemployment in Areas of Substantial Labor Surplus," BLS, Study Paper No. 23, January 1960, for the Joint Economic Committee, *Employment, Growth and Price Levels*.

18.   Joint Economic Committee, *Employment, Growth and Price Levels*, Study Paper No. 6, BLS, "The Extent and Nature of Frictional Unemployment," November 1959, 2.

19.   John T. Dunlop, "Public Policy and Unemployment," in Senate, Special Committee on Unemployment Problems, *Studies in Unemployment*, Hearings, 1960, 1–2, 14.

20.   Other important papers in the same volume included William Miernyk, "Foreign Experience with Structural Unemployment and Its Remedies," and Clyde Dankert, "Automation and Unemployment." The final *Report of the Special Committee on Unemployment Problems*, 86th Congress, March 1960, was heavily influenced by these papers. It came down in favor of a balanced program of growth and special aid in light of the "class" nature of current unemployment. These early 1960 discussions of recent unemployment trends were reflected in other professional writings as well. See, for example, George W. Wilson, "The Relationship Between Output and Employment," *Review of Economics and Statistics*, February 1960; and Harold Sylvester, "Bread and Circuses, 1984?" *IUD Digest*, Winter 1960.

21.   For a sample of important contributions see "Effects of Mechanization and Automation in Offices," *International Labour Review*, February, March, and April 1960; "Experience with the Introduction of Office Automation," *Monthly Labor Review*, April 1960; *Adjustments to the Introduction of Electronic Data Processing*, BLS Bulletin 1276, 1960; papers by Solomon Barkin, John Diebold, Eli Ginzberg, and John Dunlop in *Governor's Conference on Automation*, Cooperstown, N.Y., June 1960; Ida Hoos, "When the Computer Takes Over the Office," *Harvard Business Review*, July–August 1960; "Office Automation in the Federal Government," *Monthly Labor Review*, September 1960; Einar Hardin, "The Reaction of Employees to Office Automation," *Monthly Labor Review*, September 1960; Walter Buckingham in Joint Economic Committee, *New Views on Automation*, Hearings, 1960; and testimony by Charles Killingsworth, Frederick Harbison, and Eli Ginzberg at Senate, Committee on Labor and Public Welfare, *Manpower Problems*, Hearings, 86th Congress, 2nd Session, 1960.

22.   The quotes are from Joseph Pechman, statement, Joint Economic Committee, *Current Economic Situation and Short-Run Outlook*, Hearings, 86th Congress, 2nd Session, 1961, 114; Charles Schultz, statement, Joint Economic Committee, *Current Economic Situation*, Hearings, 1961, 120; and Pechman, 129–30, Schultz, 132, in Joint Economic Committee, *Current Economic Situation*, Hearings, 1961.

23.   Clarence D. Long, "A Theory of Creeping Unemployment and Labor Force Replacement," paper before the Catholic Economic Association, December 27, 1960, as reprinted in the *Congressional Record*, July 25, 1961, 13430.

24.   U.S. President, *Economic Report of the President*, January 1961, 15.

25.   The quote is from "When Machines Have Jobs—And Workers Do Not," *U.S. News and World Report*, February 6, 1961, 77. The intensity of popular interest in early 1961 is reflected in the many other statements of concern, including, for example, "Changes Coming in Labor Policies," "Among the Jobless—How They Live, What They Say," and "Latest on Jobs Hit by Machines," all in *U.S. News and World Report*, February 27, 1961; "The Automation Jobless: Not Fired, Just Not Hired," *Time*, February 24, 1961; Edward Townsend, "The Human Equation: Automation and Displaced Workers," *Challenge*, February 1961; J. V. McKenna, "Must Automation Destroy Jobs?" *America*, February 18, 1961; Geoffrey Cornog, "Automatic Data Processings—Dr. Jekyll or Mr. Hyde?" *Public Administration Review*, 1961; Howard Nicholson, "Problem of the 1960's—Automation, Unemployment and the Abundant Life," *Magazine of Wall Street*, March 11, 1961; "Impact of Automation Is Next Issue," *Business Week*, March 18, 1961; "Automation Deal," *Business Week*, March 25, 1961, "UAW Heats Up Automation Issue," *Business Week*, March 25, 1961; "A Cure for Automation," *Business Week*, April 29, 1961; "Automation Problem Tackled," *Business Week*, May 6, 1961; *Training and Retraining in Depressed Areas*, Bulletin T-152, March 1961, and *Training—The Key to the Future*, April 1961, both by the Department of Labor, Bureau of Apprenticeship and Training; *Factory Jobs: Employment Outlook for Workers in Jobs Requiring Little or No Experience or Specialized Training*, BLS Bulletin 1288, 1961; *Technological Change and Productivity in the Bituminous Coal Industry, 1920–60*, BLS Bulletin 1305, 1961; the entire January 1961 issue of the *Employment Security Review* on "Adapting Farm Labor Services to Changing Times"; and Carol Barry, "White-Collar Employment," *Monthly Labor Review*, January and February 1961. For later 1961 popular comments see *Unemployment—Causes and Cures*, National Association of Manufacturers, NAM Economic Series No. 83, April 1961; "Automation and Unemployment," *International Teamster*, May, June, and July 1961; Malcolm Denise, "Unemployment and Automation," *Business Topics*, Summer 1961; "When Machines Replace Men," *Newsweek*, June 19, 1961; "Help for Displaced Workers," *Business Week*, June 17, 1961; "Automation, Unemployment: Problems We Face," *Catholic World*, June 1961; William Gomberg, "Problems of Economic Growth and Automation," *California Management Review*, Summer 1961; a report on an August conference on automation in Francis X. Quinn, S. J., *The Ethical Aftermath of Automation* (Westminster, Md.: Newman Press, 1962); "The Impact of Automation—A Challenge to America," *American Federationist*, August 1961; "What Hope for the Hard-Core Jobless?" *Business Week*, May 13, 1961; and House, Committee on Education and Labor, *Impact of Automation on Employment*, Report, 87th Congress, 1st Session, June 1961.

26.   The Samuelson report was released by the Kennedy administration on January 6, 1961.

27.   *The American Economy in 1961: Problems and Policies*, "Supplement B: Unemployment and the Structure of the Labor Force," statement of the Council of Economic Advisers before the Joint Economic Committee, March 6, 1961, in *January 1961 Economic Report of the President*, Hearings, 87th Congress, 1st Session, 1961, 378.

28.   Joint Economic Committee, *January 1961 Economic Report of the President*, Hearings, 1961, 380.

29.   One of the most dramatic developments in the beginning of the debates occurred at the same *January 1961 Economic Report of the President*, 1961, hearings. Testifying on the same day as the CEA, William McChesney Martin, chairman of the Federal Reserve Board, claimed that current unemployment was mainly structural (p. 470). The

conflicting analyses of the Fed and the CEA were quickly noted by JEC members (pp. 480–81). The conflict was also noted by the popular press, and President Kennedy called both Heller and Martin in to confer on the question. The result was that statements of consensus were later submitted to the JEC by Heller and Martin. For comments in the popular press, see "The Question of Structural Unemployment," *Business Week*, March 25, 1961, and "Unemployment as Two Experts See It," *U.S. News and World Report*, March 20, 1961. The "consensus" statements were printed in the *January 1961 Economic Report of the President*, Hearings, 1961. To all who had followed the exchange, however, it was obvious that these statements of "consensus" simply reaffirmed the previous positions of the participants. See Martin's comments (pp. 486–87), Heller's comments (pp. 606–7), and Representative Curtis' note that these statements did not resolve anything (p. 570).

30.   See, for example, Paul Samuelson, statement, House, Committee on Education and Labor, *Impact of Automation on Employment*, Hearings, 87th Congress, 1st Session, 1961; Raymond Zelder, *Postwar Unemployment in the United States* (San Francisco: Bank of America, 1961); Norman Ture, "New Wine for Old Bottles?" *Challenge*, May 1961; Robert J. Myers, Deputy Commissioner of Labor Statistics, Address at Commencement Week Seminar, University of Pittsburgh, Pittsburgh, June 9, 1961; Solomon Fabricant, "Basic Facts on Productivity Change: An Introduction by Solomon Fabricant," in John Kendrick, *Productivity Trends in the United States* (New York: National Bureau of Economic Research, 1961); and statements by Otto Eckstein and Jewell Rasmussen in Senate, Committee on Labor and Public Welfare, *Emergency Employment Acceleration Act*, Hearings, 87th Congress, 1st Session, 1961.

31.   See, for example, National Planning Association, *The Rise of Chronic Unemployment*, April 1961; June Meredith, "Long-Term Unemployment in the United States," *Monthly Labor Review*, June 1961; Walter Buckingham, "The Great Employment Controversy," chapter 6 of his *Automation: Its Impact on Business and People* (New York: Harper and Brothers, 1961); John P. Henderson, *Changes in the Industrial Distribution of Employment 1919–59*, University of Illinois, Bulletin No. 87, August 1961; Morris Horowitz, "Automation and Full Employment: A Public Point of View," *Proceedings of the New York University Fourteenth Annual Conference on Labor* (New York: Bender, 1961); Clyde Dankert, "Are Shorter Hours the Answer? Problems of Technological Unemployment," *Challenge*, December 1961; and the statement by Harvey Brazer in Senate, Committee on Labor and Public Welfare, *Emergency Employment Acceleration Act*, Hearings, 1961.

32.   See, for example, Alvin Hansen, letter to the editor, *New York Times*, March 12, 1961; and Neil Chamberlain, "The Many Faces of Unemployment," *Challenge*, March 1961.

33.   There were actually three professional viewpoints argued in the structural debates—structural, deficient demand, and neoclassical. The neoclassical view was that current unemployment was not due to deficient demand or to structural change, but to the minimum wage and union activities. The strongest proponents of this view were Yale Brozen and Clarence Long. See, for example, Yale Brozen, "Why Do We Have an Unemployment Problem?" in *Employment and Unemployment: The Problem of the 1960's* (Washington, D.C.: United States Chamber of Commerce, May 1961), and Clarence Long, "Labor Force and Unemployment in the 1960's," in the same volume. Also see Brozen's testimony in Senate, Committe on Labor and Public Welfare, *Emergency Employment Acceleration Act*, Hearings, 1961. Because the neoclassical view occupied only a minor position in the debates, a recounting of its evolution is left out of the following summary of the discussions. For a detailed look at the role of the neo-

classical position in the debates, see Donald Wells, *The United States' Unemployment Problem—Structural or Lack of Demand?* (Unpublished doctoral dissertation, University of Southern California, 1966).

34.   Also see Phyllis Groom, "European Government Programs," *Monthly Labor Review*, August 1961; Phyllis Groom, "Federal and State Legislation on Retraining," *Monthly Labor Review*, September 1961; Rennard Davis, "Skill Improvement Training for Electricians and Plumbers," *Monthly Labor Review*, October 1961; Ewan Clague, *Automation and Unemployment*, statement by the Commissioner of Labor Statistics, Annual Convention, Massachusetts Labor Council, Boston, September 29, 1961; and Bureau of Employment Security, *Background Information on Impact of Automation and Technological Change on Employment and Unemployment*, BES No. R-206, September 1961.

35.   Harold Demsetz, "Structural Unemployment: A Reconsideration of the Evidence and the Theory," *Journal of Law and Economics*, October 1961, 81–83, 90, 92.

36.   Edward Kalachek, *Labor Markets and Unemployment* (Belmont, California: Wadsworth, 1973), 114.

37.   Robert Stein and Frazier Kellogg, Bureau of Labor Statistics, "Unemployment in the Early 1960's," in Joint Economic Committee, *Unemployment: Terminology, Measurement and Analysis*, Hearings, 87th Congress, 1st Session, 1961, 80.

38.   James Knowles and Edward Kalachek, *Higher Unemployment Rates, 1957–60: Structural Transformation or Inadequate Demand?* Joint Economic Committee, 87th Congress, 1st Session, 1961, 5–8.

39.   Knowles and Kalachek 9, 39, 51–52.

40.   Knowles and Kalachek 54, 73, 78–79.

CHAPTER 8

1.   Arthur Ross, "Conclusions," in Arthur M. Ross, ed., *Unemployment and the American Economy* (New York: Wiley, 1964), 202.

2.   Paul Samuelson and Robert Solow, "Analytical Aspects of Anti-Inflation Policy," *American Economic Review*, May 1960.

3.   Milton Friedman, "The Role of Monetary Policy," *American Economic Review*, March 1968.

4.   All statements were in Joint Economic Committee, *Employment and Unemployment*, Hearings, 87th Congress, 1st Session, 1962; pp. 340, 353–54, 356–57. For testimony in support of the BLS report and thus that more than demand stimulation would be needed to reduce unemployment to 4 percent, see testimony at the same hearings by Ewan Clague.

5.   Richard Wilcock and Walter Franke, "Will Economic Growth Solve the Problem of Long-Term Uemployment?" *Proceedings of the Fourteenth Annual Meeting*, IRRA, December 1961. Also see the comments by Stanley Lebergott, "Unemployment Statistics for Fiscal and Monetary Policy"; William Miernyk, "Problems and Remedies for Depressed Area Unemployment"; G. H. Borts, "Comment"; and Robert Lampman, "Comment," at the same IRRA meetings. Borts and Lebergott sided with Wilcock and Franke. Miernyk, however, was more cautious about the impact of demand policy. For other comments taking the same line as Miernyk in the same period, see Victor Fuchs, "Action Programs to Deal with Unemployment," and Stanley Ruttenberg, "Structural Unemployment—Still a Problem in Our Economy," both in *1962 Proceedings of the*

Business and Economic Statistics Section, American Statistical Association, December 1961. Also see Murray Brown and John deCanci, "Technological Changes in the United States, 1950–1960," at the same meetings.

6.   Solomon Barkin, "Comments," 25, and William Miernyk, "Labor Market Lessons from Abroad," 75, in *The Labor Market and Social Security: Proceedings of the Fourth Annual Social Security Conference* (Kalamazoo, Mich.: Upjohn Institute for Economic Research, 1962). Also see Clarence Long, "An Overview of Postwar Labor Market Developments," in the same collection.

7.   Richard Lester, "Comments"; and Charles Killingsworth, "Comments," both in *Labor Market*, 1962; quote from p. 44.

8.   U.S. President, *Economic Report of the President*, January 1962, 8, 46.

9.   See in particular the comments by Henry Wallich, Gardiner Means, Leon Keyserling, and Alvin Hansen in Joint Economic Committee, *January 1962 Economic Report of the President*, Hearings, 87th Congress, 2nd Session, 1962.

10.   Donald Michael, *Cybernation: The Silent Conquest* (Santa Barbara, California: Center for the Study of Democratic Institutions, 1962). The *Business Week* quote is from "Is Automation Really a Job Killer?" February 24, 1962, 46.

11.   For a sample of the popular debates over automation in 1962, see W. H. Ferry as quoted in "Where to Find 60,000 New Jobs Every Week," *U.S. News and World Report*, April 16, 1962; Thomas B. Curtis, *87 Million Jobs* (New York: Duell, Sloan and Pierce, 1962); Ben B. Seligman, "Man, Work and the Automated Feast," *Commentary*, July 1962; "Automation . . . And Its Real Problems," *Challenge*, February 1962; Bill François, "The Fear of Tomorrow," *The Progressive*, March 1962; "Automation Creates New Jobs," *Nation's Business*, April 1962; Frank Flick, "Does 'Automation' Cause Unemployment?" *Vital Speeches*, February 15, 1962; "The Other Side of Automation," *Dun's Review*, May 1962; Everett Kassalow, "Labor Relations and Employment Aspects after Ten Years," in Morris Philipson, ed., *Automation: Implications for the Future* (New York: Vintage Books, 1962); papers by John Snyder, Albert Hayes, and David Morse in *Focus on Automation* (New York: American Foundation on Automation and Employment, Inc., 1963); Harold Wolf and Henry Kester, "High Level Stagnation and Economic Growth," *Business Topics*, Winter 1962; and William Glazier, "Automation and Joblessness: Is Retraining the Answer?" *Atlantic Monthly*, August 1962. For commentary on the debate over administration policy, see "Critics Fire on CEA," *Business Week*, March 10, 1962.

12.   References include Walter Buckingham, "The Impending Educational Revolution," in Luther Evans and G. E. Arnstein, eds., *Automation and the Challenge to Education* (Washington, D. C.: National Education Association, 1962); Walter Buckingham, "White-Collar Automation," *The Nation*, January 6, 1962; Walter Buckingham, "The Great Employment Controversy," *Annals of the American Academy of Political and Social Science*, March 1962; Clarence Long, "Full Employment by 1963?" *Challenge*, February 1962; Leon Keyserling, "Two-Fifths of a Nation," *The Progressive*, March 1962; Solomon Fabricant, "Which Productivity? Perspective on a Current Question," *Monthly Labor Review*, June 1962; Henry Hazlitt, "Automation Makes Jobs," *Newsweek*, March 5, 1962; Daniel Diamond, "The Shift to Services: What Does It Mean?" *Challenge*, July 1962; John Diebold, "The Application of Information and Technology," *Annals of the American Academy of Political and Social Science*, March 1962; Hans Apel, "Should We Shorten the Workweek?" *Challenge*, March 1962; Harold Sylvester, "The Sweet Sound of Automation," *IUD Digest*, Summer 1962; and

Charles Killingsworth, "Forward," *Annals of the American Academy of Political and Social Science*, March 1962.

13.   Ewan Clague and Leon Greenberg, "Employment," in John Dunlop, ed., *Automation and Technological Change* (Englewood Cliffs, N. J.: Prentice-Hall, 1962), 116, 119–20, 121, 127.

14.   Joint Economic Committee, *State of the Economy and Policies for Full Employment*, Hearings, 87th Congress, 2nd Session, 1962. The one economist raising structural concerns was Raymond Saulnier, 311.

15.   See, for example, Robert M. Solow, "Investment for Growth"; Moses Abramowitz, "Sources of Productivity Gains"; and James Knowles, "Why Unemployment Stays Up"; all in the *New Republic*, October 20, 1962; and Daniel Diamond, "Automation and the Growth of the Office Labor Force," *Business Topics*, Winter 1962. See also Solomon Fabricant, "Productivity," *Challenge*, December 1962, for an analysis of recent productivity trends that reached conclusions in sharp contrast with those of Clague and Greenberg in "Employment," *Automation*. For evidence that the neoclassical view was part of the continuing debates in addition to the deficient demand and structural positions, see Herbert Stein, "Reducing Unemployment—With or without Inflation?" *Industrial Relations*, October 1962. Also see Robert M. Solow, "A Policy for Full Employment," *Industrial Relations*, October 1962.

16.   For a sample of the popular debate, see "The March of the Robots," January 1963; "The Missing Links in Automation," February 1963; and "New Directions in Production," June 1963; all in *Dun's Review*; "Labor Dilemmas—Automation and Image," *Newsweek*, March 4, 1963; and "The Technological Revolution," *Challenge*, February, March, April, May, June, and July 1963. For professional response to this debate, see Yale Brozen, *Automation: The Impact of Technological Change* (Washington, D.C.: American Enterprise Institute, March 1963); William Peterson, "Automation and Unemployment—A Myth Revisited," *Christian Economics*, February 1963; and Edward Shils, *Automation and Industrial Relations* (New York: Holt, Rinehart and Winston, 1963). Policy issues related to this debate included continuing discussions of special unemployment assistance programs. See House, Committee on Education and Labor, *Youth Conservation Corps*, Hearings, 88th Congress, 1st Session, 1963; and House, Committee on Education and Labor, *Vocational Education Act of 1963*, Hearings, 88th Congress, 1st Session, 1963.

17.   U.S. President, *Economic Report of the President*, 1963.

18.   For a sample of current professional discussions of the tax cut, see House, Committee on Ways and Means, *President's 1963 Tax Message*, Hearings, 88th Congress, 1st Session, 1963, Parts 1 to 7; and a series of articles in *Challenge*, March, April, and May, 1963. Also see the U.S. President, *Manpower Report of the President*, 1963.

19.   Walter Heller, "The Administration's Fiscal Policy," in Ross, *Unemployment*, 95, 97, 104.

20.   Otto Eckstein, "Aggregate Demand and the Current Unemployment Problem," in Ross, *Unemployment*, 121. The Denison articles referred to are "Dispersion of Unemployment by SMSA 1950–60," and "Incidence of Unemployment by States and Regions 1950–60," mimeo.

21.   Arthur Ross, "The Problem of Unemployment," in Ross, *Unemployment*, 11.

22.   Seymour Wolfbein, "The First Year of the Manpower Act"; William Haber, "Next Steps in Labor Market Policy," 34, 36; both in Ross, *Unemployment*.

23.   Arthur Ross, "Conclusions," in Ross, *Unemployment*, 199, 202.

24. A great deal of relevant empirical work was published in this period, including Gertrude Bancroft and Stuart Garfinkle, "Job Mobility in 1961," *Monthly Labor Review*, August 1963; John Lansing, Eva Mueller, William Ladd, and Nancy Barth, *The Geographic Mobility of Labor: A First Report* (Ann Arbor, Mich.: Institute of Social Research, April 1963); June Meredith, "Labor Force and Employment, 1960–62," *Monthly Labor Review*, May 1963; Richard Wilcock and Walter Franke, *Unwanted Workers: Permanent Layoffs and Long-Term Unemployment* (New York: Free Press of Glencoe, 1963); Louis Ferman, *Death of a Newspaper: The Story of the Detroit Times* (Kalamazoo, Mich.: Upjohn Institute for Employment Research, April 1963); various papers in Gerald Somers, Edward Cushman, and Nat Weinberg, eds., *Adjusting to Technological Change* (New York: Harper and Row, 1963); Bureau of Labor Statistics, *Impact of Office Automation in the Internal Revenue Service*, BLS Bulletin 1364, July 1963; Bureau of Employment Security, *Experience of Other Countries in Dealing with Technological Unemployment*, BES No. ES-220, August 1963; Conley Dillon, "Area Redevelopment Act—What Has It Accomplished?" *Challenge*, April 1963; Arnold Weber, "Automation and Retraining," *Proceedings of the New York University Sixteenth Annual Conference on Labor* (New York: Bender, 1963); and the testimony by Gerald Somers before the Senate, Committee on Labor and Public Welfare, *Nation's Manpower Revolution*, Hearings, Part 2, 88th Congress, 1st Session, 1963. Popular articles included "Unemployment in America," *Newsweek*, April 1, 1963; and "The Point of No Return for Everybody—Automation: Its Impact Suddenly Shakes Up the Whole U.S.," *Life*, July 19, 1963. Also see Victor Fuchs, "Fallacies and Facts about Automation," *New York Times Magazine*, April 7, 1963, 27; Robert Solow, "Automation: Technique, Mystique, Critique," *Journal of Business*, April 1963; and Robert Lekachman, "Automation Is Nothing New," *Challenge*, April 1963.

25. All testimony was at the Senate, Committee on Labor, *Nation's*, Hearings, Part 1, 1963; quotes from pp. 1–2, 258, 260, 268, 275–76.

26. See Sar Levitan, statement, Senate, Committee on Labor, *Nation's*, Hearings, Part 2, 1963; and William Miernyk, statement, Senate, Committee on Labor, *Nation's*, Hearings, Part 3. Haber's testimony in Part 3 was identical to his April Conference on Unemployment paper.

27. Gerald Somers, "Research on the Manpower Implications of Technological Change," *Labor Law Journal*, August 1963, 672. For other examples of "differences in shading" in this period, see Sidney Sufrin, "A Problem Prolonged, Not Solved," *Challenge*, July 1963; and George P. Schultz, "Unemployment and Labor Market Policy," *Monthly Labor Review*, July 1963.

28. Other contributions from this period include William Haber, Louis Ferman, and James Hudson, *The Impact of Technological Change* (Kalamazoo, Mich.: Upjohn Institute for Employment Research, 1963); "The Great Information Revolution," *Dun's Review*, September 1963; papers at the Joint Computer Conference as reported in Robert MacBride, *The Automated State* (Philadelphia: Chilton, 1967), 20–23; A. J. Jaffe, "What Productivity Does to Jobs," *Business Week*, September 14, 1963; Lowell Gallaway, "Labor Mobility, Resource Allocation and Structural Unemployment," *American Economic Review*, September 1963; and a speech by Gardiner Ackley of the CEA, "Does Automation Cost Many Jobs?" *U.S. News and World Report*, September 1963.

29. Leon Keyserling, statement, Senate, Committee on Labor, *Nation's*, Hearings, Part 5, 1963; and Otto Eckstein, statement, Senate, Committee on Labor, *Nation's*, Hearings, Part 5, 1963.

30.   Charles Killingsworth, statement, Senate, Committee on Labor, *Nation's*, Hearings, Part 5, 1963, 1470.
31.   Killingsworth 1475–78.
32.   Killingsworth 1475, 1479–80.
33.   See the testimony by John Diebold, Isaac Auerback, Thomas Watson, John Snyder, Leon Greenberg, and A. J. Jaffe for examples of both popular and professional views on the subject. All statements were given at the Senate, Committee on Labor, *Nation's*, Hearings, Part 5, 1963.
34.   For a summary of Heller's speech, see Senate, Committee on Labor, *Nation's*, Hearings, Part 5, 1963, 1787–88.
35.   Charles Killingsworth, "Automation, Jobs, and Manpower," in *Automation and Public Welfare: Proceedings of a Conference Sponsored by the American Foundation on Automation and Employment*, October 7–9, 1963 (New York: American Public Welfare Association, 1964).
36.   Charles Killingsworth, "Unemployment and the Tax Cut," statement at the Senate, Committee on Labor, *Nation's*, Hearings, Part 5, 1963, 1792–93.
37.   Walter Heller, statement, Senate, Committee on Labor, *Nation's*, Hearings, Part 5, 1963, 1752, 1760–61.
38.   "Why Unemployment Stays High," *Business Week*, November 16, 1963, 136, 138, 143. See also "Automation Toll: How Serious?" *U.S. News and World Report*, October 14, 1963; and "Automation: Tranquilizing Myths," *Newsweek*, October 14, 1963.
39.   The references are to Sidney Sufrin, "Spreading the Work Won't Create More Jobs," and Daniel Diamond, "New Jobs for the Structurally Unemployed," both in *Challenge*, November 1963; Gunnar Myrdal, Neil Chamberlain, and Richard Nelson, statements, in Senate, Committee on Labor, *Nation's*, Hearings, Parts 8 and 9, 1963; Leon Keyserling, statement, Senate, Committee on Public Works, *Accelerated Public Works Program*, Hearings, 88th Congress, 1st Session, 1964; Robert Stein, "Work History, Attitudes, and Income of the Unemployed," *Monthly Labor Review*, December 1963; and Richard Lester, "The Structure and Organization of the Labor Market," *Proceedings of a Symposium on Employment*, American Bankers Association, February 23, 1964. For other examples of comments from the same period, see Seymour Wolfbein, "Unemployment and Manpower Development," and Gerald Somers, "Automation, Retraining and Public Welfare," both in *Automation and Public Welfare*, 1964; Daniel Fusfield, statement, Senate, Committee on Labor, *Nation's*, Hearings, Part 6, 1963; and Murray Brown and John deCani, "A Measure of Technological Employment," *Review of Economics and Statistics*, November 1963.

CHAPTER 9

1.   For a sample of popular and professional contributions during 1964 see Otis Lipstein and Kenneth Reed, *Transition to Automation*, University of Colorado Studies, Series in Business, No. 1, January 1964; *Jobs, Machines and People* (Santa Barbara, California: Center for Democratic Institutions, 1964); "New View of Manpower Needs," February 1964, and "How to Keep Up with Technology," March 1964, both in *Nation's Business*; Grace Hull, ed., *Conference on Automation*, Ohio State University, February 21, 1964; Leon Greenberg and Ewan Clague, "Automation: A Discussion of Research Methods," *Labour and Automation*, Bulletin No. 1, 1964; The Ad Hoc Committee on

the Triple Revolution, *The Triple Revolution*, March 22, 1964, Santa Barbara, California; Gardner Ackley and John Snyder, "Automation: Threat and Promise," *New York Times Magazine*, March 22, 1964; Yale Brozen, "Putting Economics and Automation into Perspective," *Automation*, April 1964; Ewan Clague, "What Employment Statistics Show," *Automation*, April 1964; Leon Greenberg, "The Relationship of Automation, Productivity and Employment: Current Developments in the United States," *Seminars on Private Adjustments to Automation and Technological Change*, U.S. President's Advisory Committee on Labor-Management Relations, May–June 1964; Harold S. Roberts, ed., *Automation: Some of Its Effects on the Economy and Labor* (Honolulu: University of Hawaii, 1964); Robert Cooney, "Automation: The Impact on Jobs and People," *American Federationist*, May 1964; Robinson Newcomb, "Five Ways to Cut Unemployment," *Nation's Business*, July 1964; Elliott Morss, "Needed: A Smaller Labor Force," *Challenge*, July 1964; John I. Snyder, "Automation and Unemployment: Management's Quiet Crisis," *The Personnel Job in a Changing World*, AMA Report No. 80, 1964; *Automation in General Electric: The Human Side of the Story* (New York: General Electric, 1964); *Automation and Employment* (Wilmington, Delaware: DuPont, 1964); Ralph Ellis, *Is Automation Causing Unemployment?*, National Association of Manufacturers, Industrial Relations Sourcebook Series, 1964; *Research Report Number Two: Automation* (Milwaukee, Wisconsin: The Manpower Research Council, 1964); Richard Beaumont and Roy Helfgott, *Management, Automation and People* (New York: Industrial Relations Counselors, 1964); and International Brotherhood of Pulp, Sulphite and Paper Mill Workers, *Automation: Economic Implications and Impact upon Collective Bargaining*, 1964.

2.   Norman Pauling, "Some Negelected Areas of Research on the Effects of Automation and Other Technological Change on Workers," *Journal of Business*, July 1964.

3.   U.S. President, *The Manpower Report of the President*, 1964, 30, 33.

4.   Robert M. Solow, "The Nature and Sources of Unemployment in the United States," *International Trade and Finance: A Collected Volume of Wicksell Lectures 1958–1964* (Stockholm: Almquist and Wiksell, 1965).

5.   Robert Aaron Gordon, "Has Structural Unemployment Worsened?" *Industrial Relations*, May 1964, 52, 54.

6.   See Arthur Burns, "The Federal Tax Cut and the National Economy," a June 10 speech at Oregon State University, published in *Challenge*, October 1964; Garth Mangum, "Employing the Unemployed," speech at the Conference of Business Economists, May 8, 1964; Sidney Sufrin, "The Crux: Demand and Employment," *Challenge*, June 1964; Bureau of Labor Statistics, *Labor Mobility and Private Pension Plans*, BLS Bulletin 1407, June 1964; Sidney Fine, *The Nature of Automated Jobs and Their Educational and Training Requirements* (McLean: Human Sciences Research Inc., June 1964); J. M. Culbertson, *Full Employment or Stagnation?* (New York: McGraw-Hill, 1964); Paul Sultan and Paul Prasow, "The Skill Impact of Automation," reprinted in Senate, Committee on Labor and Public Welfare, *Exploring the Dimensions of the Manpower Revolution*, Vol. I, 88th Congress, 2nd Session, 1964; Bureau of Labor Statistics, *Case Studies of Displaced Workers: Experiences of Workers after Layoff*, BLS Bulletin 1408, 1964; Victor Fuchs, *Productivity Trends in the Goods and Service Sectors, 1929–61: A Preliminary Survey*, NBER Occasional Paper 89, 1964; and Bureau of Labor Statistics, *Technological Trends in 36 Major American Industries*, a report prepared for the President's Advisory Committee on Labor-Management Relations, 1964.

7.   Richard D. Lipsey, "Structural and Deficient-Demand Unemployment Reconsid-

ered," in Arthur M. Ross, ed., *Employment Policy and the Labor Market* (Berkeley: University of California Press, 1965), 221, 235.

8.   Lipsey 242.

9.   Lipsey 247, 251.

10.   Barbara Berman, "Alternative Measures of Structural Unemployment," in Ross, *Employment*.

11.   See House, Committee on Education and Labor, *To Amend the Manpower Development and Training Act of 1962, As Amended*, Hearings, 89th Congress, 1st Session, 1965, 176.

12.   The papers were Otto Eckstein, "Perspectives on Employment under Technological Change"; George H. Hildebrand, "Some Alternative Views of the Unemployment Problem in the United States"; and Charles Killingsworth, "Structural Unemployment in the United States"; all in Jack Stieber, ed., *Employment Problems of Automation and Advanced Technology* (London: Macmillan, 1966), a report of a conference held July 19–24, 1964.   See also Ewan Clague, "Measurement of Technological Change"; Margaret Gordon, "The Comparative Experience with Retraining Programmes in the United States and Europe"; and Leonora Stettner, "Survey of Literature on Social and Economic Effects of Technological Change," all in the same volume.

13.   For a sample of the popular debates, see "Study Raises Automation Warning," *Nation's Business*, August 1964; "Humanizing Technological Change," *American Federationist*, August 1964; Samuel Saben, "Geographic Mobility and Employment Status," *Monthly Labor Review*, August 1964; Edwin Dale, "The Great Unemployment Fallacy," *New Republic*, September 5, 1964; letters debating the Dale article in the *New Republic* by Senator Clark (September 26), Lawrence Berlin (September 26), Oscar Gass (September 19), Stanley Sheinbaum (September 26), W. H. Ferry (September 19), William Miernyk (September 19), and Alvin Hansen (September 26); and J. James Miller, "Automation, Job Creation, and Unemployment," *Academy of Management Journal*, December 1964.   The professional articles referred to are Richard Pasternak, "Unemployment: A Crisis in Economic Theory," *Challenge*, October 1964; Margaret Gordon, "U.S. Manpower and Employment Policy," *Monthly Labor Review*, November 1964; Stanley Lebergott, "Unemployment: A Perspective," in Stanley Lebergott, ed., *Men without Work* (Englewood Cliffs, N. J.: Prentice-Hall, 1964); Charles Killingsworth, "Discussion," in *The Requirements of Automated Jobs*, North American Joint Conference, Washington, D.C., December 1964 (OECD; Paris, 1965); Barbara Berman and David Kaun, "Characteristics of Cyclical Recovery and the Measurement of Structural Unemployment," *Proceedings of the Business and Economic Statistics Section*, American Statistical Association, December 1964; and N. J. Simler, "Long-Term Unemployment, The Structural Hypothesis, and Public Policy," *American Economic Review*, December 1964.   For other comments from the same period, see William Miernyk, "Area Redevelopment Programs at Home and Abroad," *Proceedings of the Seventeenth Annual Meeting*, IRRA, December 1964; Leon Greenberg, "Technological Change, Productivity and Employment in the United States"; Seymour Wolfbein, "The Pace of Technological Change and the Factors Affecting It"; Ewan Clague, "Effects of Technological Change on Occupational Employment Patterns in the United States"; Louis Levine, "Effects of Technological Change on the Nature of Jobs"; and Robert C. Goodwin, "The Labor Force Adjustment of Workers Affected by Technological Change"; all in *The Requirements*.

14.   William Haber, *Business Topics*, November 1964.

15.   Charles Silberman, "Automation and the Labor Market," *Fortune*, January, February, April, May, and August, 1965; and Peter Drucker, "Automation Is Not the Vil-

lain," *New York Times Magazine*, January 10, 1965. Two other optimistic attacks were "Automation—We Can Handle It," *Look*, January 1965; and Virgil Day, "Automation, Employment and Unemployment," speech delivered February 15, 1965 at the Great Decisions Public Affairs Forum, Bloomington, Illinois. For a structuralist reply see "Jeremiahs and Pacifiers," *Nation*, February 8, 1965, 127.

16. U.S. President, *Economic Report of the President*, January 1965.

17. Joint Economic Committee, *January 1965 Economic Report of the President*, Hearings, Parts 1–4, 89th Congress, 1st Session, 1965.

18. All statements were in House, Committee on Education and Labor, *To Amend the Manpower Development and Training Act of 1962, as Amended*, Hearings, 89th Congress, 1st Session, 1965; Miernyk quotes from p. 176.

19. Charles Killingsworth, "Comment," *The Measurement and Interpretation of Job Vacancies* (New York: National Bureau of Economic Research, 1966).

20. For a sample of contemporary contributions, see Michael Borus, "Has Structural Unemployment Worsened?" and R. A. Gordon, "Reply to Mr. Borus," both in *Industrial Relations*, February 1965; Yale Brozen, "Automation: A Job Creator—Not a Job Destroyer," *U.S. News and World Report*, March 8, 1965; Clyde Dankert, "Automation, Unemployment and Shorter Hours," in Clyde Dankert, Floyd Mann, and Herbert Northrup, eds., *Hours of Work* (New York: Harper and Row, 1965); Robert Cissell and Helen Cissell, "Automation and Jobs," *America*, April 3, 1965; Bureau of Labor Statistics, *Outlook for Numerical Control of Machine Tools: A Study of a Key Technological Development in Metalworking Industries*, BLS Bulletin 1437, March 1965; and *Manpower Planning to Adapt to New Technology at an Electric and Gas Utility—A Case Study*, BLS Report No. 293, 1965. The reference is to U.S. President, *Manpower Report of the President*, 1965. Also see "Labor Force and Unemployment in 1964," *Monthly Labor Review*, April 1965.

21. Harold Taylor, statement, Joint Hearings, Senate Committee on Labor and Public Welfare, and House, Committee on Education and Labor, *1965 Manpower Report of the President*, Hearings, 89th Congress, 1st Session, 1965, 62; and Eli Ginzberg, statement, Joint Hearings, *1965 Manpower Report*, 1965.

22. Otto Eckstein, statement, Joint Hearings, *1965 Manpower Report*, 1965; and Charles Killingsworth, statement, Joint Hearings, *1965 Manpower Report*, 1965, 248, 270.

23. Denis Johnston, "Educational Attainment of Workers, March 1964," *Monthly Labor Review*, May 1965. For other relevant contributions see Lester Thurow, "The Changing Structure of Unemployment," *Review of Economics and Statistics*, May 1965; Vladimir Stoikov, "Structural Unemployment: Comment," and Lowell Gallaway, "Reply," *American Economic Review*, June 1965; and *The Effects of Automation on Occupations and Workers in Pennsylvania*, Pennsylvania State Employment Service, May 1965.

24. Arthur Okun, "The Role of Aggregate Demand in Alleviating Unemployment," in William Bowen and Frederick Harbison, *Unemployment in a Prosperous Economy*, A Report on the Princeton Manpower Symposium, May 13–14, 1965 (Princeton: Princeton University Press, 1965). The other papers were William Bowen, "Unemployment in the United States: Quantitative Dimensions"; and Charles Killingsworth, "Unemployment after the Tax Cut," both in Bowen and Harbison, *Unemployment*.

25. Richard Musgrave, "Demand versus Structural Unemployment," in Bowen and Harbison, *Unemployment*.

26. Robert Aaron Gordon, "The Current Business Expansion in Perspective," in

Robert Aaron Gordon and Margaret Gordon, *Prosperity and Unemployment* (New York: Wiley, 1966). Also see R. A. Gordon, "Introduction"; Otto Eckstein, "Discussion"; Joseph Pechman, "Discussion"; and Martin Gainsbrugh, "Discussion"; all in the same volume.

27. Margaret Gordon, "The Behavior of Employment, 1961–65"; Solomon Fabricant, "Discussion"; and Stanley Lebergott, "Discussion"; all in Gordon and Gordon, *Prosperity*.

28. Gertrude Bancroft, "Lessons from the Patterns of Unemployment in the Last Five Years"; Edward Kalachek, "The Composition of Unemployment and Public Policy"; Lester Thurow, "Discussion"; and Charles Killingsworth, "Discussion," 252; all in Gordon and Gordon, *Prosperity*.

29. Killingsworth 253–54.

30. Albert Rees, "Economic Expansion and Persisting Unemployment: An Overview," in Gordon and Gordon, *Prosperity*, 328.

31. Included among these were Seymour Wolfbein, *Employment, Unemployment and Public Policy* (New York: Random House, 1965); George Terborgh, *The Automation Hysteria* (New York: Norton, 1965); and Herbert Simon, "The Long-Range Economic Effects of Automation," in Herbert Simon, *The Shape of Automation for Men and Management* (New York: Harper Torch Books, 1965).

32. Gilpatrick, *Structural Unemployment*. Also see the introduction by William Miernyk in Gilpatrick, *Structural Unemployment*; and Gilpatrick, "On the Classification of Unemployment: A View of the Structural-Inadequate Demand Debate," *Industrial and Labor Relations Review*, January 1966.

33. The references are to George Hildebrand, "Reducing Unemployment: Problems and Policies," *Labor Law Journal*, August 1965; Robert M. Solow, "Technology and Unemployment," *Public Interest*, Fall 1965; Robert J. Flanagan, "Disguised Unemployment and the Structural Hypothesis," *Industrial Relations*, October 1965; Garth Mangum, "Economic Growth and Unemployment," in Juanita Kreps, *Technology, Manpower and Retirement Policy* (Cleveland: World, 1966); Otto Eckstein, "Employment and Retirement of Older Workers and National Economic Development," and Joseph Froomkin, "Implications of Technological Change for Jobs," both in Kreps, *Technology*; Clyde Dankert, "Comment," *Labor Law Journal*, August 1965; Robert L. Heilbroner, "Men and Machines in Perspective," *Public Interest*, Fall 1965; and William Gruber, "The Use of Labor Force Participation and Unemployment Rates as a Test for Structural Difficulties," in *Proceedings of the Eighteenth Annual Winter Meeting*, IRRA, December 1965. Also see Susan Holland, "Long-Term Unemployment in the United States," *Monthly Labor Review*, September 1965; M. C. Urquhart, in *The Requirements of Automated Jobs*, OECD, 1965; William Miernyk, statement, Senate, Committee on Labor and Public Welfare, *Employer Encouragement for On-the-Job-Training*, Hearings, 89th Congress, 1st and 2nd Sessions, 1965–66; Leon Greenberg, "Productivity Trends and Unemployment," in Kreps, *Technology*; Bernard Corry, "The Role of Technological Innovation in Theories of Income Distribution," *American Economic Review*, May 1966; Arnold Weber, "The Role and Limits of National Manpower Policies," and comments by Garth Mangum, both in *Proceedings*, IRRA, December 1965.

34. The references are to "Consumers on Upbeat" and "Forecasters Look Again—Upward," both in *Business Week*, October 9, 1965; "Help-Wanted—Almost Everywhere," *Business Week*, October 16, 1965; *Time*, November 12, 1965, 103; "Hitting a Faster Beat," *Business Week*, November 27, 1965; and *Business Week*, December 4, 1965, 27.

CHAPTER 10

1. U.S. President, *Economic Report of the President*, January 1966.

2. *Technology and the American Economy*, report of the National Commission on Technology, Automation and Economic Progress, February 1966. For reaction to the NCT report see Robert Lekachman, "The Automation Report," *Commentary*, May 1966; A. H. Raskin, "The Great Society: The Impact of Automation," *Vital Speeches*, July 1, 1966; "Machines Won't Take Over After All," *Business Week*, October 8, 1966; and Herbert Striner, "An Evaluation of the Report of the National Commission on Technology, Automation and Economic Progress," in *Proceedings of the Nineteenth Annual Winter Meeting*, IRRA, December 1966. The appendix papers were Walter Buckingham, "The Poverty and Unemployment Crisis," and Clyde Dankert, "Technological Change—Past and Present," both in NCT Appendix Vol. VI, *Statements Relating to the Impact of Technological Change*, February 1966.

3. Vladimir Stoikov, "Increasing Structural Unemployment Re-examined," *Industrial and Labor Relations Review*, April 1966; Robert Lekachman, "The Automation Report," *Commentary*, May 1966; and Barbara Bergmann and David Kaun, *Structural Unemployment in the United States* (Washington D.C.: Brookings Institution, 1966). Also see Robert Aaron Gordon, "Introduction," in Robert Aaron Gordon, ed., *Toward a Manpower Policy* (New York: Wiley, 1967).

4. George Iden, *The Determinants of Persistent High Unemployment in Major Labor Market Areas of the United States from 1950 to 1963* (Unpublished doctoral dissertation, Harvard University, 1966). See also George Iden, "Unemployment Classification of Major Labor Areas: 1950–65," *Journal of Human Resources*, Summer 1967. Donald Wells, *The United States' Unemployment Problem—Structural or Lack of Demand?* (Unpublished doctoral dissertation, University of Southern California, 1966). Mamoru Ishikawa, *Relevance of the Structural Hypothesis in Long-Term Unemployment* (Unpublished doctoral dissertation, Vanderbilt University, 1966).

5. Murray Brown, *On the Theory and Measurement of Technological Change* (Cambridge: Cambridge University Press, 1966), 165, 177.

6. See, for example, Edward Chase, "The Manpower Debate," *The Reporter*, October 20, 1966; Lloyd Ulman, "Automation in Perspective," in John R. Coleman, *The Changing American Economy* (New York: Basic Books, 1967); Richard Nelson, Merton Peck, and Edward Kalachek, *Technology, Economic Growth and Public Policy* (Washington, D.C.: Brookings Institution, 1967); Robert Aaron Gordon, *The Goal of Full Employment* (New York: Wiley, 1967); A. J. Jaffe and Joseph Froomkin, *Technology and Jobs: Automation in Perspective* (New York: Praeger, 1968); and Walter Heller, ed., *Perspectives on Economic Growth* (New York: Random House, 1968). The few other relevant comments included Arthur D. Butler, "Identifying Structural Unemployment," and Vladimir Stoikov, "Reply," both in *Industrial and Labor Relations Review*, April 1967; Einar Hardin, "Full Employment and Workers' Education," *Monthly Labor Review*, May 1967; Lowell Gallaway, *Interindustry Labor Mobility in the United States 1957 to 1960*, Social Security Administration, Research Report No. 18, 1967; and Robert McBride, *The Automated State: Computer Systems as a New Force in Society* (Philadelphia: Chilton, 1967).

7. Gerald Somers, *Retraining the Unemployed* (Madison: University of Wisconsin Press, 1968), 12; and Eli Ginzberg, *Manpower Agenda for America* (New York: McGraw-Hill, 1968).

8.   Charles Killingsworth, "Full Employment and the New Economics," May 16, 1968 speech at the University of Glasgow, printed in the *Scottish Journal of Political Economy*, February 1969, 4–5, 7, 10, 13, 18.

9.   Denis Johnston, "Education and the Labor Force," *Monthly Labor Review*, September 1968, 4.

10.   Johnston 11.

11.   Charles Killingsworth, "The Continuing Labor Market Twist," *Monthly Labor Review*, September 1968, 13.

12.   See Robert Aaron Gordon, "Unemployment Patterns with 'Full Employment,'" *Industrial Relations*, October 1968; Mahood Zaidi, "Structural Unemployment, Labor Market Efficiency and the Intrafactor Allocation Mechanism in the United States and Canada," *Southern Economic Journal*, January 1969; Lawrence Fulco, "How Mechanization of Harvesting Is Affecting Jobs," March 1969; Chester Myslicki, "Report on Productivity in the Automobile Industry," March 1969; John Henneberger, "Productivity Rises as Radio-TV Output Triples in 8 Years," March 1969; Joseph Ullman, "Helping Workers Find Jobs after a Shutdown," April 1969; Lawrence Fulco and Shelby Herman, "Productivity and Unit Labor Costs in 1968," June 1969; Herman Rothenberg, "Office Automation and the IRS," October 1969; Morton Lewis, "Adjusting to Technology on the Railroads," November 1969; and "Automation: Measuring Its Social Cost," August 1969; all in the *Monthly Labor Review*; and Betty Fishman and Leo Fishman, *Employment, Unemployment and Economic Growth* (New York: Crowell, 1969).

13.   Eva Mueller, *Technological Advance in an Expanding Economy: Its Impact on a Cross-Section of the Labor Force* (Ann Arbor, Mich.: Institute for Social Research, 1969), iii, 10–12, 70. Another study producing relevant data was Lowell Gallaway, *Geographic Labor Mobility in the United States 1957 to 1960*, Social Security Administration, Research Report No. 28, 1969, 110.

14.   Richard Perlman, *Labor Theory* (New York: Wiley, 1969).

15.   The papers referred to are Charles Killingsworth, "Fact and Fallacy in Labour Market Analysis," *Scottish Journal of Political Economy*, February 1970; Charles Killingsworth, "Rising Unemployment: A 'Transitional' Problem?" Senate, Committee on Labor and Public Welfare, *Manpower Development and Training Legislation, 1970*, Hearings, Part 3, 91st Congress, 1st and 2nd sessions, 1970; Charles Killingsworth, statement, Joint Economic Committee, *Current Labor Market Developments*, Part 1, Hearings, 92nd Congress, 1st Session, 1972; C. Duncan MacRae and Stuart O. Schweitzer, "Help-Wanted Advertising, Aggregate Unemployment, and Structural Change," *Proceedings of the Twenty-Third Annual Winter Meeting*, IRRA, December 1970; Lowell Gallaway, *Manpower Economics* (Homewood, Ill.: Richard D. Irwin, 1971); Denis Johnston, "The Labor Market 'Twist' 1964–69," *Monthly Labor Review*, July 1971; Ray Marshall and Richard Perlman, *An Anthology of Labor Economics: Readings and Commentary* (New York: Wiley, 1972); Edward Kalachek, *Labor Markets and Unemployment* (Belmont, California: Wadsworth, 1973); and Charles Killingsworth, "The Outlook for the Economy," *Proceedings of the New York University Twenty-Eighth Annual Conference on Labor* (New York: Bender, 1976). Also see Rajesh Kiran Mohindru, *A Study of Cyclical and Structural Unemployment in the United States in the Post-War Period* (Unpublished doctoral dissertation, University of Pennsylvania, 1969); Mordecai Lando, "Full Employment and the New Economics—A Comment," *Scottish Journal of Political Economy*, February 1970; A. M. Sum and T. P. Rush, "The Geographic Structure of Unemployment Rates," *Monthly Labor Review*, March 1975; U.S. President, *Manpower Report of the President*, 1973; Bureau of Labor

Statistics, *Technological Change and Manpower Trends in Six Industries*, BLS Bulletin 1817, 1974; *Technological Change and Manpower Trends in Five Industries*, BLS Bulletin 1856, 1975; Alan Fechter, *Forecasting the Impact of Technological Change on Manpower Utilization and Displacement: An Analytical Summary*, The Urban Institute, March 1974; and Larry Blair, *Technological Impact in the Labor Market: Conceptual Issues and State of the Art Study*, Human Resources Institute, University of Utah, no date.

CONCLUSION

1.   For a list of major European contributions in the early 1980s debates, see the references in Katsoulacos, *Employment Effect*, 156–59. For an excellent review of the issues raised by these debates, see Vivarelli, *Economics of Technology and Employment*. Following the same pattern as in the late years of the technological unemployment and structural unemployment debates, both Katsoulacos' and Vivarelli's books are revisions of Ph.D. theses and provide a thorough evaluation of the issues addressed in recent discussions. A new British journal, *Structural Change and Economic Dynamics*, devoted its first issue of June 1990 to the topic of structural change and unemployment. A review of the issues debated in the European discussions is included in "One Lump or Two," *The Economist*, November 25, 1995, 67–68.

2.   See, for example, Katherine G. Abraham, "Structural/Frictional v. Deficient Demand Unemployment: Some New Evidence," *American Economic Review*, September 1983; Eli Ginzburg, Thierry J. Noyelle, and Thomas M. Starbuck, Jr., *Technology and Employment: Concepts and Clarifications* (Boulder, Colorado: Westview Press, 1986); Stephen M. Hills, ed., *The Changing Labor Market: A Longitudinal Study of Young Men* (Lexington: Lexington Books, 1986); and Richard Cyert and David Mowery, eds., *The Impact of Technological Change on Employment and Economic Growth* (Cambridge, Mass.: Ballinger Publishing Co., 1988).

Selected Bibliography

Ackley, Gardiner, and John Snyder. "Automation: Threat and Promise." *New York Times Magazine*, 22 March 1964, 16.

Ad Hoc Committee on the Triple Revolution. *The Triple Revolution*. Santa Barbara: Ad Hoc Committee on the Triple Revolution, 1964.

Alexander, Magnus. "Unemployment Not Machine-Made." *Iron Age* 121 (15 March 1928): 733–34.

American Management Association. *The Personnel Job in a Changing World*. AMA Report No. 80. New York: American Management Association, 1964.

"The Automation Jobless: Not Fired, Just Not Hired." *Time* 77 (24 February 1961): 69.

"Automation Toll: How Serious?" *U.S. News and World Report* 55 (14 October 1963): 103.

Backhouse, Roger E., ed. *New Directions in Economic Methodology*. London: Routledge, 1994.

Baker, Elizabeth. "Machinery versus Trade Skills." In *Unemployment and Adult Education: A Symposium*, ed. Morse A. Cartwright, 27–30. New York: American Association for Adult Education, 1931.

———. "Discussion." *Bulletin of the Taylor Society* 15 (December 1930): 261–63.

———. "Unemployment and Technical Progress in Commercial Printing." *American Economic Review* 20 (September 1930): 442–66.

Bancroft, Gertrude. "Lessons from the Patterns of Unemployment in the Last Five Years." In *Prosperity and Unemployment*, ed. Robert Aaron Gordon and Margaret Gordon, 191–226. New York: Wiley, 1966.

Barnett, George E. *Chapters on Machinery and Labor*. Cambridge, Mass.: Harvard University Press, 1926.

Belfer, Nathan. "The Theory of the Automatic Reabsorption of Technologically Displaced Labor." *Southern Economic Journal* 16 (July 1949): 35–43.

———. "Technical Change and Technological Unemployment." Ph.D. diss., Harvard University, 1946.

Bell, Spurgeon. *Productivity, Wages and National Income*. Washington, D.C.: Brookings Institution, 1940.

Berg, Maxine. *The Machinery Question and the Making of Political Economy, 1815–1848*. Cambridge: Cambridge University Press, 1980.

Bergmann, Barbara, and David Kaun. *Structural Unemployment in the United States*. Washington, D.C.: Brookings Institution, 1966.

Berman, Barbara. "Alternative Measures of Structural Unemployment." In *Employment Policy and the Labor Market*, ed. Arthur M. Ross, 256–68. Berkeley: University of California Press, 1965.

———, and David Kaun. "Characteristics of Cyclical Recovery and the Measurement of Structural Unemployment." In *Proceedings of the Business and Economics Section*, American Statistical Association, 2. December 1964.

Black, John D. "Discussion." *American Economic Review, Supplement* 18 (March 1928): 171–72.

Blair, John M. "Labor Productivity and Industrial Prices." Ph.D. diss., The American University, 1941.

———, and Ruth Aull. "Technology and Economic Balance." U.S. Senate, Temporary National Economic Committee, *Technology in Our Economy*. Monograph No. 22. 76th Cong., 3rd Sess., 1941. 85–220.

Blaug, Mark. *The Methodology of Economics: Or How Economists Explain*. 2nd ed. Cambridge: Cambridge University Press, 1992.

Borus, Michael. "Has Structural Unemployment Worsened?" *Industrial Relations* 4 (February 1965): 111–14.

Bouniatian, Mentor. "Technical Progress and Unemployment." *International Labour Review* 22 (March 1933): 327–48.

Bowen, William. "Unemployment in the United States: Quantitative Dimensions." In *Unemployment in a Prosperous Economy*, ed. William Bowen and Frederick Harbison, 15–44. Princeton: Princeton University Press, 1965.

———, and Frederick Harbison, eds. *Unemployment in a Prosperous Economy*. Princeton, N. J.: Princeton University Press, 1965.

Bratt, Elmer. "Did Productivity Increase in the Twenties?" *Journal of the American Statistical Association* 34 (June 1939): 326–32.

Bright, James R. "Thinking Ahead." *Harvard Business Review* 33 (November–December 1955): 27–32, 156–66.

Brown, Murray. *On the Theory and Measurement of Technological Change*. Cambridge: Cambridge University Press, 1966.

———, and John deCani. "A Measure of Technological Unemployment." *Review of Economics and Statistics* 45 (November 1963): 386–94.

Brozen, Yale. *Automation: The Impact of Technological Change*. Washington, D.C.: American Enterprise Institute, 1966.

———. "Automation: A Job Creator—Not a Job Destroyer." *U.S. News and World Report* 58 (March 8, 1965): 94–100.

———. "Why Do We Have an Unemployment Problem?" In *Employment and Unemployment: The Problem of the 1960's*, Chamber of Commerce of the United States, 20–32. Washington, D.C.: Chamber of Commerce of the United States, 1961.

———. "The Economics of Automation." *American Economic Review* 47 (May 1957): 339–50.

———. "Some Economic Aspects of Technological Change." Ph.D. diss., University of Chicago, 1942.

Buckingham, Walter. "The Great Employment Controversy." *Annals of the American Academy of Political and Social Science* 340 (March 1962): 46–52.

————. *Automation: Its Impact on Business and People.* New York: Harper and Brothers, 1961.

Butler, Arthur D. "Identifying Structural Unemployment." *Industrial and Labor Relations Review* 20 (April 1967): 441–44.

Butler, Harold. *Unemployment Problems in the United States.* Geneva: International Labour Office, 1931.

Caldwell, Bruce. *Beyond Positivism: Economic Methodology in the Twentieth Century.* London: Allen and Unwin, 1982.

Cartwright, Morse A., ed. *Unemployment and Adult Education: A Symposium.* New York: American Association for Adult Education, 1931.

Chamber of Commerce of the United States. *Employment and Unemployment: The Problem of the 1960's.* Washington, D.C.: Chamber of Commerce of the United States, 1961.

Chamberlain, Neil. "Statement." U.S. Joint Economic Committee, *Employment, Growth and Price Levels.* Hearings. Part 8, 86th Cong., 1st Sess., 1959. 2703–7.

Clague, Ewan. "Statement." U.S. Joint Economic Committee, *Employment and Unemployment.* Hearings. 87th Cong., 1st Sess., 1962. 64–72, 92–97.

————, and Leon Greenberg. "Employment." In *Automation and Technological Change,* ed. John Dunlop, 114–31. Englewood Cliffs, N. J.: Prentice-Hall, 1962.

————, and Leon Greenberg. "Technological Change and Employment." *Monthly Labor Review* 85 (July 1962): 742–46.

————. "Automation and Unemployment." Statement by the Commissioner of Labor Statistics. Annual Convention, Massachusetts Labor Council. Boston, 29 September 1961.

————. "Productivity, Employment and Living Standards." Statement by the Commissioner of Labor Statistics. Conference on Productivity. Milwaukee: University of Wisconsin Industrial Relations Center, 4 June 1949.

————. "Memorandum on Technological Unemployment." U.S. Bureau of Labor Statistics. *Report of the Advisory Committee on Employment Statistics.* Bulletin 542, May 1931. 16–31.

————, and W. J. Couper. "The Readjustment of Workers Displaced by Plant Shutdowns." *Quarterly Journal of Economics* 45 (February 1931): 309–46.

————. "Productivity and Wages." *American Federationist* 34 (March 1927): 285–96.

Coleman, John R., ed. *The Changing American Economy.* New York: Basic Books, 1967.

Committee on Recent Economic Changes. *Recent Economic Changes in the United States.* 2 vols. New York: McGraw-Hill, 1929.

Committee on Technological Employment. "Report of the Committee on Technological Employment to the Secretary of Labor." U.S. Select Committee on Unemployment Insurance, *Unemployment Insurance.* Part 2, 72nd Cong., 1st Sess., 1931. 543–644.

Corey, Lewis. "An Estimate of Unemployment: Cyclical Idleness Added to Technological." *The Annalist* 31 (9 March 1928): 443–44.

Curtis, Thomas B. *87 Million Jobs.* New York: Duell, Sloan and Pierce, 1962.

Cyert, Richard, and David Mowery, eds. *The Impact of Technological Change on Employment and Economic Growth.* Cambridge, Mass.: Ballinger Publishing Co., 1988.

Dale, Edwin. "The Great Unemployment Fallacy." *New Republic* 151 (5 September 1964): 1–12.

Dalmulder, J. J. J. *On Econometrics: Some Suggestions Concerning the Method of Econometrics and Its Application to Studies Regarding the Influence of Rationalisation on Employment in the U.S.A.* Haarlem: De Erven F. Bohn N.V., 1937.

Dankert, Clyde. "Automation, Unemployment and Shorter Hours." In *Hours of Work*, ed. Clyde Dankert, Floyd Mann, and Herbert Northrup, 161–78. New York: Harper and Row, 1965.

————, Floyd Mann, and Herbert Northrup, eds. *Hours of Work*. New York: Harper and Row, 1965.

————. "Automation and Unemployment." U.S. Senate, Special Committee on Unemployment Problems, *Studies in Unemployment*. 86th Cong., 2nd Sess., 1960. 225–50.

————. "Technological Change and Unemployment." *Labor Law Journal* 10 (June 1959): 393–404.

————. *Sharing the Gains of Technological Change*. Hanover, Mass.: Amos Tuck School of Business Administration, Dartmouth College, 1955.

————. "Views on Machinery and Unemployment." *Scientific Monthly* 50 (February 1940): 155–62.

————. "Unemployment and Machinery." *Dalhousie Review* 13 (October 1933): 313–24.

Day, E. E., and Woodlief Thomas. *The Growth of Manufactures 1899–1923*. U.S. Bureau of the Census, Monograph VIII. Washington, D.C.: GPO, 1928.

Demsetz, Harold. "Structural Unemployment: A Reconsideration of the Evidence and the Theory." *Journal of Law and Economics* 4 (October 1961): 80–92.

Douglas, Paul. *Controlling Depressions*. New York: Norton, 1935.

————. "Technological Aspects of Unemployment." *Bulletin of the University of Georgia* (August 1933): 150–61.

————. "Technocracy." *The World Tomorrow* 16 (18 January, 1933): 59–61.

————. "Technological Unemployment." *American Federationist* 37 (August 1930): 923–50.

————. "Technological Unemployment: Measurement of the Elasticity of Demand as a Basis for Prediction of Labor Displacement." *Bulletin of the Taylor Society* 15 (December 1930): 254–61.

————. "Machinery and Unemployment." *Current History* 33 (October 1930): 42–46.

Drucker, Peter. "Automation Is Not the Villain." *New York Times Magazine* (10 January 1965): 26.

Dunlop, John T. *Automation and Technological Change*. Englewood Cliffs, N. J.: Prentice-Hall, 1962.

————. "Public Policy and Unemployment." U.S. Senate, Special Committee on Unemployment Problems, *Studies in Unemployment*. 86th Cong., 2nd Sess., 1960. 1–16.

Durand, E. Dana. "Progress in National Efficiency." In *The Fifteenth Annual Report of the Secretary of Commerce*, U.S. Department of Commerce, xxvii–xxxiii. Washington, D.C.: GPO, 1927.

Eckstein, Otto. "Discussion." In *Prosperity and Unemployment*, ed. Robert Aaron Gordon and Margaret Gordon, 48–56. New York: Wiley, 1966.

————. "Perspectives on Employment under Technological Change." In *Employment Problems of Automation and Advanced Technology*, ed. Jack Stieber, 86–104. London: Macmillan, 1966.

————. "Statement." U.S. Senate, Committee on Labor and Public Welfare, *Nation's Manpower Revolution*. Hearings. Part 5, 88th Cong., 1st Sess., 1963. 1406–13.

Eisermann, Gottfried, ed. *Wirtschaft und Kultursystem*. Stuttgart: Eugen Rentsch Verlag, 1955.

Ezekiel, Mordecai. "Productivity, Wage Rates and Employment." *American Economic Review* 30 (September 1940): 507–23.

————. "Population and Unemployment." *Annals of the American Academy of Political and Social Science* 188 (November 1936): 230–42.

Fabricant, Solomon. "Productivity and Prices." *Challenge* 11 (December 1962): 35–39.

————. "Basic Facts on Productivity Change: An Introduction by Solomon Fabricant." In *Productivity Trends in the United States*, John Kendrick, xxxv–lii. New York: National Bureau of Economic Research, 1961.

————. *Labor-Savings in American Industry, 1899–1939*. National Bureau of Economic Research Occasional Paper No. 23. New York: National Bureau of Economic Research, 1945.

————. *Employment in Manufacturing, 1899–1939: An Analysis of Its Relation to the Volume of Production*. New York: National Bureau of Economic Research, 1942.

————. *The Relation between Factory Employment and Output since 1899*. National Bureau of Economic Research Occasional Paper No. 4. New York: National Bureau of Economic Research, 1941.

Fackler, Walter. "Statement." U.S. Senate, Special Committee on Unemployment Problems, *Unemployment Problems*. Hearings. 86th Cong., 1st Sess., 1959. 44–75.

Feyerabend, Paul. *Against Method: Outline of an Anarchistic Theory of Knowledge*. London: New Left Books, 1975.

Fisher, Irving. "Full Employment: Prosperity's Problem." *Magazine of Wall Street* (7 April 1928): 1024–25.

Flanagan, Robert J. "Disguised Unemployment and the Structural Hypothesis." *Industrial Relations* 5 (October 1965): 23–36.

Froomkin, Joseph. *Technology and Jobs: Automation in Perspective*. New York: Praeger, 1968.

Fuchs, Victor. "Fallacies and Facts about Automation." *New York Times Magazine* (7 April 1963): 27.

Fukuoka, Masao. "Full Employment and Constant Coefficients of Production." *Quarterly Journal of Economics* 69 (February 1955): 23–44.

Gallaway, Lowell. "Labor Mobility, Resource Allocation and Structural Unemployment." *American Economic Review* 53 (September 1963): 694–716.

Garver, F. B. "Discussion." *Journal of the American Statistical Association, Supplement* 28 (March 1933): 39–41.

Gill, Corrington. "Statement." U.S. Senate, Temporary National Economic Committee, *Technology and Concentration of Economic Power*. Hearings. Part 30, 76th Cong., 3rd Sess., 1940. 17220–42.

Gilpatrick, Eleanor G. *Structural Unemployment and Aggregate Demand: A Study of Employment and Unemployment in the United States, 1948–1964*. Baltimore: Johns Hopkins University Press, 1966.

Ginzburg, Eli, Thierry J. Noyelle, and Thomas M. Starbuck, Jr. *Technology and Employment: Concepts and Clarifications*. Boulder, Colorado: Westview Press, 1986.

Glass, J. C., and W. Johnson. *Economics: Progression, Stagnation or Degeneration?* Ames: Iowa State University Press, 1989.

Gordon, Robert Aaron. "Unemployment Patterns with 'Full Employment'." *Industrial Relations* 8 (October 1968): 46–72.

————. *The Goal of Full Employment*. New York: Wiley, 1967.

————. "Introduction." In *Toward a Manpower Policy*, ed. Robert Aaron Gordon, 1–10. New York: Wiley, 1967.

————, ed. *Toward a Manpower Policy*. New York: Wiley, 1967.

————. "The Current Business Expansion in Perspective." In *Prosperity and Employment*, ed. Robert Aaron Gordon and Margaret Gordon, 14–47. New York: Wiley, 1966.

————. "Introduction." In *Prosperity and Unemployment*, ed. Robert Aaron Gordon and Margaret Gordon, 1–12. New York: Wiley, 1966.

————, and Margaret Gordon, eds. *Prosperity and Unemployment*. New York: Wiley, 1966.

————. "Reply to Mr. Borus." *Industrial Relations* 4 (February 1965): 114–15.

————. "Has Structural Unemployment Worsened?" *Industrial Relations* 3 (May 1964): 53–77.

Gourvitch, Alexander. *Survey of Economic Theory on Technological Change and Employment*. Washington, D.C.: GPO, May 1940.

Greenberg, Leon. "Productivity Trends and Unemployment." In *Technology, Manpower and Retirement Policy*, ed. Juanita Kreps, 33–38. Cleveland: World, 1966.

————. "Technological Change, Productivity, and Employment in the United States." In *The Requirements of Automated Jobs, Supplement*, North American Joint Conference on the Requirements of Automated Jobs, 13–36. Paris: Organisation for Economic Co-operation and Development, 1965.

Grether, Ewald, ed. *Essays in Social Economics in Honor of Jessica Blanche Peixotto*. Berkeley: University of California Press, 1935.

Gruber, William. "The Use of Labor Force Participation and Unemployment Rates as a Test for Structural Difficulties." In *Proceedings of the Eighteenth Annual Winter Meetings*, Industrial Relations Research Association, 220–32. December 1965.

Haber, William. "Next Steps in Labor Market Policy." In *Unemployment and the American Economy*, ed. Arthur M. Ross, 31–53. New York: Wiley, 1964.

————, Louis Ferman, and James Hudson. *The Impact of Technological Change*. Michigan: Upjohn Institute for Employment Research, 1963.

————. "The Persistence of Unemployment." *Labor Law Journal* 10 (July 1959): 451–54.

Haberler, Gottfried. "Some Remarks on Professor Hansen's View on Technological Unemployment." *Quarterly Journal of Economics* 46 (May 1932): 558–62.

Hagen, E. E. "Savings, Investment and Technological Unemployment." *American Economic Review* 32 (September 1942): 553–55.

Hamberg, Daniel. "Full Capacity versus Full Employment Growth." *Quarterly Journal of Economics* 66 (August 1952): 444–49.

Hansen, Alvin. "Institutional Frictions and Technological Unemployment." *Quarterly Journal of Economics* 46 (May 1932): 62–65.

————. "The Theory of Technological Progress and the Dislocation of Employment." *American Economic Review, Supplement* 22 (March 1932): 25–31.

————. "Institutional Frictions and Technological Unemployment." *Quarterly Journal of Economics* 45 (August 1931): 684–97.

Hausman, Daniel. *The Inexact and Separate Science of Economics*. Cambridge: Cambridge University Press, 1992.

Heller, Walter. "The Administration's Fiscal Policy." In *Unemployment and the American Economy*, ed. Arthur M. Ross, 93–115. New York: Wiley, 1964.

———. "Statement." U.S. Senate, Committee on Labor and Public Welfare, *Nation's Manpower Revolution*. Hearings. Part 5, 88th Cong., 1st Sess., 1963. 1751–69.

———. "The American Economy in 1961: Problems and Policies." U.S. Joint Economic Committee, *January 1961 Economic Report of the President*. Hearings. 87th Cong., 1st Sess., 1961. 309–419.

Hildebrand, George. "Some Alternative Views of the Unemployment Problem in the United States." In *Employment Problems of Automation and Advanced Technology*, ed. Jack Stieber, 105–27. London: Macmillan, 1966.

———. "Reducing Unemployment: Problems and Policies." *Labor Law Journal* 16 (August 1965): 477–85.

Iden, George. "The Determinants of Persistent High Unemployment in Major Labor Market Areas of the United States from 1950 to 1963." Ph.D. diss., Harvard University, 1966.

International Trade and Finance: A Collected Volume of Wicksell Lectures, 1958–64. Stockholm: Almquist and Wiksell, 1965.

Ishikawa, Mamoru. "Relevance of the Structural Hypothesis in Long-Term Unemployment." Ph.D. diss., Vanderbilt University, 1966.

Jaffe, A. J. "Statement." U.S. Senate, Committee on Labor and Public Welfare, *Nation's Manpower Revolution*. Hearings. Part 5, 88th Cong., 1st Sess., 1963. 1596–1613.

———. "What Productivity Does to Jobs." *Business Week* (14 September 1963): 188–89.

Jerome, Harry. *Mechanization in Industry*. New York: National Bureau of Economic Research, 1934.

———. "The Measurement of Productivity Changes and the Displacement of Labor." *American Economic Review, Supplement* 22 (March 1932): 32–40.

Johnston, Denis. "The Labor Market 'Twist' 1964–69." *Monthly Labor Review* 94 (July 1971): 26–36.

———. "Education and the Labor Force." *Monthly Labor Review* 91 (September 1968): 1–11.

———. "Educational Attainment of Workers, March 1964." *Monthly Labor Review* 88 (May 1965): 517–27.

Kahler, Alfred. "The Problem of Verifying the Theory of Technological Unemployment." *Social Research* 2 (November 1935): 439–60.

Kalachek, Edward. "The Composition of Unemployment and Public Policy." In *Prosperity and Unemployment*, ed. Robert Aaron Gordon and Margaret Gordon, 227–45. New York: Wiley, 1966.

Kaldor, Nicholas. "A Case against Technical Progress?" *Economica* 12 (May 1932): 180–96.

Katsoulacos, Y. S. *The Employment Effect of Technical Change*. Lincoln: University of Nebraska Press, 1986.

Keller, L. E. "Efficiency and Unemployment." *American Federationist* 37 (June 1930): 676–80.

Kendrick, John. *Productivity Trends in the United States*. New York: National Bureau of Economic Research, 1961.

Keyserling, Leon. "Statement." U.S. Senate, Committee on Public Works, *Accelerated Public Works Program*. Hearings. 88th Cong., 1st Sess., 1964. 199–242.

————. "Statement." U.S. Senate, Committee on Labor and Public Welfare, *Nation's Manpower Revolution*. Hearings. Part 5, 88th Cong., 1st Sess., 1963. 1349–93.

————. "Statement." U.S. Joint Economic Committee, *January 1962 Economic Report of the President*. Hearings. 87th Cong., 2nd Sess., 1962. 553–79.

Killingsworth, Charles. "The Outlook for the Economy." In *Proceedings of the New York University Twenty-Eighth Annual Conference on Labor*, 3–18. New York: Bender, 1976.

————. "Statement." U.S. Joint Economic Committee, *Current Labor Market Developments*. Hearings. Part 1, 92nd Cong., 1st Sess., 1972. 187–94.

————. "Rising Unemployment: A 'Transitional' Problem?" U.S. Senate, Committee on Labor and Public Welfare, *Manpower Development and Training Legislation, 1970*. Hearings. Part 3, 91st Cong., 1st and 2nd Sess., 1970. 1254–67.

————. "Fact and Fallacy in Labour Market Analysis." *Scottish Journal of Political Economy* 17 (February 1970): 95–107.

————. "Full Employment and the New Economics." *Scottish Journal of Political Economy* 16 (February 1969): 1–19.

————. "The Continuing Labor Market Twist." *Monthly Labor Review* 91 (September 1968): 12–17.

————. "Discussion." In *Prosperity and Unemployment*, ed. Robert Aaron Gordon and Margaret Gordon, 246–55. New York: Wiley, 1966.

————. "Structural Unemployment in the United States." In *Employment Problems of Automation and Advanced Technology*, ed. Jack Stieber, 128–56. London: Macmillan, 1966.

————. "Discussion." In *The Requirements of Automated Jobs, Supplement*, North American Joint Conference on the Requirements of Automated Jobs, 73–75. Paris: Organisation for Economic Co-operation and Development, 1965.

————. "Unemployment after the Tax Cut." In *Unemployment in a Prosperous Economy*, ed. William Bowen and Frederick Harbison, 82–92. Princeton, N. J.: Princeton University Press, 1965.

————. "Statement." U.S. Joint Hearings, Senate, Committee on Labor and Public Welfare, and House, Committee on Education and Labor, *1965 Manpower Report of the President*. Hearings. 89th Cong., 1st Sess., 1965. 248–52.

————. "Automation, Jobs and Manpower." In *Automation and Public Welfare*. Proceedings of a Conference sponsored by the American Foundation on Automation and Employment, Inc., October 7–9, 1963. New York: American Public Welfare Association, 1964. Reprinted in U.S. Senate, Committee on Labor and Public Welfare, *Nation's Manpower Revolution*. Hearings. Part 5, 88th Cong., 1st Sess., 1963. 1461–83.

————. "Unemployment and the Tax Cut." U.S. Senate, Committee on Labor and Public Welfare, *Nation's Manpower Revolution*. Hearings. Part 5, 88th Cong., 1st Sess., 1963. 1787–94.

————. "Foreword." *Annals of the American Academy of Political and Social Science* 342 (March 1962): viii–x.

————. "Automation in Manufacturing." In *Proceedings of the Eleventh Annual Meeting*, Industrial Relations Research Association, 20–32. December 1958.

King, Willford I. "The Relative Volume of Technological Unemployment." *Journal of the American Statistical Association, Supplement* 28 (March 1933): 33–41.

————. "The Effects of the New Industrial Revolution upon Our Economic Welfare." *Annals of the American Academy of Political and Social Science* 149 (May 1930): 165–72.

Knowles, James. "Why Unemployment Stays Up." *New Republic* 147 (20 October 1962): 18–19.

————, and Edward Kalachek. *Higher Unemployment Rates, 1957–60: Structural Transformation or Inadequate Demand?* U.S. Joint Economic Committee, 87th Cong., 1st Sess., 1961. 3–79.

Kreps, Juanita, ed. *Technology, Manpower and Retirement Policy.* Cleveland, Ohio: World, 1966.

Kuhn, Thomas. *The Structure of Scientific Revolutions.* Chicago: University of Chicago Press, 1962.

Lakatos, Imre, and A. Musgrave, eds. *Criticism and the Growth of Knowledge.* Cambridge: Cambridge University Press, 1970.

Lange, Oscar. *Price Flexibility and Employment.* Bloomington: Principia Press, 1945.

Lebergott, Stanley. "Unemployment: A Perspective." In *Men without Work,* ed. Stanley Lebergott, 1–53. Englewood Cliffs, N. J.: Prentice-Hall, 1964.

————, ed. *Men without Work.* Englewood Cliffs, N. J.: Prentice-Hall, 1964.

Lederer, Emil. "Technical Progress and Unemployment." *International Labour Review* 22 (July 1933): 1–25.

Lester, Richard. "Comments." In *The Labor Market and Social Security: Proceedings of the Fourth Annual Social Security Conference,* Upjohn Institute for Economic Research, 111–32. Kalamazoo, Mich.: Upjohn Institute for Economic Research, July 1962.

Lipsey, Richard D. "Structural and Deficient-Demand Unemployment Reconsidered." In *Employment Policy and the Labor Market,* ed. Arthur M. Ross, 210–55. Berkeley: University of California Press, 1965.

Long, Clarence. "Labor Force and Unemployment in the 1960's." In *Employment and Unemployment: The Problem of the 1960's,* Chamber of Commerce of the United States, 3–13. Washington, D.C.: Chamber of Commerce of the United States, 1961.

————. "A Theory of Creeping Unemployment and Labor Force Replacement." U.S. *Congressional Record.* 87th Cong., 1st Sess., 25 July 1961. 13430–38.

————. "Prosperity Unemployment and Its Relation to Economic Growth and Inflation." *American Economic Review* 50 (May 1960): 145–61.

————. "Statement." U.S. Senate, Special Committee on Unemployment Problems, *Unemployment Problems.* Hearings. 86th Cong., 1st Sess., 1959. 173–77.

Lonigan, Edna. "The Effects of Modern Technological Conditions on the Employment of Labor." *American Economic Review* 29 (June 1939): 246–59.

Lorwin, Lewis. "The Problem of Technological Unemployment—A Historical Survey." U.S. Temporary National Economic Committee, *Technology in Our Economy.* Monograph No. 22. 76th Cong., 3rd Sess., 1941. 3–83.

Lowe, Adolph. "Technological Unemployment Reexamined." In *Wirtschaft und Kultursystem,* ed. Gottfried Eisermann, 229–54. Stuttgart: Eugen Rentsch Verlag, 1955.

Lubin, Isador. "Statement." U.S. Senate, Temporary National Economic Committee, *Technology and Concentration of Economic Power.* Hearings. Part 30, 76th Cong., 3rd Sess., 1940. 17242–67.

————. "Finding the New Job." In *Unemployment and Adult Education: A Symposium,* ed. Morse A. Cartwright, 23–26. New York: American Association for Adult Education, 1931.

————. "Measuring the Labor Absorbing Power of American Industry." *Journal of the American Statistical Association, Supplement* 24 (March 1929): 27–32.

————. *The Absorption of the Unemployed by American Industry.* Washington, D.C.: Brookings Institution, 1929.

Mann, Lawrence B. "Occupational Shifts since 1920." *Journal of the American Statistical Association, Supplement* 24 (March 1929): 42–47.

Marshall, Ray, and Richard Perlman. *An Anthology of Labor Economics: Readings and Commentary.* New York: Wiley, 1972.

Martin, William McChesney. "Statement." U.S. Joint Economic Committee, *January 1961 Economic Report of the President.* Hearings. 87th Cong., 1st Sess., 1961. 462–501.

McCloskey, Donald N. *The Rhetoric of Economics.* Madison: University of Wisconsin Press, 1985.

Michael, Donald. *Cybernation: The Silent Conquest.* Santa Barbara: Center for the Study of Democratic Institutions, 1962.

Miernyk, William. "Statement." U.S. House, Committee on Education and Labor, *To Amend the Manpower Development and Training Act of 1962, As Amended.* Hearings. 89th Cong., 1st Sess., 1965. 176–79.

————. "Statement." U.S. Senate, Committee on Labor and Public Welfare, *Nation's Manpower Revolution.* Hearings. Part 3, 88th Cong., 1st Sess., 1963. 907–12.

Mills, Frederick C. *Employment Opportunities in Manufacturing Industries in the United States.* National Bureau of Economic Research Bulletin No. 70. New York: National Bureau of Economic Research, 1938.

————. "Industrial Productivity and Prices." *Journal of the American Statistical Association* 32 (June 1937): 247–62.

————. "Man and the Machine." *Today* 7 (28 November 1936): 6–7, 30.

————. *Prices in Recession and Recovery.* New York: National Bureau of Economic Research, 1936.

————. "Industrial Change and Unemployment." In *Essays in Social Economics in Honor of Jessica Blanche Peixotto,* ed. Ewald Grether, 227–45. Berkeley: University of California Press, 1935.

————. *Aspects of Manufacturing Operations during Recovery.* National Bureau of Economic Research Bulletin No. 56. New York: National Bureau of Economic Research, 1935.

————. *Changes in Prices, Manufacturing Costs and Industrial Productivity.* National Bureau of Economic Research Bulletin No. 53. New York: National Bureau of Economic Research, 1934.

————. *Economic Tendencies in the United States.* New York: National Bureau of Economic Research, 1932.

Mitchell, Wesley C. "Machines Make Jobs." *Nation's Business* 17 (September 1929): 43–45, 110–12.

————. "A Review." In *Recent Economic Changes,* ed. Committee on Recent Economic Changes, vol. II, 841–910. New York: McGraw-Hill, 1929.

Mohindru, Rajesh Kiran. "A Study of Cyclical and Structural Unemployment in the United States in the Post-War Period." Ph.D. diss., University of Pennsylvania, 1969.

Mueller, Eva. *Technological Advance in an Expanding Economy: Its Impact on a Cross-Section of the Labor Force.* Ann Arbor: Institute for Social Research, University of Michigan, 1969.

Musgrave, Richard. "Demand versus Structural Unemployment." In *Unemployment in a Prosperous Economy*, ed. William Bowen and Frederick Harbison, 93–97. Princeton, N. J.: Princeton University Press, 1965.

Myers, Robert J. "Occupational Readjustment of Displaced Skilled Workers." *Journal of Political Economy* 37 (August 1929): 473–89.

National Commission on Technology, Automation and Economic Progress. *Technology and the American Economy*. Princeton, N. J.: Princeton University Press, 1965.

Neisser, Hans. "'Permanent' Technological Unemployment: 'Demand for Commodities Is Not Demand for Labor.'" *American Economic Review* 32 (March 1942): 50–71.

North American Joint Conference on the Requirements of Automated Jobs. *The Requirements of Automated Jobs*. 2 vols. Paris: Organisation for Economic Cooperation and Development, 1965.

Okun, Arthur. "The Role of Aggregate Demand in Alleviating Unemployment." In *Unemployment in a Prosperous Economy*, ed. William Bowen and Frederick Harbison, 67–81. Princeton, N. J.: Princeton University Press, 1965.

Parnes, Herbert. "Statement." U.S. Senate, Special Committee on Unemployment Problems, *Unemployment Problems*. Hearings. 86th Cong., 1st Sess., 1959. 177–82.

Pasternak, Richard. "Unemployment: A Crisis in Economic Theory." *Challenge* 13 (October 1964): 17–19.

Patinkin, Don. "Price Flexibility and Full Employment." *American Economic Review* 38 (September 1948): 43–64.

Pauling, Norman. "Some Neglected Areas of Research on the Effects of Automation and Other Technological Change on Workers." *Journal of Business* 37 (July 1964): 261–73.

Pechman, Joseph. "Statement." U.S. Joint Economic Committee, *Current Economic Situation and Short-Run Outlook*. Hearings. 86th Cong., 2nd Sess., 1961. 108–9.

Perlman, Richard. *Labor Theory*. New York: Wiley, 1969.

"The Point of No Return for Everybody—Automation: Its Impact Suddenly Shakes up the Whole U.S.," *Life* 55 (19 July 1963): 68A–88.

Popper, Karl. *Conjectures and Refutations: The Growth of Scientific Knowledge*. 4th ed. London: Routledge and Kegan Paul, 1972.

President's Research Committee on Social Trends. *Recent Social Trends in the United States*. 2 vols. New York: McGraw-Hill, 1933.

"Productivity of Labor in Eleven Industries." *Monthly Labor Review* 24 (January 1927): 35–49.

Pu, Shou Shan. "Technological Progress and Employment." Ph.D. diss., Harvard University, 1949.

"The Question of Structural Unemployment." *Business Week* (25 March 1961): 52.

Rees, Albert. "Economic Expansion and Persisting Unemployment: An Overview." In *Prosperity and Unemployment*, ed. Robert Aaron Gordon and Margaret Gordon, 327–48. New York: Wiley, 1966.

Ross, Arthur M., ed. *Employment Policy and the Labor Market*. Berkeley: University of California Press, 1965.

———. "Conclusions." In *Unemployment and the American Economy*, ed. Arthur M. Ross, 199–211. New York: Wiley, 1964.

———. "The Problem of Unemployment." In *Unemployment and the American Economy*, ed. Arthur M. Ross, 1–27. New York: Wiley, 1964.

———, ed. *Unemployment and the American Economy*. New York: Wiley, 1964.

Roylance, William G. "Significance of Nonmechanical Factors in Labor Productivity and Displacement." *Monthly Labor Review* 37 (November 1933): 1028–38.

Ruttenberg, Stanley. "Structural Unemployment—Still a Problem in Our Economy." In *1961 Proceedings of the Business and Economics Statistics Section*, American Statistical Association, 156–61. December 1961.

Samuelson, Paul. "Statement." U.S. Joint Committee on Education and Labor, *Impact of Automation on Employment*. Hearings. 87th Cong., 1st Sess., 1961. 130–46.

Schultz, Charles. "Statement." U.S. Joint Economic Committee, *Current Economic Situation and Short-Run Outlook*. Hearings. 86th Cong., 2nd Sess., 1961. 114–22.

Seligman, Ben B. "Man, Work and the Automated Feast." *Commentary* 34 (July 1962): 9–19.

Silberman, Charles. "Automation and the Labor Market." *Fortune* 71 (January 1965): 124–27, 220–28; (February 1965): 153–55, 210–16; (April 1965): 130–33, 228–34; (May 1965): 112–15, 218–22; (August 1965): 156–61, 218–26.

Simler, N. J. "Long-Term Unemployment, the Structural Hypothesis, and Public Policy." *American Economic Review* 54 (December 1964): 985–1001.

Slichter, Sumner. "Implications of the Shorter Hour Movement." *Proceedings of the Academy of Political Science* 15 (January 1934): 63–75.

———. "Technological Unemployment: Lines of Action, Adaptation and Control." *American Economic Review, Supplement* 22 (March 1932): 41–54.

———. "The Problem of Technological Unemployment." In *Unemployment and Adult Education: A Symposium*, ed. Morse A. Cartwright, 31–39. New York: American Association for Adult Education, 1931.

———. "Discussion." *Bulletin of the Taylor Society* 15 (December 1930): 264–66.

———. "Market Shifts, Price Movements and Employment." *American Economic Review, Supplement* 19 (March 1929): 5–22.

———. "The Price of Industrial Progress." *New Republic* 53 (8 February 1928): 316–17.

Snyder, John I. "Automation and Unemployment: Management's Quiet Crisis." In *The Personnel Job in a Changing World*, American Management Association Report No. 80, 9–18. New York: American Management Association, 1964.

Somers, Gerald. "Research on the Manpower Implications of Technological Change." *Labor Law Journal* 14 (August 1963): 669–76.

Solow, Robert M. "Technology and Unemployment." *Public Interest* 1 (Fall 1965): 17–26.

———. "The Nature and Sources of Unemployment in the United States." In *International Trade and Finance: A Collected Volume of Wicksell Lectures, 1958–1964*, 253–91. Stockholm: Almquist and Wiksell, 1965.

———. "A Policy for Full Employment." *Industrial Relations* 2 (October 1962): 1–14.

Staehle, Hans. "Employment in Relation to Technical Progress." *Review of Economic Statistics* 22 (May 1940): 94–100.

Stein, Herbert. "Reducing Unemployment—With or without Inflation?" *Industrial Relations* 2 (October 1962): 15–27.

Stern, Boris. "Technological Displacement of Labor and Technological Unemployment." *Journal of the American Statistical Association, Supplement* 28 (March 1933): 42–47.

———. "Discussion." *American Economic Review, Supplement* 22 (March 1932): 55–62.

Stettner, Leonora. "Survey of Literature on Social and Economic Effects of Technological Change." In *Employment Problems of Automation and Advanced Technology*, ed. Jack Stieber, 451–79. London: Macmillan, 1966.

Stieber, Jack, ed. *Employment Problems of Automation and Advanced Technology*. London: Macmillan, 1966.

Stoikov, Vladimir. "Increasing Structural Unemployment Re-examined." *Industrial and Labor Relations Review* 19 (April 1966): 368–76.

———. "Structural Unemployment: Comment." *American Economic Review* 55 (June 1965): 527–31.

Sufrin, Sidney. "The Crux: Demand and Employment." *Challenge* 12 (June 1964): 6–9.

———. "Spreading the Work Won't Create More Jobs." *Challenge* 12 (November 1963): 29–31.

———. "A Problem Prolonged, Not Solved." *Challenge* 11 (July 1963): 8–10.

Taft, Philip, and Merton Stoltz. "Statement." U.S. Joint Economic Committee, *Employment, Growth and Price Levels*. Hearings. Part 8, 86th Cong., 1st Sess., 1959. 2707–32.

Taylor, Harold. "Statement." U.S. Joint Hearings, Senate, Committee on Labor and Public Welfare, and House, Committee on Education and Labor, *1965 Manpower Report of the President*. Hearings. 89th Cong., 1st Sess., 1965. 59–66.

Terborgh, George. *The Automation Hysteria*. New York: Norton, 1965.

Tinbergen, Jan. "The Influence of Productivity on Economic Welfare." *Economic Journal* 62 (March 1952): 68–86.

———, and Paul de Wolff. "A Simplified Model of the Causation of Technological Unemployment." *Econometrica* 7 (July 1939): 193–207.

Townsend, Edward. "The Human Equation: Automation and Displaced Workers." *Challenge* 9 (February 1961): 16–20.

Tugwell, Rexford G. "Occupational Obsolescence." In *Unemployment and Adult Education: A Symposium*, ed. Morse A. Cartwright, 20–22. New York: American Association for Adult Education, 1931.

———. "The Theory of Occupational Obsolescence." *Political Science Quarterly* 46 (June 1931): 171–227.

Ulman, Lloyd. "Automation in Perspective." In *The Changing American Economy*, ed. John R. Coleman, 182–200. New York: Basic Books, 1967.

United States. Bureau of Labor Statistics. "The Extent and Nature of Frictional Unemployment." U.S. Joint Economic Committee, *Employment, Growth and Price Levels*. Study Paper No. 6. 86th Cong. 1st Sess., 19 November 1959.

———. Congress. House. Committee on Education and Labor. *To Amend the Manpower Development and Training Act of 1962, As Amended*. Hearings. 89th Cong., 1st Sess., 1965.

———. Congress. House. Committee on Labor. *Investigation of Unemployment Caused by Labor-Saving Devices in Industry*. Hearings. 74th Cong., 2nd Sess., 1936.

———. Congress. Joint Committee on Education and Labor. *Impact of Automation on Employment*. Hearings. 87th Cong., 1st Sess., 1961.

———. Congress. Joint Economic Committee. *Current Labor Market Developments*. Hearings. 3 parts. 92nd Cong., 1st and 2nd Sess., 1972.

———. Congress. Joint Economic Committee. *Employment and Unemployment*. Hearings. 87th Cong., 1st Sess., 1962.

———. Congress. Joint Economic Committee. *January 1962 Economic Report of the President*. Hearings. 87th Cong., 2nd Sess., 1962.

——. Congress. Joint Economic Committee. *Current Economic Situation and Short-Run Outlook.* Hearings. 86th Cong., 2nd Sess., 1961.

——. Congress. Joint Economic Committee. *January 1961 Economic Report of the President.* Hearings. 87th Cong., 1st Sess., 1961.

——. Congress. Joint Economic Committee. *Employment, Growth and Price Levels.* Hearings. 10 parts. 86th Cong., 1st Sess., 1959.

——. Congress. Joint Hearings, Senate, Committee on Labor and Public Welfare, and House, Committee on Education and Labor. *1965 Manpower Report of the President.* Hearings. 89th Cong., 1st Sess., 1965.

——. Congress. Senate. Committee on Labor and Public Welfare. *Manpower Development and Training Legislation, 1970.* Hearings. 4 parts. 91st Cong., 1st and 2nd Sess., 1970.

——. Congress. Senate. Committee on Labor and Public Welfare. *Nation's Manpower Revolution.* Hearings. 10 parts. 88th Cong., 1st and 2nd Sess., 1963–64.

——. Congress. Senate. Committee on Public Works. *Accelerated Public Works Program.* Hearings. 88th Cong., 1st Sess., 1964.

——. Congress. Senate. Select Committee on Unemployment Insurance. *Unemployment Insurance.* Hearings. 2 parts. 72nd Cong., 1st Sess., 1931.

——. Congress. Senate. Special Committee on Unemployment Problems. *Studies in Unemployment.* 86th Cong., 2nd Sess., 1960.

——. Congress. Senate. Special Committee on Unemployment Problems. *Unemployment Problems.* Hearings. 7 parts. 86th Cong., 1st Sess., 1959.

——. Congress. Senate. Temporary National Economic Committee. *Technology in Our Economy.* Monograph No. 22. 76th Cong., 3rd Sess., 1941.

——. Congress. Senate. Temporary National Economic Committee. *Technology and Concentration of Economic Power.* Hearings. 31 parts. 76th Cong., 3rd Sess., 1940.

——. Department of Commerce. *The Fifteenth Annual Report of the Secretary of Commerce.* Washington, D.C.: GPO, 1927.

——. National Resources Committee. *Technological Trends and National Policy.* Washington, D.C.: GPO, 1937.

——. President. *Economic Report of the President.* Washington, D.C.: GPO, 1961; 1962; 1963; 1964; 1965; 1966.

——. President. *The Manpower Report of the President.* Washington, D.C.: GPO, 1963; 1964; 1965.

——. President's Advisory Committee on Labor–Management Policy. *Seminars on Private Adjustments to Automation and Technological Change.* Washington, D.C.: GPO, 1964.

Upjohn Institute for Economic Research. *The Labor Market and Social Security: Proceedings of the Fourth Annual Social Security Conference.* Kalamazoo, Mich.: Upjohn Institute for Economic Research, July 1962.

Vinogradoff, D. I. "Effects of a Technological Improvement on Employment." *Econometrica* 1 (October 1933): 410–17.

Vivarelli, Marco. *The Economics of Technology and Employment.* Aldershot, England: Edward Elgar, 1995.

Weintraub, David, and Irving Kaplan. *Summary of Findings to Date, March 1938.* National Research Project Report G-3. Washington, D.C.: National Research Project, 1938.

——, and Lewis Hine. *Technological Change.* Washington, D.C.: National Research Project, 1937.

————, and Harold Posner. *Unemployment and Increasing Productivity*. National Research Project Report G-1. Washington, D.C.: National Research Project, 1937.

————. "The Displacement of Workers through Increases in Efficiency and Their Absorption by Industry." *Journal of the American Statistical Association* 27 (December 1932): 383–400.

Wells, Donald. "The United States' Unemployment Problem—Structural or Lack of Demand?" Ph.D. diss., University of Southern California, 1966.

"When Machines Have Jobs—And Workers Do Not." *U. S. News and World Report* 50 (6 February 1961): 76–78, 87–90.

White, R. C. "Technological Unemployment." *Social Forces* 9 (June 1931): 572–81.

"Why Unemployment Stays High." *Business Week* (16 November 1963): 133–43.

Wilcock, Richard, and Walter Franke. "Will Economic Growth Solve the Problem of Long-Term Unemployment?" In *Proceedings of the Fourteenth Annual Meeting*, Industrial Relations Research Association, 37–49. December 1961.

Witte, James G. "Automatic Production and Unemployment: A Theoretical Analysis." Ph.D. diss., Indiana University, 1956.

Wolman, Leo. "Machinery and Unemployment." *The Nation* 136 (22 February 1933): 202–4.

Woytinski, Vladimir. *Three Sources of Unemployment*. International Labour Office, Studies and Reports, Series C, No. 20. Geneva: International Labour Office, 1935.

Wright, Chester M. "A Nation of Men—Or Machines?" *Nation's Business* 16 (September 1928): 39–40.

Wright, James L. "Is the Machine Replacing Man?" *Nation's Business* 15 (September 1927): 78–80.

————. "Need We Be Afraid of a Job Famine?" *Nation's Business* 15 (January 1927): 22–24.

Wubnig, Arthur. "The Measurement of the Technological Factor in Labor Productivity." *Journal of the American Statistical Association* 34 (June 1939): 19–25.

Index

Ackley, Gardner, 97, 118; changes in views, 139–40

Adams, Arthur B., 44

Ad Hoc Committee on the Triple Revolution, 8

AFL-CIO, 112, 118

Alexander, Magnus, 36

American Assembly, papers at meetings of, 96–97

American Association for Adult Education, papers at meetings of, 37–38, 49–50

American Bankers Association, on structural unemployment, 112

American Council on Education, papers at meetings of, 105

American Economic Association, papers at meetings of, 32, 40–41, 80

American Economic Review, articles in, 38

American Federationist, The, articles in, 37

American Federation of Labor, 37; new wage policy, 23

American Foundation on Automation and Employment, papers at meetings of, 105–106

American Statistical Association, papers at meetings of, 27, 64–65

American Technotax Society, 59

America's Capacity to Produce (Brookings Institution), 62

Annalist, The, articles in, 25

Apel, Hans, on automation, 9

Area Development Assistance Act, 97

Austrian School, 21

automation: Congressional hearings on, 77, 100–101; origin of term, 77, 160 n.1; as a popular issue, 77–78, 84, 93, 95–99, 112, 161–62 nn.2, 3; studies of effects, 78–79, 127–28, 133–36, 164 n.7

Automation Hysteria, The (Terborgh), 8

Automation: The Awesome Servant, 96

Babbage, Charles, 17

Baker, Elizabeth, 38, 76; 1930s displaced workers study, 48–50, 52, 57, 64, 67

Bakke, E. Wight, 99

Baltimore Sun, 7

Bancroft, Gertrude, on structural unemployment, 122

Barkin, Solomon, on structural unemployment, 94

Barnett, George E., case studies of technological change, 23, 30, 49–51

Barton, John, 17
Bayesian learning-from-experience, 4,
    9, 13, 74–75, 138–40
Beard, Charles, 38
Belfer, Nathan, 12, 72; on
    technological unemployment, 71
Bell, Spurgeon, 67, 76; Ezekiel on,
    66–67; on technological
    unemployment, 66
Bergmann, Barbara, on structural
    unemployment, 129
Berman, Barbara, 7, 114, 124, 135,
    137, 141; on structural
    unemployment, 116–18
Beveridge, William, on
    unemployment, 21
Black, John D., 26; on 1920s
    productivity advances, 27, 29
Blair, John M., 65; on technological
    unemployment, 67
Blaug, Mark, 3, 15
Borus, Michael, 141
Bouniatian, Mentor: on compensation
    argument, 42; on Lederer, 42; on
    Say's Law, 42
Bowen, William, on structural
    unemployment, 121
Brookings Institution, 70, 75;
    publications by, 30–31, 61–62, 66
Brown, Murray, 7, 9, 141; on
    structural unemployment, 129
Brozen, Yale, 139; changes in views,
    138
Buckingham, Walter, 134; on
    automation, 96, 128; changes in
    views, 138
Bureau of Commerce, 1920s
    productivity studies, 23–24, 28–30,
    33, 50, 74
Bureau of Employment Security, 101
Bureau of Labor Statistics, 10, 63, 96,
    121; early productivity studies, 23–
    24, 27–28, 32–33, 49–52, 55–56,
    74, 150 nn.2, 3, 5; studies of
    structural unemployment, 80–81,
    88–89
Bureau of the Census, 90; 1920s
    productivity studies, 23–24, 33, 74
business cycles, theories of, 44

Business Week, articles in, 96, 108,
    124–25
Butler, Harold, 76, 141; on
    technological unemployment, 50–
    51

Caldwell, Bruce, 3, 15
Census of Occupations, 27, 29
Census of Unemployment, 55, 57
Challenge, articles in, 108–109
Chalmers, Thomas, 17
Chamberlain, Neil, 141–42; changes in
    views, 139–40; on structural
    unemployment, 79, 109
changes in views of economists, 4, 9,
    13, 74–75, 138–40
Chase Manhattan Bank, survey of
    professional opinion, 117, 123
Clague, Ewan, 10, 13, 136; changes in
    views, 138; on empirical
    methodology, 51, 62; on 1920s
    productivity advances, 24; 1930s
    displaced workers study, 48–51,
    54, 57, 64, 67, 73, 76; on structural
    unemployment, 96; on
    technological unemployment, 28–
    29
Clark, John Bates, 21
Clark, John Maurice, 44
Classical School, 2, 37, 39; on
    technological change and
    employment, 17–20
Collander, David, 15; on economics as
    a discipline, 13
Committee on Education and Labor, 30
Committee on Labor and Public
    Welfare, testimony at hearings,
    100–109
Commons, John R., on technological
    unemployment, 27
compensation argument, 2, 40, 44;
    Bouniatian on, 42; Douglas on, 37;
    Hansen on, 39; Say's Law and, 17–
    19; Schumpeter on, 22; Tugwell
    on, 38; Vivarelli on, 5; wages fund
    and, 18–19
Conference on Unemployment, papers
    at, 98–100, 107
Corey, Lewis, on technological

unemployment, 25
Council of Economic Advisers, 85–87,
    98, 100, 103, 105, 107, 113, 122–
    23, 128, 135, 139, 141; members
    of, 85, 95, 97, 114, 117–18, 120–
    21; on structural unemployment,
    84–86, 95–96, 102, 108, 111–12;
    on unemployment, 97–98, 102,
    106, 121, 127
Couper, W. J., 1930s displaced
    workers study, 48–51, 64, 67, 73,
    76
Current Economic Situation, hearings,
    82–83
Curtis, Thomas, 84; on structural
    unemployment, 83, 112, 118
Cybernation: The Silent Conquest
    (Michael), 95

Dalmulder, J. J. J., on technological
    unemployment, 65
Dankert, Clyde: changes in views, 138;
    history of technological
    unemployment debates, 128; on
    structural unemployment, 124
data limitations, problems of, 6, 145;
    in structural unemployment
    debates, 99, 108, 121, 141–42; in
    technological unemployment
    debates, 32–33, 47, 50, 57, 59, 75–
    76, 137–38, 140–42, 158 n.6
Davis, James J., on technological
    unemployment, 24–25
Day, E. E., 32
Demsetz, Harold, 88, 114, 129, 137,
    141; on structural unemployment,
    86–87, 89
Denison, Edward, 98, 101, 107, 113–
    14, 135
Dennison, Henry, 31, 33
Department of Labor, 101; on
    structural unemployment, 102, 108,
    111–13
de Wolff, Paul, on technological
    unemployment, 65
Diamond, Daniel: on automation, 96;
    on structural unemployment, 109
Diebold, John, on automation, 96
displaced workers studies, 73, 75; in

1920s, 30–31, 78; in 1930s, 48–52,
    57, 64, 67, 157 n.12; in 1950s, 78–
    79, 164 n.7; in 1960s, 133–35
doctoral dissertations, significance of,
    6, 9, 71, 124, 129, 181 n.1
Douglas, Paul, 9, 14, 27, 39–41, 43–
    44, 50–51, 71–73, 76; changes in
    views, 74; on 1920s productivity
    advances, 26; on Say's law, 37, 43;
    on Technocracy, 43; on
    technological unemployment, 37–
    38, 43, 47–48, 151 n.15
Drucker, Peter, 119; on structural
    unemployment, 118
Dunlop, John, on structural
    unemployment, 81–82, 101
Durand, E. Dana, 26, 51

Eckstein, Otto, 10, 99, 107, 113–14,
    118, 135, 137; changes in views,
    139–40; on structural
    unemployment, 98–99, 117, 120,
    122, 124; on unemployment, 97,
    102–103
Econometrica, articles in, 65
econometrics: in structural
    unemployment debates, 88, 90,
    115, 124; in technological
    unemployment debates, 65, 68
Economic Report of the President, 94;
    hearings, 84–86, 95, 98, 112–13,
    118, 123, 127, 130; on policy, 98,
    127; on structural unemployment,
    84, 95, 111–12, 118
Economic Tendencies in the United
    States (Mills), 53, 60
Effects of Machinery on Wages, The
    (Nicholson), 20
empirical studies: adequacy of
    theoretical foundations for, 6–7,
    13, 51–52, 62, 64, 87–88, 115,
    117, 120–21, 124, 129, 135, 137,
    141–42; 1920s conflict with
    professional expectations, 26, 29,
    31–33, 62; initial approaches in
    1920s, 29–31, 47; new approaches
    in 1930s, 47–50; importance in
    1960s, 82, 88, 94, 115–17, 135–38,
    140–42; and progress in debates,

76, 142

Employment Act of 1946, symposium on, 128

Employment and Unemployment, hearings, 88

Employment in Manufacturing (Fabricant), 89

Employment Problems of Automation and Advanced Technology, conference papers, 117

Employment Stabilization Research Institute, 48

Europe, technological unemployment debates in, 42, 143, 181 n.1

Ezekiel, Mordecai, 61, 76; on Bell, 66–67; changes in views, 75

Fabricant, Solomon, 63, 67, 89, 97, 137; changes in views, 138; on structural unemployment, 122; on technological unemployment, 65–66

Fackler, Walter, on structural unemployment, 112

falsifiability, 3, 10; evidence for, 12–13

Federal Reserve Board, 24, 54, 63, 118; on structural unemployment, 102

Fellner, William, on stagnation thesis, 45

Feyerabend, Paul, 3, 10. *See also* methodological pluralism

Fisher, Irving, on technological unemployment, 28

Flakner, R. P., 27

Flanagan, Robert, on structural unemployment, 124

Fortune, articles in, 118

Franke, Walter, on structural unemployment, 94

frictional unemployment, definition of, 80; extent of, 80–81, 83

Friedman, Milton, 93

Froomkin, Joseph, on structural unemployment, 124

Fukuoka, Masao, 9

full employment, unemployment at, 83, 85, 89, 95, 104–106, 113, 120,

123, 128, 130–31, 139, 142

Gainsbrugh, Martin, on structural unemployment, 122

Galbraith, John Kenneth, 4; on structural unemployment, 118

Gallaway, Lowell, 141; changes in views, 139–40; on structural unemployment, 135

Garver, F. B., 76; on Say's Law, 55; on technological unemployment, 55–56

General Glut controversy, 19

General Theory of Employment, Interest and Money (Keynes), 44, 70

Gill, Corrington, 65

Gilpatrick, Eleanor, 9, 10, 13–14, 135, 137, 141–42; on structural unemployment, 6–7, 123–24

Ginzberg, Eli, 142; changes in views, 139–40; on structural unemployment, 101, 119–20, 130

Glass, J. C., 3, 15

Goldfinger, Nat, 99

Gordon, Kermit, 85, 95, 97

Gordon, Margaret, on structural unemployment, 118, 122

Gordon, Robert Aaron, 10, 135–36, 141; changes in views, 139–40; on structural unemployment, 114, 122

Great Depression, 25, 33, 35–36, 59, 153 n.1

Great Society program, 112

Green, William, on technological unemployment, 35

Greenberg, Leon, 136; changes in views, 139–40; on structural unemployment, 96

Gruber, William, on structural unemployment, 124

Haber, William, 9, 100; changes in views, 138; on structural unemployment, 99, 101, 118

Haberler, Gottfried, 43, 72, 74; on technological unemployment, 41

Hadley, Arthur, 20

Hagen, Everett E., 12, 69, 71–72; on

technological unemployment, 70
Hamberg, Daniel, 9
Hansen, Alvin, 43, 72, 74, 141;
    changes in views, 75, 138; on price
    flexibility, 40–41; on Say's Law,
    39; on technological
    unemployment, 39–41; stagnation
    thesis, 45
Harris, Seymour, on structural
    unemployment, 118
Hausman, Daniel, 3, 15; on economics
    as a discipline, 13–14
Hazlitt, Henry, on automation, 96
Heilbroner, Robert, on structural
    unemployment, 124
Heller, Walter, 9, 14, 85, 95, 97, 99,
    103, 113–14, 136–37, 140–41, 168
    n.29; changes in views, 139–40;
    Killingsworth on, 105–106, 108; on
    Killingsworth, 105, 107–108, 112;
    on structural unemployment, 98,
    105, 107, 112
Hicks, John R., 4; on Kaldor, 44
Hildebrand, George, 9, 142; changes in
    views, 139, on structural
    unemployment, 117, 124
histories of economic ideas, reasons to
    read, 2–4

Iden, George, on structural
    unemployment, 129
Industrial and Labor Relations
    Review, articles in, 128–29
Industrial Relations Research
    Association, papers at meetings of,
    94
Industrial Revolution, 17
inflation, and demand policy, 84, 94,
    98, 114, 116, 127, 138–39, 141
innovations, product and process, 4–5,
    144
International Institute of Social
    Research, 48
International Labour Office,
    publications of, 50–51, 117
Interstate Commerce Commission, 27
interviews, 148 n.19
Ishikawa, Mamoru, on structural
    unemployment, 129

Italy, technological unemployment in,
    7–8

Jaffe, A. J., 113; changes in views,
    139–40
Jerome, Harry, 10, 13, 61, 76; on
    empirical methodology, 52, 62;
    impact of work, 73; on
    technological unemployment, 60
Johnson, Lyndon, 112
Johnson, W., 3, 15
Johnston, Denis: on Killingsworth,
    132–33; on structural
    unemployment, 121, 131–32, 135
Joint Economic Committee, 128; staff
    study of structural unemployment,
    88–91, 95; testimony at hearings,
    79–80, 82–86, 88–91, 94–95, 97–
    98, 112, 118, 127
Journal of Commerce, articles in, 25
Journal of the American Statistical
    Association, articles in, 54–56, 76

Kahler, Alfred, 63–64, 76; on
    technological unemployment, 61
Kalachek, Edward, 14, 101; changes in
    views, 139–40; Knowles-Kalachek
    study, 90, 93–100, 107, 114–15,
    120, 130, 135–37, 141–42; on
    structural unemployment, 88–91,
    122, 135
Kaldor, Nicholas, 43, 72: Hicks on, 44;
    on price flexibility, 42; on
    technological unemployment, 42
Katsoulacos, Y. S., 4, 6, 14, 181 n.1;
    theoretical conclusions, 4–5
Kaufman, Jacob, on structural
    unemployment, 80
Kaun, David, on structural
    unemployment, 118, 129
Keller, L. E., on technological
    unemployment, 35
Kendrick, John, 89, 96, 97, 101; on
    structural unemployment, 94
Kennedy, John F., 84, 96, 102, 168
    n.29
Keynes, John Maynard, 2, 70; theory
    of business cycles, 44
Keynesian economics, 2, 4, 10–12; and

structural unemployment debates, 78, 81–83, 85, 93, 97, 100, 122, 129–31, 136–37, 144; and technological unemployment debates, 69–73

Keyserling, Leon: changes in views, 139–40; on unemployment, 97, 102, 109, 112, 118

Killingsworth, Charles, 14, 136–37, 141–42; on automation, 96, 103; changes in views, 139–40; Heller on, 105, 107–108, 112; on Heller, 105–106, 108; Johnston on, 132–33; on structural unemployment, 94–95, 103–107, 117–23, 130–33, 135

Kimball, Dexter, 31

King, Willford, 55–56, 76; changes in views, 75; on technological unemployment, 54–55, 57

Knappen, Theodore, on technological unemployment, 36

Knowles, James, 14, 101; Knowles-Kalachek study, 90, 93–100, 107, 114–15, 120, 130, 135–37, 141–42; on structural unemployment, 88–91

Korean War, 77; recessions after, 78

Kuhn, Thomas, 3, 10–12

Labor Market and Social Security, conference papers, 94–95

Laidler, Harry, on technological unemployment, 35

Lakatos, Imre, 3, 10, 11–12

Lange, Oscar, 12, 72; on technological unemployment, 71

Lauck, W. Jett, on technological unemployment, 28

Lausanne School, 21

Lebergott, Stanley, on structural unemployment, 118, 122

Lederer, Emil, 43; Bouniatian on, 42; changes in views, 75; on technological unemployment, 42–43

Leiserson, William, on technological unemployment, 28–29

Lekachman, Robert, on Keynesian economics, 128–29

Lester, Richard, on structural unemployment, 94–95, 109, 119

Lipsey, Richard, 7, 10, 13, 114, 123–24, 129, 135, 137, 141–42; on empirical studies, 115; on Phillips Curve, 115; on structural unemployment, 115–17

Long, Clarence: changes in views, 139; on structural unemployment, 80, 83–84

Lonigan, Edna, 72–73; on price flexibility, 44–45; on technological unemployment, 44–45

Lubin, Isador, 14, 38; changes in views, 75; 1920s displaced workers study, 30–31, 33, 48–51, 54, 57, 64, 67, 73, 76; on technological unemployment, 49, 65

Machinery and Allied Products Institute, 36, 61

machinery and unemployment debates, 1–2, 149 n.7; empirical evidence in, 20; history of, 17–22

Machinery, Employment, and Purchasing Power (National Industrial Conference Board), 8, 36, 61

machine tax movement, 36, 59, 154 n.3

MacRae, C. Duncan, on structural unemployment, 135

Magdoff, Harry, 64

Malthus, Thomas Robert, 17, 19, 21

Mangum, Garth, 128; on structural unemployment, 124

Mann, Lawrence, 1920s occupations flows study, 29–30, 33

Manpower Development and Training Act, 94, 97–98; hearings on, 119

Manpower Report of the President, 94, 98, 111, 121, 130; hearings on, 119–20; on policy, 98, 112–14, 119–20, 128

Marcet, Jane, 17

Marshall, Alfred, 2, 21

Marshall, Ray, on structural unemployment, 135

Martin, William McChesney, 140; on
    structural unemployment, 118, 168
    n.29
Marx, Karl, 17, 21, 129; on machinery
    and unemployment, 19, 21
McCloskey, Donald, 3, 15
McCracken, Paul, 99; on
    unemployment, 97
McCulloch, John Ramsey, 17–18, 71;
    and Ricardo, 19
Means, Gardner, 73
Mechanization in Industry (Jerome),
    60, 61
Menger, Carl, 2
methodological pluralism, 3; evidence
    for, 10
methodology of economics, 3–4, 8–14
methodology of scientific research
    programs, 3, 10; evidence for, 11–
    12
Michael, Donald, on automation, 95–
    96, 100–101
Miernyk, William, 142; changes in
    views, 138; on structural
    unemployment, 94, 101, 119
Mill, John Stuart, 2, 17–18, 21, 39–40,
    43; on machinery and
    unemployment, 19
Mills, Frederick C., 44, 54, 56, 64, 73,
    76; changes in views, 75; on
    empirical methodology, 62; on
    price flexibility, 53, 60; on
    technological unemployment, 53,
    57, 60–63
Mitchell, Wesley C., on technological
    unemployment, 28–29, 31–33
Monthly Labor Review, articles in, 24,
    79, 109, 121, 131
Mueller, Eva, displaced workers study,
    133–35
Musgrave, Richard, 7, 124, 137; on
    structural unemployment, 121
Myers, Robert J., 1920s displaced
    workers study, 30–31, 33, 48–51,
    54, 57, 64, 67, 73, 76
Myrdal, Gunnar, on structural
    unemployment, 109

Nathan, Robert, on structural

unemployment, 112
National Bureau of Economic
    Research, 61, 67; publications by,
    28, 31, 60, 65–66, 119
National Commission on Technology,
    Automation and Economic
    Progress, 8; reports of, 127–28
National Industrial Conference Board,
    36, 54, 61, 63, 122
National Organization for the Taxation
    of Labor-Saving Devices, 36, 59
National Research Project on
    Reemployment Opportunities and
    Recent Changes in Industrial
    Techniques, 8, 10, 62–63, 65, 67–
    68, 75–76, 127–28, 145
National Resources Committee, 62, 68;
    on technological unemployment,
    63–64
Nation's Business, articles in, 24–25
Nation's Manpower Revolution,
    hearings, 100–109
Neisser, Hans, 8–9, 12, 71–72; on
    technological unemployment, 69–
    70, 129
Nelson, Richard, on structural
    unemployment, 109
Neoclassical School, 2, 37; on
    technological change and
    employment, 21–22
New Republic, 25
new wage policy, 23
Nicholson, John Shield, 20, 25
normal vs. revolutionary science, 10,
    12; evidence for, 11

Okun, Arthur, 118; on structural
    unemployment, 121
*On the Principles of Political Economy
    and Taxation* (Ricardo), 1, 18–19

Parnes, Herbert, on structural
    unemployment, 79
Pasternak, Richard, on structural
    unemployment, 118
Pauling, Norman, 10; on automation,
    112
Pechman, Joseph, 84; on structural
    unemployment, 82–83, 122; on

unemployment, 97
Perlman, Richard, 13, 137, 141; changes in views, 139–40; on structural unemployment, 135
Perry, Arthur, 20
Phillips Curve, 4; Lipsey on, 115; and structural unemployment debates, 93–94
Pigou, A. C., 4, 44
policy statements, and structural unemployment debates, 87, 102, 111, 140, 145
Popper, Karl, 3, 10, 12–13
Posner, Harold, 76; on technological unemployment, 63–64
President's Conference on Unemployment, papers at, 31
price flexibility: Hansen on, 40–41; Kaldor on, 42; Long on, 84; Lonigan on, 44–45; Mills on, 53, 60; and technological unemployment, 4–5, 7–8, 40–45, 69–73, 160 n.2
Price Flexibility and Employment (Lange), 71
productivity data, 10; first comprehensive in U.S., 23–24, 31, 150 nn. 2, 3, 5; and structural unemployment debates, 89–90, 96–98, 137; and technological unemployment debates, 24–26, 159 n.12
Productivity Trends in the United States (Kendrick), 89
progress in debates: on aggregate level, 9, 72–73, 76, 136–38, 140–42; on individual level, 9, 73–76, 138–40; in theoretical vs. empirical literatures, 73–76, 136–38, 141–42, 145
Pu, Shou Shan, 12, 72; on technological unemployment, 71
Public Works Acceleration Act, 97

Railroad Trainman, 25
Recent Economic Changes, articles in, 28, 31–32, 153 n.36
recessions: of 1927, 23, 25; of 1937, 59; in 1950s, 78

Rees, Albert, 99; on structural unemployment, 123
Relation between Factory Employment and Output since 1899, The (Fabricant), 65
Research Program on Unemployment, papers at, 114–17, 121–23
Reuther, Walter, on structural unemployment, 112, 118
revolutionary vs. normal science, 10, 12; evidence for, 11
Reynolds, Lloyd, on structural unemployment, 94
Ricardo, David, 1, 2, 17, 21, 39; on machinery and unemployment, 18–19
Robinson, Joan, 44
Ross, Arthur, 98, 103; on the structural unemployment debates, 95, 99–100
Roylance, William, 10

Samuelson, Paul, 141, 149 n.7; on unemployment, 84–85, 94
Say, J. B., 17–18; and Say's Law, 18
Say's Law, 21, 40, 43; Bouniatian on, 42; Douglas on, 37, 43; Garver on, 55; Hansen on, 39; and labor displacement, 17–19; Slichter on, 40; and the technological unemployment debates, 29, 32, 38, 71–72; Tugwell on, 38
Scheler, Michael, on technological unemployment, 35
Schultz, Charles, 84; on structural unemployment, 83
Schumpeter, Joseph, 44; on compensation argument, 22
Schweitzer, Stuart O., on structural unemployment, 135
Scottish Journal of Political Economy, articles in, 131
Senior, Nassau, 17–18
Silberman, Charles, 119; on structual unemployment, 118
Simler, N. J., 135; on structural unemployment, 118
Sismondi, J. C. L., 17, 19
Slichter, Sumner, 26–27, 38–39, 48, 63, 71, 76; changes in views, 74–

75; on Say's Law, 40; on technological unemployment, 27–29, 32–33, 38, 40–41

Smith, Adam, 1

Social Aspects of Rationalisation, The (International Labour Office), 50

Solow, Robert, 120, 128, 137, 141–42; changes in views, 139–40; on structural unemployment, 114, 124

Somers, Gerald, 130; on the structural unemployment debates, 101–102

Soule, George, 27

Special Committee on Unemployment Problems, studies for, 81–82, 167 n.20

stagnation thesis, 45

State of the Economy, hearings, 97

Stein, Robert, on structural unemployment, 109

Stern, Boris, 10, 13, 57, 61, 64, 76; on empirical methodology, 52, 62; impact of work, 74; on technological unemployment, 55–56

Stettner, Leonora, 10

Stoikov, Vladimir, 141; changes in views, 139–40; on structural unemployment, 128

Stoltz, Merton, on structural unemployment, 79

Striner, Herbert, on structural unemployment, 101

structural unemployment debates, 2; beginning of, 77, 79–80, 84, 86; as a case study, 3–15; comparisons with technological unemployment debates, 8–9, 82, 117, 127, 137, 140, 143–45; econometrics in, 88, 90, 115, 124; empirical studies' problems, 115, 117, 120–21, 124, 129, 135, 137, 141–42; end of, 8, 123, 125, 127–35; evaluation of, 135–45; importance of Keynesian ideas in, 78, 81–83, 85, 93, 97, 100, 122, 129–31, 136–37, 144; inaccuracies in histories of, 111, 119, 120, 123; major positions in, 139, 169 n.33; and Phillips Curve, 93–94; and policy statements, 87,

102, 111, 140, 145; reduced intensity period, 91, 93–97; revival of, 100–109, 114, 117. *See also* automation

Sufrin, Sidney, on structural unemployment, 109

Suits, Daniel, on unemployment, 97

survey of professional opinion, 117, 123

Sylvester, Harold, on automation, 96

Taft, Philip, on structural unemployment, 79

Taylor, Harold, on structural unemployment, 120

Taylor Society, papers at meetings of, 48

tax cut policy, 97–98, 108, 111–12, 118, 120, 123

Technocracy, 8, 36; Douglas on, 43

Technological Trends and National Policy (National Resources Committee), 63

technological unemployment debates, 2; beginning of, 23–26; as a case study, 3–15; comparisons with structural unemployment debates, 8–9, 82, 117, 127, 137, 140, 143–45; early 1930s theoretical debates, 38–40, 154 n.8; end of, 8, 11, 68–73; evaluation of, 72–76, 143–45; first professional responses in 1920s, 26–33; first use of econometrics in, 65, 68; influence of Keynesian ideas on, 69–73; initial theoretical approaches, 37–38; late 1930s empirical work, 62–68; neoclassical theoretical approaches, 43–45; new empirical approaches in 1930s, 47–50; as a popular issue in 1920s, 25–26, 151 nn.10, 11; as a popular issue in early 1930s, 35–36; as a popular issue in late 1930s, 62. *See also* price flexibility

Technology and Concentration of Economic Power, 65

Temporary National Economic Committee, 62, 65, 67, 75

Terborgh, George, 8
Theobald, Robert, on automation, 100–101
Theory of Unemployment (Pigou), 4
Theory of Value (Hicks), 4
Theory of Wages (Hicks), 44
Thomas, Woodlief, 26, 32
Thurow, Lester, on structural unemployment, 122
Time, articles in, 125
Tinbergen, Jan, on technological unemployment, 65, 71–72
Tobin, James, 85, 95
Tugwell, Rexford, 38, 71; changes in views, 75; on 1920s productivity advances, 26; on Say's Law, 38; on technological unemployment, 38–39

Ulman, Lloyd, 9
unemployment. *See* automation; frictional unemployment; full employment; structural unemployment debates; technological unemployment debates
Unemployment: A Problem of Industry (Beveridge), 21
Unemployment Problems in the United States (Butler), 50–51
United States Chamber of Commerce, on structural unemployment, 112
United States Employment Service, 97, 101
United States House, proposals to tax machines, 36
United States Senate: proposals to tax machines, 36; report on technological unemployment, 36
U. S. News and World Report, articles in, 84

Vietnam War, and the structural unemployment debates, 8, 11, 78, 111, 118, 122, 125, 127, 130, 133, 136, 138, 141
Vinogradoff, D. I., 65
Vivarelli, Marco, 4, 6, 14, 181 n.1; empirical findings, 7–8; theoretical conclusions, 5, 7

wages fund, 21; and labor displacement, 18
Walras, Léon, 2
Walrasian equilibrium, 5
Webb, Sidney, 21
Webster, Donald, on structural unemployment, 112
Weintraub, David, 57, 64, 76; changes in views, 75; on technological unemployment, 54, 63–64
Wells, David, 20
Wells, Donald, on structural unemployment, 129
White, R. C., 63, 76; on technological unemployment, 51
Wilcock, Richard: changes in views, 138; on structural unemployment, 94
Wirtz, Willard, 100
Wolfbein, Seymour, 99
Wolman, Leo, on technological unemployment, 56–57
World War I, 31; productivity advances after, 24
World War II, 83, 103–104; and automation, 77; and the technological unemployment debates, 8, 11, 68–69, 71; trends after, 78, 96, 121, 137
Woytinsky, Wladimir, 61, 76
Wubnig, Arthur, on empirical methodology, 64

About the Author

GREGORY R. WOIROL is Professor of Economics and holder of the Richard and Bille Diehl Distinguished Chair at Whittier College. Dr. Woirol has published numerous books and journal articles dealing with subjects in economics.